Pastor Jim Bakker is a living example of how Christians should live out Ephesians 6:10–20—not just in taking up the full armor of God but in following Paul's exhortation to stand, stand, *stand* against the schemes of the devil. Well, Satan has taken his best shots at Jim Bakker, and Pastor Jim is still standing. This book is an honest, open, inspiring message of redemption, salvation, and Christ's ultimate triumph. We are honored to stand with him.

—Derek and Sharon Gilbert
SkyWatchTV
Hosts, *Unraveling Revelation* and
The Bible's Greatest Mysteries

Jim Bakker's new book, *You Can Make It*, will give anyone who has ever gone through any type of hardship or struggle a renewed hope and encouragement. If there has ever been a story of a comeback kid—that would make not only a great story but also a great movie—this book is it! Jim is not only a patient of mine but a friend, and I endorse this book completely.

—Don Colbert, MD

I have known Jim and Lori Bakker for many years. I have stood by them through the mountains and the valleys of life. And through it all they have remained faithful servants of Jesus Christ. This book takes you on a journey through the most difficult year of Jim's life, both personally and in ministry. From persecution, to almost losing the ministry, to the stroke and other family health issues, to the triumph of recovery and restoration, this book makes you feel as if you are right there with him every step of the way. I'm so proud of Jim and Lori Bakker. They are amazing people and dear friends.

—Tommy Barnett
Global Pastor, Dream City Church;
Chancellor, Southeastern University;
Co-pastor, The Dream Center

Jim Bakker is an American icon that I am glad to call a friend. He is also an enabler of the end-time watchmen and himself a prophet who—like those Old Testament seers that were persecuted and slain for showing "before of the coming of the Just One" (Acts 7:52, KJV)—has been relentlessly persecuted over the past twenty years to silence his growing voice and platform. If for no other reason than that, you should pay close attention to what he says is coming next.

—DR. THOMAS HORN
TELEVISION AND RADIO PERSONALITY;
BEST-SELLING AUTHOR; PUBLISHER

Pastor Jim Bakker's *You Can Make It* is an engrossing prophetic saga. His consistent words of biblical forewarning have been documented in several venues, and he's often been spot-on throughout the years. As Pastor Jim says, "We entered the Revelation Generation a short time ago. All I can do is point to the Scriptures and the events of today and say that time is running out....We are living in the days that Jesus foretold." This latest offering from Jim Bakker illuminates our times, informs, inspires, and profoundly encourages—all at once. This is a book of divine perspective. This is a book for our generation!

—CARL GALLUPS
SENIOR PASTOR SINCE 1987; TOP 60 AMAZON BEST-SELLING
AUTHOR; CHRISTIAN MEDIA PERSONALITY

Jim Bakker is a watchman prophet for America! I believe this book is truly a "times and seasons" wake-up call and prophetic warning to a church that demands awakening. Early in *You Can Make It*, Pastor Jim paints the following picture: "Yes, there is revival. Yes, revival can continue to push back the judgment. But it will take more than revival now. We must have a great awakening larger than anything this country has ever seen." I believe we need a landscape-changing awakening, as in the days of Jonathan Edwards and Charles Finney, to spiritually shake the nation to its core. The good news: I believe we are hearing some early rumblings of this awakening and that spiritual generals and fathers such as Pastor Jim Bakker are blowing the trumpet and sounding the alarm. God is raising up those willing to stand in an hour of compromise, moral relativism, and biblical illiteracy. Truly, *You Can Make It* will call you to spiritual attention, give you an accurate prophetic evaluation of where we are on God's end-time clock, and help position you to stand strong in this time of intense shaking and great awakening!

—LARRY SPARKS, MDIV
PUBLISHER, DESTINY IMAGE

Jim Bakker has been a faithful watchman on the wall for decades. Watchmen are the first soldiers an enemy tries to take out, for obvious reasons. To see Jim stay at his post for as long as he has under the relentless fire is a marvel. I have to be thankful for such a faithful witness, but even more importantly we need to hear his message. Jim Bakker's life is part of the message, and this book is a unique mixture of testimony and prophecy.

—RICK JOYNER
COFOUNDER, MORNINGSTAR MINISTRIES

The book that you are holding in your hands is not just another book to be read and placed on a bookshelf. Jim Bakker's life has been a combination of heartache, joy, and lessons learned in the crucible of God's love and revelation knowledge. I encourage you to prayerfully listen with your heart as you read and discuss the contents written as inspired not only by Jim Bakker's experiences but by the warnings of God spoken through him for us today! I am honored to know Jim Bakker and to call him my friend and brother.

—MARY ANN PELUSO-MCGAHAN
MCGAHAN PELUSO MINISTRIES

YOU CAN MAKE IT

YOU CAN MAKE IT

JIM BAKKER
A WATCHMAN
WITH ANDREW LIETZEN

FRONT
LINE

Scripture quotations marked TLB are from The Living Bible. Copyright © 1971. Used by permission of Tyndale House Publishers, Inc., Wheaton, IL 60189. All rights reserved.

Visit the author's website at jimbakkershow.com, JimBakkerBooks.com.

Library of Congress Cataloging-in-Publication Data:
An application to register this book for cataloging has been submitted to the Library of Congress.
International Standard Book Number: 978-1-63641-047-0
E-book ISBN: 978-1-63641-048-7

While the author has made every effort to provide accurate internet addresses at the time of publication, neither the publisher nor the author assumes any responsibility for errors or for changes that occur after publication. Further, the publisher does not have any control over and does not assume any responsibility for author or third-party websites or their content.

21 22 23 24 25 — 9 8 7 6 5 4 3 2 1
Printed in the United States of America

CONTENTS

ACKNOWLEDGMENTS

I T IS ONLY by the absolute grace of God and the call He has placed upon my life that I am able to boldly declare that I am still standing! I could not have done this alone. More than ever, I am deeply thankful to my wife, Lori, who has not left my side throughout this storm. Not only is she my best friend; she is my partner, my caretaker, my sounding board, the love of my life, and so much more.

It is through my wife, Lori, that God has grafted together a dynamic family. Each and every one of my children and grandchildren have helped to reenergize my soul, no matter where God has placed them throughout this ministry and the world. I especially want to thank Tammy Sue, Mondo, Maricela, and Lil' Lori for their tireless devotion to cohosting *The Jim Bakker Show* in my absence, as well as continuing to maintain our television ministry and operations at Morningside. I also wish to thank Lori's mother, Char Graham, the matriarch of our family, for her many conversations and encouraging words throughout my recovery, as well as my sister Donna for her continued support and love. And how could I forget our two dogs, Lucky and Snowball, for their unconditional love!

I especially want to express my never-ending gratitude to the many doctors, nurses, and medical professionals who have helped to save my life and aid me in navigating my road to recovery.

There are many at Morningside I must also thank, including our faithful Executive Board of Directors, including Philip Cameron, Rick Joyner, Char Graham, Dr. James Lukavksy, Tommy Reid, Charles Smith, Bishop Ron Webb, and Dr. Tom Horn. Each of these leaders stood by my side throughout our litigation, operational struggles, and health issues. Words cannot express my utmost gratitude for Pastor Joe

Campbell; his wife, Becky; and his family who continue to look after our Morningside family, as well as Lori's House, a place of hope and healing for expectant mothers. Through their efforts several babies who would have been aborted were brought into this world and provided joy for many. I also thank the residents at Morningside, along with our faithful staff and volunteers who have continued to pray for me and my family through this difficult season in addition to working together and standing with us at every opportunity. I have special thanks to our production team, including Kimberly, our producer of *The Jim Bakker Show*. I want to give proper thanks to Bishop Ron Webb for his faithful visits and phone calls to keep me encouraged while I was fighting for my life. I also thank him for his heart for our community and the world.

The year 2020 was difficult, and though we saw great hardship, we also saw great miracles. I want to thank Jim and Julie Pigg not just for their continued support but for their role in helping restore the PTL Television Network around the world. I also thank Stephen Strang, Pat Robertson and the CBN News team, Tom Horn, Derek and Sharon Gilbert, and Zach Drew for standing by our side and our television ministry as we were attacked on all sides for sharing the gospel of Jesus Christ around the world. It is because of their efforts and their support that we were able to endure a difficult season as agents of cancel culture attempted to shut down our ministry.

Lori and I both want to thank Tiffany, who has become more than our assistant. She has become an essential part of our lives. We also want to thank our chefs at Morningside, Vasken and Staci, who have worked hard with my doctors to help restore my health.

Finally, I must thank the fantastic team at Charisma Media as well as our team who helped edit and proofread every word, including Maricela, Mondo, Kimberly, and Cousin Pat. I especially want to thank Andrew Lietzen, without whom this book would not have been possible. He worked tirelessly to capture all that I have said in the last fourteen years and more, as well as the experiences I have endured for the sake of the gospel, and transcribed them into this incredible book.

Most of all, I want to thank my Lord and Savior, Jesus Christ. He has never, ever, ever left me or forsaken me. Because of Him I know that my story isn't over yet.

FOREWORD

THE BOOK YOU are about to read is a treasure. Jim Bakker has withstood storms that the usual Christian would have buckled under and is still standing. As I read the many trials, challenges, victories, and yes, by his own admission, ways he has missed the Lord, I simply was amazed. I couldn't help but think of the number of times that I have whined about small things and compare them with what Jim has gone through, overcome, and lived! There is no comparison.

I have personally known Jim and Lori Bakker since they were newly married. All that's to say they are the real deal. There is no pretense about them. The crucible they have survived and come out of still loving each other, their humility, and their gratitude to God cannot be faked. Why do I include both of them in this foreword? In order to really know someone, at least if the person is married, you need to know the inner workings of his or her life, and that also involves the person's private life. Jim and Lori love each other.

Why should you take the time to read *You Can Make It*? It is profound and life changing. Jim has lived what amounts to many lives and writes from the perspective of a leader who has distilled the wisdom garnered from his hard-won experience. That is why I called it a treasure.

Many people today are crying out for mentorship. As one devours the contents of his story, he shares how to keep persisting before God and never ever give up. I was fortified in my walk with God through learning from him. He is quite transparent in telling about his own struggles during the times of refining. Jim went through the loss of one of the greatest ministries that has ever been built for God's kingdom, then prison, divorce, financial problems, the loss of dignity, renown, and a life-threatening stroke.

At the writing of this book, Jim is eighty-one years old. As we say here in Texas, where I live, "He ain't no spring chicken." Most people who are eighty-one are retired, in a retirement home, or not alive at all! Not only is he alive, but he is building a major network for the prophets to have a voice and building a Hall of the Prophets. That should be encouraging to anyone past fifty! (I simply can't find retirement in the Bible! We need to refire and allow God to use us in new and vibrant ways as we age.)

You might know that he wrote a book titled *I Was Wrong*. For anyone trying to point a finger at him for various events in his past, in all good faith, I recommend you take the time to read it before forming an opinion.

One of the sweetest portions of the book is the one in which some of his children and his wife, Lori, write what they feel about Jim. You can also tell what a deep love for the Lord each of them has.

Not only is Jim Bakker a media genius and pioneer; he deeply loves each and every one of his family members. Most of all, he loves God and His Word. That is a powerful combination indeed!

Not only is he a master builder, entrepreneur, and Bible teacher; he is a true prophet. God has given him the hard assignment, as He did David Wilkerson, of sharing the hard things. There is a suffering in that kind of calling. It is not in Jim's personality to be such a person. He does it out of his love for truth and God's people.

Jim Bakker is my hero. He is not only *my* hero but one to hundreds of thousands, perhaps millions, around the world, and he has earned it.

—Cindy Jacobs
Generals International
Dallas

INTRODUCTION

THE YEAR 1976 was marked by, among other things, the nation's celebration of its bicentennial—two hundred magnificent years of freedom. I myself have always been patriotic, with an undying love for the United States of America, but that year I had something else to celebrate.

I had had the privilege of serving as president of the PTL Television Network since 1974. We were just beginning to settle into our brand-new facilities at Heritage Village in North Carolina. Before that we had operated out of an old furniture store we'd converted into a studio, which we had greatly outgrown. Heritage Village itself spanned twenty-five beautiful acres. The entire campus had been modeled after Colonial Williamsburg, a perfect example of what I had hoped to accomplish with Heritage. The church always had a rich history and few people to tell the tale. Not only did Christians need to be reminded of where they and their country came from, but also they needed to be empowered with the Holy Spirit, educated on the Word of God, and prepared to be disciples for Him. We were building a center where Christians could learn about their spiritual heritage, a place of history for the church to remember from whence it came. To show how revivals had been conducted at the turn of the twentieth century, we had plans to bring one of Billy Sunday's last surviving tabernacles, along with many other artifacts from the history of the American church, to Heritage Village.

Not everyone could come to the village, and we knew that. The crux of my calling was to reach the world for Christ, and the most effective way I could do that was through the means of television.

Work was already underway building the PTL Satellite Network.

We would tape our daily show, and we'd send copies on videotape all around the nation for syndication. The network was rapidly expanding. IBM once reported to us that in the formative years of our ministry we experienced over 3,000 percent growth! It was amazing to see all the people God brought to our daily show, *The PTL Club*. The who's who of the church, politics, and secular entertainment appeared on *PTL*. We made it a point every day to give a salvation call and invite viewers to phone in for prayer. We featured one of the largest and grandest live Christian orchestras daily, which even top secular performers would use as a backdrop while they performed Christian songs. Our program even won a Dove Award for a television program in 1977. We were overjoyed with what God was doing.

On July 4, 1976, we committed our studio and efforts to God. In attendance were many of the founders of Christian television from around the nation. Life had been a whirlwind up to that day, and it only intensified after that. It was everything we could do to keep up with the expansion. We were adding counselors left and right. We were creating materials for our partners to build their faith and their knowledge of the Word. We were constructing new buildings to house classes and our staff. Work had begun on PTL University and PTL School of Evangelism.

I loved every minute of it! I loved seeing God work in my life and the lives of others. No matter what happened, I simply could not get enough of doing the Lord's work.

In November of that year I welcomed David Wilkerson to the *PTL Club* broadcast at Heritage Village. I had always admired David for his work in New York City, and who wouldn't? He founded an incredible addiction-recovery program named Teen Challenge, which still endures to this day. He was already known worldwide for the best-selling book *The Cross and the Switchblade*, published in 1962. His passion for God was contagious, and I loved nothing more than talking about the work of the Lord with Christians such as him.

If there was one thing David knew well, it was that the church's work was only just beginning. America may have hit its two hundredth milestone, but its people had already started to turn away from the Lord.

American Christianity needed more than just salvation. It needed something else entirely; it needed to stay saved.

David and I were kindred spirits in this regard. Shortly before I began my ministry, I had received seven different prophetic words over my life, given to me by Brother Phil Halverson while I was attending North Central Bible College in Minnesota at nineteen years old. Each of these words was profound in its own right (including one warning that I would ignore on two occasions and would later pay a large price for each time). Two of the words he had given to me that day were that I would go places no one else had gone to and that I would "help usher in the coming of the Lord Jesus Christ."

Both were incredibly tall orders. Where could I go that no one else had gone to? And how exactly do you usher in the coming of our Lord and Savior? It became clear to me years later. In the mid-1960s I was a traveling evangelist, going from church to church, city to city, state to state. One evening I'd returned to my hotel room from preaching at a revival, and I was exhausted. The room had a television. Being on the road all the time meant that I had rarely used one of these, but I was not unfamiliar with the device. I figured now was a good time to see what Americans were watching and what forces were coming against Christians when they weren't in the pews or at the altar.

I was shocked to find out that there was hardly anything uplifting or edifying for Christians! It sickened me, and I couldn't help but wonder how many seeds sown from the pulpit had fallen and not taken root because of this invention.

Channel after channel, I kept searching for hope. I landed on the NBC network and *The Tonight Show Starring Johnny Carson*. I watched for a few minutes, and then I knew what I had to do. Christians needed their own talk show. More than that, they needed their own programming, and even networks, if they were going to be fed daily with the Word of God. The pursuit of this goal led me to come alongside Pat Robertson at CBN in Virginia. There I was able to launch a program for kids called *Come on Over* and then later a show that became *The 700 Club*, among several other opportunities throughout eight years of service. From there God moved me to California to take part in founding

TBN with Paul and Jan Crouch. I helped start many other television networks before finally landing in North Carolina with the PTL Network. I was living my dream, living my calling, and broadcasting the gospel of Jesus Christ to the ends of the earth. As Brother Halverson would put it, Christianity was going to new places.

Ten years had passed since I had started, but even though entire channels and networks dedicated to Christian television had sprung up, Christian broadcasting and programming was still a brand-new concept to the American people and the world. I knew that I was living the Great Commission. We were standing on Mark 16:15: "He said to them, 'Go into all the world, and preach the gospel to every creature.'" The only way we thought—we *knew*—that was possible was through television and satellite broadcasting.

Even as we struggled and believed God to bring His light to television every day, we knew that the world was starting to grow dark. David Wilkerson also knew this. I can attest that he knew far better than I did. This was one reason I had invited him to join me for a broadcast that day in 1976.

David had just released his latest book, and it had the most intriguing title, *Racing Toward Judgment*. We sat next to each other and talked for more than an hour. He shared how he'd been ostracized by his closest and dearest friends for publishing such a serious and sobering book. Many had celebrated David for the marvelous work he'd performed in New York City, risking his life to be a light for Christ to the ghettos and the addicts through Teen Challenge. But those who had celebrated him started to turn away, one by one, when he began to preach and publish prophetic words of judgment. At the time, I didn't care what others had said. It was my duty to share the message of the Lord, no matter what He had to say.

On the broadcast, Wilkerson gave a multitude of examples of how rampantly sin was sweeping our great nation. Among his observations were "a flood of filth on television," earthquakes throughout the world, looming economic depressions, a rise in pornography, a rise in divorce rates and broken homes, and many other milestones that were hard to fathom at the time. He shared that the Lord was ready to judge America at that moment and that this judgment had been suspended. The church was in the middle of a revival, a great renewal that was sweeping the world. The Lord had seen a great measure of repentance in churches, politics, sports, and entertainment. The key to keeping judgment suspended would be integrating Christ into our governments and worldview. And he warned that the moment we broke His commandments and became ashamed of His testimony, that restraint would end.[1]

His words grieved me. It was such a powerful, heavy word, and I could feel the Holy Spirit nudge me to give assurance and direction to the television audience.

I turned to the camera and shared that I had previously sought the Lord on this very subject. I repeated the questions to the television audience that I had asked God. "What is the answer?" I asked. "What is the key, Lord? How are we going to make it through? What is going to happen?"[2]

I smiled and told them, "He turned me to that portion of Scripture, and He told me that the body [the church] was going to take care of itself. He said the place of security is being in the body of Christ, the assembling of ourselves together, not on the outside."[3]

And then I said something even more profound. To this day I believe it wasn't me speaking but the Holy Spirit speaking through me. "It's amazing how many of those little old grandmas got chickens in the coop." As I said that, I was reminded of my grandma Irwin and the many chicken dinners that came from her chicken coop. I looked out to the studio audience to several blank stares. Even my staff gave me strange looks. I smiled and said, "Some of you don't even know what I'm talking about. But someday you will."[4]

The show ended, and I thanked David Wilkerson for joining me on the broadcast. But then I did the worst thing imaginable. I didn't listen to the watchman. I didn't stop to heed, much less incorporate, the warning given by God.

For me life continued to move forward. I maintained the mission that I'd been given by God, following Him to the four-square-mile campus we named Heritage USA on a mission to collect and share the heritage of the Christian church with all believers. My plate was full, and I focused on delivering messages that would make parishioners and viewers happy. My focus was on soul winning, but I realized later that I was not teaching full biblical truth. Had I listened to the watchman then, I would have adjusted the messages on our daily broadcasts. I would have fought harder to keep American Christians from going astray.

David Wilkerson and I would cross paths decades later but not in person. It was our messages that had started to synchronize. The Lord was showing many of the same things now to me that He had been showing to David Wilkerson for many years. My life had been transformed. Because of my experiences I no longer taught a message of prosperity or that everything would be all right. I preached a message of the power of restoration, the Book of Revelation, and the true gospel, which Jesus revealed to me through my darkest days. This was a message God had given me through five years in prison. I was again building a television ministry from nothing but this time near Branson, Missouri. I had gone through the valley.

I now, more than ever, see the perversion that has gripped this country. I see how much America has forsaken the One who ordained its foundation. I see everything that David Wilkerson and many other prophets warned America not to do—and Americans are doing these things without remorse or guilt. I had to go through the deepest valleys and travel roads through hell in order to start listening to God and His watchmen. Because I can now listen, I can now heed the warning. It is time for you to do the same.

America has turned from God, and judgment is now upon this great nation. The church has been lulled to sleep. Its most profound voices are being silenced one by one.

Yes, there is revival. Yes, revival can continue to push back the judgment. But it will take more than revival now. We must have a great awakening larger than anything this country has ever seen.

Can America be saved? I wholeheartedly believe that it can. We must repent. We must reform our ways. We must take up our cross and follow Him. And we must never, never, never take our eyes off Him. The writer of Hebrews tells us:

> Do not despise the chastening of the LORD, nor be discouraged when you are rebuked by Him; for whom the

LORD loves He chastens, and scourges every son whom He
receives.

—HEBREWS 12:5–6, NKJV

Judgment isn't about punishment. Judgment isn't about revenge. Our God so greatly loves His creation; He deeply loves you! He is preparing a new heaven and a new earth and is preparing to reunite us with Him in a world free from sin. And He so deeply wants each one of us to join Him there.

As I believed back at Heritage, even on that significant day in 1976, there is security in the body of Christ. I firmly believe that we are living in the church's greatest hour. The Lord has never kept His plan a secret.

Surely the Lord GOD does nothing without revealing His
purpose to His servants the prophets.

—AMOS 3:7

He uses the office of the prophets to share what He is about to do so that we will stay firmly founded on God and His Word and not be led astray. And Jesus gave us one of the most important reminders:

You are the salt of the earth. But if the salt loses its saltiness, how shall it be made salty? It is from then on good for
nothing but to be thrown out and to be trampled under-
foot by men.

—MATTHEW 5:13

Why would the Lord compare Christians to salt? Our Father designed each of our bodies perfectly, and our bodies rely on salt to function properly. It's been scientifically proved that our bodies use salt to balance our nervous and cardiovascular systems. If there isn't enough salt, then our bodies cannot function. Can you see an instance in your community, or even the world, where a little more Jesus could bring balance?

Because Jesus knew the church would not heed that word, He warned in one of His final and most important addresses,

> Because iniquity will abound, the love of many will grow
> cold.
> —Matthew 24:12

Merriam-Webster defines *iniquity* as "gross injustice; a wicked act."[5] The Greek word here is ἀνομία, or *anomia*, which means lawlessness, an utter disregard for God's law.[6] Are we not seeing this world grow colder and darker because of the absence of the church?

The church is still very capable of action. We acted in 2016 to elect the forty-fifth president of the United States, Donald J. Trump. However, the voices of darkness grow louder every day. In the year 2020 alone we continually saw the darkness grow with each passing moment.

- What is happening?
- What will happen next?
- What is the key to salvation, Lord?
- How are we going to make it through?

The answers to these questions and more lie in the pages ahead. First, I'll share with you several warnings that the Lord has given to me throughout my decades as a watchman. Second, my family and I will pull back the curtain and recount many struggles we experienced in 2020, including attacks on our ministry and platform, as well as my physical struggles through a life-changing stroke. Finally, I will stress the importance of listening to the prophets and watchmen as we enter the final hour. And I'll share a few things that will soon envelop both our nation and the world.

Join me on this journey. Though life continues to unfold around us all, do not ignore or dismiss the warnings from the Lord. He loves you deeply, and He wants you to stand amid the storm, functioning as a lighthouse for both the saved and the unsaved. Yet you can stand only if you are fully aware of what the Lord expects from you. The day and the hour are growing short. Time is running out for you to heed the word of the Lord.

CHAPTER 1

THE WATCHMAN'S CALL

A T AGE TWENTY-ONE I began my ministry as a traveling evangelist before finding my true calling in front of a television camera. I was privileged to pioneer Christian television among several great men and women of God, and years later I was substantially blessed with a second chance at life. Multiple times in my more than a decade of service at PTL and Heritage USA did I live under a microscope. That pressure continues today, and so does the campaign to discredit me and the work I have been called to do for the Lord.

I am far from perfect. Who hasn't made mistakes? My mistakes just happened to be paraded on the national stage. These pitfalls, their consequences, and even the lessons I learned were detailed in my book *I Was Wrong*. For five years I served in federal prison for a crime I did not commit. In the beginning I could not understand why a soul-winning preacher such as myself would be thrown out into the cold and locked inside a prison cell, seemingly doomed to live out the remainder of my days there. At the time, I was condemned to serve forty-five years, with my release set for 2034.

They say that hindsight is twenty-twenty, and I tend to agree. I often say that I never lost a friend in all my years of tribulation; I just discovered who they were. I came to realize that the same is true for things. I may have lost everything in the physical world, but I didn't lose anything in the spiritual self. In fact, I rediscovered Jesus and my true calling.

The Bible is filled with stories of those in prison. Joseph in Pharaoh's dungeon, Samson in Philistine captivity, Daniel in the lions' den, His prophets in exile, Jesus at the hands of Pilate, and Peter and Paul in several Roman prisons. The apostle John even wrote the entire Book of Revelation on the island of Patmos, living out the rest of his days as an inmate in a prison colony. How wrong I had been to focus on select passages of Scripture and ignore the entirety of His Word!

David Wilkerson was not the only one to bring a warning of judgment to *The PTL Club*, but I never stopped long enough to truly listen. I unashamedly continued preaching the gospel of Jesus Christ from the pulpit and television stage for decades. Heritage USA was part of the greatest undocumented revival America had ever experienced. At the last count, over ten million people gave their hearts to Christ through our ministry. The response was so great that we had nearly one thousand People That Love centers throughout the country to follow up on every single one of these salvations to provide for them and get them plugged in to a nearby church. Our ministry either hosted or sponsored a multitude of ministries, ranging from marriage counseling conferences to our girls' home for unwed, pregnant mothers to Kevin's House, for those with special needs, to name a few. We were always building, always expanding.

But in all the years I had preached the gospel with fervor and passion, I had failed those who were watching and relying on me for the full biblical truth because I was selective with Scripture. I had only wanted to focus on what was good and happy because that drove the expansion.

My dreams had become so big that they began to break me down. Throughout the 1980s I grew exhausted and weary in well-doing. On the day I was called into ministry, Brother Halverson warned me never to become overtired, for the enemy would use that exhaustion to destroy me.

Consider this: Have you ever been on a stage in front of a large audience? Often the stage lighting is so bright that all you can see is what's directly in front of you or whatever and whoever is sharing the stage with you. If there's an audience of thousands in front of you, it's impossible to see each person. If you're lucky, you can see those in the front row. Only if you focus can you filter out the spotlights and see everything. I hadn't focused when I'd received the warning signs, but once I had been removed from the spotlight, I could see them clearly.

I grieved every day inside my prison cell. Heritage USA had nearly three thousand employees at its height, and we affected millions of people every year. When my world came crashing down, so did theirs. Every single ministry that operated because of Heritage USA disappeared almost overnight. I never got to say goodbye to Heritage, nor did I ever get to apologize to every single person that I had hurt through my actions. I asked God inside my cell, "Do You hate me? Did You bring me here to punish or get even with me?"

"No, Jim," God answered me. "I got even with you on the cross. I brought you here to know Me!"

I soon disappeared into the pages of my Bible. I began at Genesis and slowly worked my way through. When I hit the end of Revelation, I went back to the beginning and went through again. I filled more notebooks than I could count with the lessons I had learned. The margins on each page of my Bible shrank each time too. As I continued to dive deeper and deeper, I understood more and more how much I had overlooked in the last two decades. Passages such as Matthew 24, Mark 13, and Luke 21 (the Olivet Discourse), Daniel 7 and 12 (the Antichrist and the Great Tribulation), 1 Thessalonians 5 (the Day of the Lord), and even 2 Timothy 3 (a picture of perilous times) shook my spirit as if it were a divine tuning fork, resonating in perfect synchronization with the Holy Spirit. With a renewed passion I pursued God as never before.

Day after day, night after night I continued to receive more and more revelations. Nothing could match my hunger or zeal for the Word of the Living God, yet I couldn't help but wonder what I was to do with this intense and personal knowledge of the Scriptures. The voice of the Lord had often been clear to me, and one particular day it rang deeper than ever before.

I had been searching the Word, attempting to decode chapters 17 and 18 of Revelation and the great harlot doomed to fall. I was led to Isaiah 21, which started remarkably as a complement to those chapters, recounting a deep and dark prophecy against the Babylon of the day. But when I got to verse 6, I froze.

> For thus hath the LORD said unto me, Go, set a watchman,
> let him declare what he seeth.
>
> —ISAIAH 21:6, KJV

Like Elijah's experience on the mountain in 1 Kings 19, the Lord wasn't speaking to me in loud and mighty acts. He wasn't speaking through an emboldened evangelist behind a church pulpit. God wasn't locking eyes with me through a camera lens on television. He wasn't coming through the earpiece on my transistor radio that I'd purchased at the prison's commissary. He was in the quiet Word on the page. The Lord told me that I was to be a watchman.

I read the verse again. And again. Be a watchman? "Lord, just how exactly am I supposed to do that?" I would often ask.

I would sit in the prison yard on occasion and look past the fence capped with spools of razor wire, unable to do anything but reflect on what I had done for decades on television. It didn't matter that I had led millions to Christ. It didn't matter that I had supported various world missions and humanitarian efforts, including hospitals in Calcutta, India, with Mark Buntain and in Tenwek, Kenya, with Franklin Graham and Samaritan's Purse. I once influenced millions of believers. But now I'd been reduced to a laughingstock and cast out by the very church I helped cultivate and grow, many of them cleaving to what I once had— prosperity. I had been effectively canceled by society and doomed to be forgotten.

Just how exactly could God use me? Who would listen to a disgraced man trapped behind cold prison bars? God continued to show me that He hadn't forgotten me. All my years on television were not worthless. He had used me to build a platform for salvation, and those salvations were eternal. The Lord showed me that my time in prison was a time of renewal, a spiritual reset. Before prison I was so distracted by busily working on His behalf that I hadn't taken the proper time to listen. I had to be removed from everything so that my attention could focus on nothing else but Him and I could relearn the full gospel. Nowhere else could I have learned and studied the Book of Revelation the way I did in prison, carefully examining one word at a time.

RECOMMISSIONED

Because I had recommitted, rededicated, and refocused my life on Him and the complete truth, I was released after serving five years instead of the forty-five I'd been sentenced to. On July 1, 1994, I walked out of the prison gates into the waiting arms of my eldest children, Tammy Sue and Jamie Charles. I was once again a free man. But for all my renewed dedication, I had nowhere to go and no idea how I would fulfill the new call on my life. Very few knew I had been released, and most still did not care to look past my sin and public disgrace.

God demonstrated His mighty power soon enough. He used Billy, Ruth, and Franklin Graham to begin the restoration process. He used Ron Blackwood to ensure I wouldn't leave the Lord's side while in prison. He used Pastor Tommy Barnett to keep my son Jamie from falling into the devil's hands. He used Pastor Matthew Barnett and the Dream Center to remind me what it meant to serve the church. He used Pastor Tommy Reid and more than a dozen other pastors to recommission me into the ministry, doing so over the very first pulpit I ever preached from during my days as an evangelist. I developed deep friendships with many great men and women of God, such as my dear friend Pastor Dan Betzer of First Assembly of God in Fort Myers, Florida, who accepted me for who I was, not who I had been.

The journey ahead would be challenging, but I didn't know yet how difficult it would prove to be. When I returned to speaking from the pulpit, I was invited all across the world to share my testimony. I was welcomed by many wonderful people, a group too numerous to count or name lest I accidently overlook a friend. The Lord brought me all around the world, but it was not all wonderful. I wanted to preach what I had learned from Revelation everywhere, but most only wanted to hear my testimony. My heart broke, and I wept for those who would not allow me to share the warnings I had received from Revelation. In several cases I was rebuked for heresy, condemned for being a prophet of doom, and sometimes discarded much as one might do to a street-corner preacher warning that the end was near.

I lamented their actions. The words from Ezekiel 33:1–9, having long been burned into my spirit, echoed in my mind. Here they are from the King James Version:

> Again the word of the LORD came unto me, saying, Son of man, speak to the children of thy people, and say unto them, When I bring the sword upon a land, if the people of the land take a man of their coasts, and set him for their watchman: If when he seeth the sword come upon the land, he blow the trumpet, and warn the people; then whosoever heareth the sound of the trumpet, and taketh not warning; if the sword come, and take him away, his blood shall be upon his own head. He heard the sound of the trumpet, and took not warning; his blood shall be upon him. But he that taketh warning shall deliver his soul. But if the watchman see the sword come, and blow not the trumpet, and the people be not warned; if the sword come, and take any person from among them, he is taken away in his iniquity; but his blood will I require at the watchman's hand.
>
> So thou, O son of man, I have set thee a watchman unto the house of Israel; therefore thou shalt hear the word at my mouth, and warn them from me. When I say unto the wicked, O wicked man, thou shalt surely die; if thou dost not speak to warn the wicked from his way, that wicked man shall die in his iniquity; but his blood will I require at thine hand. Nevertheless, if thou warn the wicked of his way to turn from it; if he do not turn from his way, he shall die in his iniquity; but thou hast delivered thy soul.

I was grieved by how much blood would be on my hands if I didn't obey and share the warnings I'd been given. My spirit was even more troubled for those who deliberately chose to disregard the warning from above. I wept for the pastors who even forced me not to share a single word of Revelation with their congregations, knowing that their massive flocks would continue to be led astray. I still weep for them.

But there were always those who were willing to hear it. When I began living at the Dream Center in Los Angeles, I would, with permission, teach an hour a day (sometimes more). I thank Pastors Tommy and Matthew Barnett for their encouragement during my time there, as well as many others who helped me find my confidence once again. When I wasn't teaching, I was doing what I could for the Dream Center, whether painting, making repairs, or even sharing a plate of food or Christ's love with the locals. There at the Dream Center, I met and married the love of my life, Lori Graham, in 1998.

Lori and I were broken pots—like Humpty Dumpty, as I affectionately called us. Whereas I had fallen from the public spotlight, Lori had lived a life filled with drugs and five abortions. By the time I first saw her, she had already been transformed by the Holy Spirit and was involved in multiple ministries, including one called Mourning to Joy, a postabortion recovery program. Bad choices had shattered both our lives, yet the Lord had pieced us back together. Our cracks and fractures were not hidden, and they served as examples of His power of restoration, grace, and love. We traveled throughout the United States and abroad, sharing what the Lord had done in our lives as a testimony to Him. We were living life happily ever after. But it seemed that our story was only beginning.

VISIONS OF THE FUTURE

One night in 1998, while sleeping peacefully in a hotel room, I found myself in a vision. All around me was mud. I had never seen so much mud in my life. I heard screams unlike I'd ever heard. These were screams of terror. People were crying out for loved ones. I was standing on top of the mud, and I could hear screaming, thousands of voices, coming up to me from underneath the mud. There was so much pain, so much sorrow. My spirit began to fall, weighed down by insurmountable grief.

I closed my eyes and wept. When I opened them again, I could not see what I'd seen before. All I could see was the darkness of the hotel room. The screams were gone, and only the memory remained. I was surprised to see that my new bride was also awake, having sensed that something was wrong. I shared what I'd seen, and neither one of us knew what to do with it but pray. I had no doubt that this event was very real.

It wasn't the first time I had a shocking vision. Just a year prior, in 1997, upon a visit to Los Angeles to be part of Larry King's broadcast by myself, I had a vision of a great earthquake in Los Angeles. Great boulders had been pushing against each other as if they were two fists. The Lord told me I had seen the pressure of the ages, and it was going to let go. A scientific report published in a newspaper a couple of years later confirmed what I had seen and even provided illustrations to demonstrate exactly what God had shown me: Los Angeles sat on a blind thrust fault.[1] Two plates were pushing together with great force. Whenever that force finally relents, one plate will thrust upward and will devastate the metropolis above it.

While the Los Angeles earthquake prophecy remains unfulfilled, my vision of the mud and screams would eventually be realized. Starting on December 14, 1999, and lasting for fifty-two hours, torrential rains flooded Vargas State in Venezuela. Over thirty-five inches of rain fell on the land. The storm was devastating, causing flash floods and mudslides that devastated entire neighborhoods. Two towns almost disappeared. Not only had the state's infrastructure been utterly destroyed, but around thirty thousand people also perished.[2] When I first saw these images, I was shocked.

All throughout 1999 the Lord awakened me night after night, telling me things that would soon come upon the world. At the end of the year, on December 31, 1999, I stood in front of a crowd of people at MorningStar Ministries under Rick Joyner's direction and shared multiple events that the Lord had shown me. Some were grand achievements from the church, such as mighty leaders rising from minorities. Others were mysterious, such as computer warfare and out-of-control weather. Others were simply words of caution, such as watching countries such as Turkey, China, Russia, and North Korea.

Of these "31 Things" I shared, three stood out. The first was there would be terrible explosions in New York City and Washington, DC. I couldn't see what had exploded in New York City, but I saw thousands of people running away as fast as they could from the explosion. Two details that stuck out to me the most were that each person was gray, covered head to toe in ash, and that they were fleeing in terror. I also had trouble seeing what had been attacked in DC, but the Lord told me it was a major defense location.

More than a year had passed before this event played out on the national stage, and it is remembered most as the day it had occurred: September 11, 2001. Both towers of the World Trade Center, as well as the Pentagon, had been hit by airplanes. I still remember turning on my TV that day (we were now living at Camp of Hope in Florida) and hearing my daughter, Tammy Sue, cry on the other end of the telephone as we watched this terrible attack unfold live in front of us. For me, it was just a replay of everything I had seen almost two years prior, right down to the ashen bystanders fleeing in terror.

After this event I soon discovered that a new hunger was growing in the church for those with prophetic gifts—especially for those looking ahead to what was to come, performing the Old Testament role of the watchman. The Lord had told me in prison, just as I sought clarity for how best to execute the calling He'd placed on my life, that I was to build a platform for the prophets, a place where their voices could be heard throughout the world. This, God told me, would need to be an entire television network. Building this network seemed to be an impossible task at the time, but we had to start somewhere, moving forward one step at a time.

What was certain was that the time had come to go back on television. God moved us from Camp of Hope to Branson, Missouri. On my sixty-third birthday, January 2, 2003, we taped our first broadcast of *The New Jim Bakker Show*. Thanks to the generosity of people such as Bob D'Andrea and the Christian Television Network, I returned to the airwaves. I wanted to ensure that we would be set apart from what I had done in the 1970s and '80s. To do so, we did our best to avoid the subject I'd been most ridiculed for—raising funds. Not only did I want to shake my prior reputation, I knew that there was only one reason to be back on television, and that was to sound the watchman's trumpet.

I used every opportunity on this daily broadcast to preach and teach, bringing the Book of Revelation in every chance I could, and sharing the signs of things to come. Over the next couple of years, we would see several of the "31 Things" come to pass, including churches starting to close their doors, deterioration of the most trusted stocks in the market, and great betrayals throughout the world.

TWO MORE MAJOR EVENTS

It wouldn't be until 2005 that a second major event from the "31 Things" would come to pass. Back on that night in 1999 the words that the Lord had given me were "death by water." It was a simple phrase, really, and most thought it had to do with flooding. This word would be repeated to me by the Lord on July 14, 2005. I was sitting next to Lori, hosting an episode of *The New Jim Bakker Show*, and I was sharing a message from the Lord. Suddenly words came out of my mouth declaring that New Orleans would be underwater. Just seven weeks later, Hurricane Katrina, a Category 3 storm, made landfall in Louisiana. More than eighteen hundred people were killed in just a few days, and over $160 billion in damage was recorded.[3]

And New Orleans was underwater, just as the Lord had shown me.

The third event was a great earthquake in Japan. At that time, the island nation was overdue for a massive earthquake, much like California is now. This earthquake, however, would signal the beginning of a total collapse of the world economy. Back in 1999, just after I'd given this prophecy, Bob Jones told me that not only was my sense of what the Lord had shown me accurate, but the Japanese earthquake would precede one coming to Los Angeles.

In February 2011 the Holy Spirit took control while I was taping a broadcast and released through me a word that a nine-point earthquake was coming. A couple of days later, the Holy Spirit did it again in the middle of another taping. Everyone around me was shocked, especially since this had never happened before. We assumed that this was an urgent word, and we began to look closely for it.

On March 11, 2011, an earthquake triggered a massive tsunami off the coast of Japan. This tsunami quickly swept Japan's eastern coast, destroying farmland, moving homes, damaging nuclear reactors, and killing more than nineteen thousand people.[4]

The initial reports claimed that this quake was only an 8.9. Rather than think that this was just a precursor to a larger quake, I firmly believed that this was the quake I had foreseen just days before. Even my staff began to doubt me, but news reports later confirmed that the quake was indeed a 9.0.[5]

WOUNDING ON THE LEFT

Several items on the list of "31 Things" remain unfulfilled, but it is clear that the Lord has continued to give me far more to be attentive to. Most times when He gives me a word, I try to take great care to ask for His timing. I carefully pray for guidance on delivering that message. However, there have been instances when I received a word and felt the need to test it before other prophets to seek more understanding of it.

On several occasions I have been invited to join Rick Joyner at Heritage International in Charlotte, North Carolina. I've joined him for many events, ranging from the annual Prophetic Roundtable to speaking during conferences in the former Heritage Grand Hotel.

On one such occasion, on December 31, 2007, I was taping several broadcasts with Rick Joyner and several others. In between tapings we were chatting while the crew reset the cameras and other equipment. I turned to Rick and shared that the Lord told me that there would be a "great wounding on the left." I had always looked to Rick as a respected prophetic voice, and I hoped he could provide some insight. Rick and the other prophets discussed it, but none of us knew what it meant. Could it be political? Could it be religious? All we could tell was that it would be severe. Thankfully the recorders hadn't been shut off, and every single word of our valuable discussion was captured.

Fulfillment wouldn't come until 2016. Our country was undergoing one of the most intense and critical election cycles I had ever seen in my life. Every single poll, media outlet, and physical sign pointed to and declared that the forty-fifth president of the United States of America would be Hillary Clinton.

That year, I had decided to watch the election results from our stage, consult with many of our show's well-known guests through their homes around the nation, and stream the results live on our website. We watched for the first couple of hours as the results came in. Hillary would win a couple of states, and her competitor, the Republican candidate, Donald J. Trump, would win a couple. The night unfolded exactly how the analysts thought it would—until the first battleground state turned red on the map. The map continued to turn red over the next hour until it ultimately stopped.

For more than an hour absolutely no updates came from the mainstream media. Our team monitored several websites and news feeds. Each source's map looked nearly identical. One source would have an extra state that would turn red. Another map wouldn't have that state, but it would have another. A third source showed the same thing. We did the math live on television and determined that not only had Donald Trump won the election, but absolutely no one wanted to be the first to admit it. We wound up being among the first on television to declare that Trump had been elected president.

I believe that without a doubt this election was the great wounding on the left. All the proof I need is everything that has transpired throughout President Trump's four-year administration, as well as the impeachments and great legal battles that have taken place in the highest levels of government. The rage, the anger, the looting, the riots, the burning, the slander, and the fury have been like nothing I have ever seen before. No one wanted to acknowledge all the good he had accomplished, only that he had to be removed from office as quickly as possible.

There are many other words, ranging from smaller events to fires in cities to drastic weather changes and so much more. Not all of them have been directly tied to singular events, and some are still in effect as our nation continues to transform around us. I continue to serve as a watchman, positioned high above the gates, looking ahead for what is to come.

And when the new warnings come, I often find that the message grows more and more sobering each time. I often worry about whether I should share them, lest they strike fear in the hearts of those listening or cause people to turn off the message, blinding themselves to what is to come. But I always have no choice. These words are not for me; they are for everyone. Sharing the message is not a privilege; it's a calling—one that I must perform no matter the cost.

CHAPTER 2

THE FOUR HORSEMEN OF THE APOCALYPSE NOW UNITED

N OCTOBER 2019 a series of events began to unfold. None of these were of any surprise to me, but I still found myself shocked, shaken to my very core. I awoke again in the middle of the night. The Lord had downloaded to my mind not one thing but several. In the darkness I reached for the pad of paper I keep near my bedside and began to write as fast as I could. I sat there for several minutes, staring at the items in my hand. The darkness in the room made them unreadable. I knew this message was too important to wait until morning. I had to make sure I had transcribed this download accurately. I also knew that the moment I turned on the lamp, I would wake Lori.

I rose from the bed and carefully made my way into Lori's dressing room, where we had set up an office area for her. I turned on the light and sat in her chair. Slowly I read each item on the list, adding a word or correction to make sure I could read the items again later. To my surprise there were more than a dozen items on this list. I felt my hands start to tremble as I realized that while I had experienced this before, it had been twenty years since I had such a major download from God.

This routine continued for two more nights as the Lord would give me more and more. The list itself was quite overwhelming. At the time, Morningside was holding a Prophetic Conference. Speaking in front of a live audience and recording shows for our network were several people whom I'd come to trust over the last few years, including Rick Joyner. I wanted to test these words with him, but the Lord did not permit me to share all of them. The time to reveal them all hadn't yet come.

For the next few weeks, I sought the Lord in prayer. I asked for more knowledge about these words, and I sought confirmation for others. As before, the Lord gave me knowledge on select words, as well as a plan for handling some of the things He told me. He also gave me a date for delivering these words: December 31, 2019—New Year's Eve. Ever since my delivery of the original "31 Things" in 1999, God had continued to give me a prophetic word to be issued each year on New Year's Eve. This process had long become a tradition, but none of the previous New Year's Eve words would be as significant as the "31 Things." This new download, however, would be as important, if not more so, as the original 1999 address.

As critical as this message was, there was just one problem. I didn't feel well, and I hadn't for several months. I was nearly eighty years old, and while my mind was still young, my physical body was starting to show its age.

A few years before, I'd been so tired at the start of a year that Lori and I took a brief sabbatical from the ministry to rest and seek the Lord. We were both amazed at how effective and impactful this was for our lives, and we quickly made this part of our yearly plan. We were now nearing the end of October, and while my body was tired, I knew I had no choice but to push through pain and sickness to complete the calendar year.

The year 2020 would be a landmark year for me, and I had been looking forward to it for some time. I was going to turn eighty, and already several of the guests and prophets on our broadcasts were reminding me that I was like Moses, who didn't start his ministry until he was eighty years old. In some ways, I was encouraged by this word. But many of my dear friends had already been called home, and as the years continued to pass me by, all I could feel was my age and this weight I still had to carry. And this weight was now heavier than ever before, thanks to this fresh download from God.

I knew I needed to share these words that the Lord had given me, and I couldn't very well do it on my birthday, January 2. After all, my staff had begun to plan a big event in my honor, and it wouldn't do to deliver a series of heavy words on what should be a day of celebration. It was clear I needed to do this on New Year's Eve. Then all I had to do was make it past my birthday, and Lori and I could take our sabbatical as planned.

Weeks later New Year's Eve had arrived. The ministry had been operating in high gear as we entered the Christmas season and began preparations for the new year, and I kept in step with the staff the whole time. When I awoke that Tuesday morning, to say that I didn't feel well was an absolute understatement. It would take another drastic event a few months later, in the coming year, for me to realize what I was truly going through. At the time, I believed that I was suffering from a massive sinus infection. The Ozark Mountains are quite lovely, and I'm happy to have a majestic view of them and Table Rock Lake from my living room window. Still, the climate has caused many in my family, including me, to develop allergies.

I lay in bed all day, and Lori did her best to check on me and try to get me moving for the message that I had to deliver that night. By now she knew some of the things I was planning to say and some of the events that I was required to share, but I just couldn't move. We had a large audience for that evening, and several hundred people had already begun to assemble on Grace Street. My friend Lance Wallnau was going to share a message with the congregation, and we planned to ring in the new year with a prayer session in our newly constructed Prayer Mountain Chapel. As they say in show business, "The show must go on!"

The clock ran out, and I reluctantly told Lori that I wouldn't be able to make it. I couldn't do what the Lord had asked me to do. Lori understood, and she left for the studio. It was time for her to get dressed and prepared for the events that evening.

Silence entered my home. Lucky and Snowball, our faithful terrier and shih tzu, curled up beside me on the bed, hoping I would rest. No matter how much I tried, sleep would not come. Minute after minute passed, and I continued to feel worse than before. I wondered if I would need to see a doctor that evening, and I started to wonder how I would, or if I could, get there and back. It wasn't long before I realized that my pain was not from the sickness. This pain was familiar, too familiar. It was rooted in anguish—the same anguish I had felt when first starting to travel and preach the Book of Revelation. I had been entrusted with some of the most prophetic and earth-shaking events that would soon come to pass. I was the watchman, and the time had come to sound the trumpet.

It took everything I had to get out of bed. Our dogs watched me prepare for the evening. I couldn't just put on a suit and tie either. As with many of our New Year's services, we look to the stroke of midnight to begin deep prayer and worship for His will to be done in the new year. It had long been customary for our staff, our congregation, visitors, and even those on stage to wear their best, "dressed to the nines," as some would say.

I arrived in my office an hour later, donning a full tuxedo and carrying my sermon notes in my shoulder bag. Lori was still in her makeup room with her assistant, Tiffany. She had already been preparing to host the evening and had informed the staff that I would not be there. I stopped in her makeup room, where both she and Tiffany looked at me in total shock. Lori did not expect me to show up at all that night. But we locked eyes with each other, and we knew that this was the right thing to do. "I have to deliver the Word," I told her, confirming with my own admission.

By now worship had begun on Grace Street. My daughter, Tammy Sue, led the congregation in some of the most impactful worship I'd heard her perform in years. The production team quickly returned to the original plan and schedule and prepared the stage while the music continued. At 8:15 p.m. I stood behind the pulpit and thanked Tammy Sue for her worship.

I looked out at the congregation and then the red light on the center camera. Beyond the lens that night was a live television audience, joining us as part of the prophetic network God had called me to build. Many of those present in the room and the audience watching from home had heard me deliver urgent words of warning before. This evening, for all intents and purposes, would prove to be quite different. The time had come to share the most sobering of words.

"The Four Horsemen of the Apocalypse," I declared to the audience with a tone as solid as I could muster, "are a worldwide event."[1]

THE FIRST HORSE

In prison I first learned that the four horsemen had been riding for some time, circling the globe to unleash their unique talents and duties to those who were the most unsuspecting. I often tell my audience that the four horsemen are out of the barn and riding throughout the world.

But what had caught my attention and the audience's attention that night were two simple words: "worldwide event." Until 2020 the horsemen roamed the earth, instigating smaller events that didn't attract much attention. I've called these particular events practice runs, much like soldiers training in boot camp for the real war. Starting that night, I declared that the horsemen would no longer be simply manipulating smaller stages. They would be front and center, in direct control of larger events that would each sweep the world by storm.

To understand what has come to pass since I shared these words, as well as what is still yet to come, we need to understand the horsemen.

> And I saw when the Lamb opened one of the seals, and I heard, as it were the noise of thunder, one of the four beasts saying, Come and see. And I saw, and behold a white horse: and he that sat on him had a bow; and a crown was given unto him: and he went forth conquering, and to conquer.
>
> —Revelation 6:1–2, kjv

White is normally associated with the Lamb of God, our Lord and Savior. However, I have long believed that this is not Jesus Christ returning for the church. I am convinced that this is none other than the antichrist spirit. I believe this for several reasons. First, we never see the riders dismount in Scripture. We see the horsemen unleashed one by one, each given a directive by the Lord to perform a specific task. Therefore, this rider cannot be the "abomination of desolation" prophesied in Daniel 9 and 11 and Matthew 24. Nor can this be the beast (Antichrist) that rises out of the sea and unites with the false prophet from Revelation 13. This is, in fact, the spirit of the Antichrist who was released to prepare the world for the greatest enemy the church shall ever know.

This rider, however, has one of the most incredible possessions of all the horsemen: a bow. Throughout history, literature, and mythology, we usually see the simple weapon paired with familiar ammunition. We read, and we almost always say, "bow and arrows." Note that arrows aren't mentioned here. The rider has a useless weapon, yet his mission is to conquer, and he is successful. How is this possible? Unlike with modern firearms, you can instantly tell by looking at the bow that it is a harmless instrument without its sharp arrows. I attest that the rider's true power, in fact, lies in his appearance.

Look at how he is presented in the scripture. The rider sits on a white horse, the color commonly associated with the purity and majesty of our Lord Jesus Christ. On his head is a crown, signifying that the rider has the highest of authorities. And he carries a bow but not arrows. This rider has the appearance of a conqueror, and with that image he subjugates those he encounters.

Many scriptures in both the Old and New Testaments warn that there will be a great deception. Jesus mentions deception three times in the Olivet Discourse of Matthew 24. It is His first warning in verse 4. He mentions it again in association with "false prophets" in verse 11—and a final time in verse 24, along with "false christs"! With each mention, Jesus ramps up the intensity of the warning. The deceptions will be so convincing, according to verse 24, that Jesus declares it will be "possible to deceive the elect," those who are already committed entirely to Jesus!

Is this really possible? How does one deceive another? One must present a false appearance and show an item as something else. Have you ever played a trick on a friend or loved one? Did that involve deception? I'm reminded of the classic cookie tin trick from my childhood. You would hand a friend a simple tin can and try not to snicker when they pulled away the lid, only to be surprised by spring-loaded snakes as they shot out of the can and into your friend's face. This harmless trick is accomplished with just a small reliance on deception. However, the rider on the white horse now employs a deception on a much larger scale. His deception begins with concealment, or twisting, of truth and replacing that truth with a lie so real it begs to be believed.

This deception has been at work for the past two decades, and we are just now starting to see the strength of that deception. I told my television audience that night, on New Year's Eve 2019, that this rider's true function was to start a War on Words.

A War on Words?

Would you not agree that today there is a war on both words and principles? America is now seeing the greatest War on Words that it has ever seen. Political correctness has twisted popular phrases and idioms. We are told to be extremely careful what we say to avoid offending even one person in a crowd of thousands. Have we not seen a single phrase, or sometimes even a single word or action, plucked out of context and spun into a completely different and falsified narrative? This has happened to me far more times than I dare to count.

America is firmly entrenched in the middle of a culture war, and its battleground isn't in the public squares. It isn't in the riots that rippled through the country in the summer of 2020. The war is being played out in front of our eyes through media platforms. Social media, television, news outlets, radio, music, and movies have been slowly changing how we speak and how we interact with one another. This movement has a label we are now all too familiar with: cancel culture. This movement has sought to relabel all good as evil and vice versa.

Consider movies and television for a moment. I remember watching *I Love Lucy* in the fifties. It was taboo then for an on-screen husband and wife to share the same bed, so Ricky and Lucy had two twin beds in their bedroom, one for each of them. If both of them would have entered the same bed, the viewers would have been indignant. Now we watch teenagers casually kiss and share a bed on many programs, and not just online. These are casually played on broadcast television in prime time in front of large audiences. Many music videos have become sexually charged, and profanity continues to run rampant in mass media. On the internet, where content is far less regulated, sex and violence are present in exponential factors, with each new show pushing the boundaries further. These are just a few examples of how the war on principles has eroded our generation.

Aside from principles, the War on Words continues to rage. Its battleground can't be found on regular terrain. In fact, many of you carry this battleground on the phones you keep in your pockets or purses, and just as many of you actively participate in it as frontline soldiers. This satanic warfare, this antichrist spirit, is rocking America. Share an opinion on social media, for example. You can have both supporters and detractors writing responses within seconds from strangers and also those you know and love. I have watched people I love staring at their phones and computers for hours and hours, participating in these heated debates. At the very end they walk away neither defeated nor victorious but exhausted and frayed. The war never ends. It just moves to the next post in the line and the next one after that.

But the end result is still achieved. Anxiety and frustration fester and grow, and a person's desperation intensifies. Desperate people rarely make the right decision and will rush headfirst into a crisis that often requires careful planning. Desperate people, I have learned, are easily manipulated and easily convinced. It is this group of people who will fall the hardest for deceiving spirits. Again, Jesus says:

> And Jesus answered and said unto them, Take heed that no man deceive you. For many shall come in my name, saying, I am Christ; and shall deceive many.
> —Matthew 24:4–5, KJV

See that? Jesus didn't just warn of deception; He *promised* that it would happen. How could someone come in the name of Christ and deceive so many people? Those who do not present a true image of Christ only enable the antichrist spirit to perform its masterful work on society. Those who seek signs and miracles more than the Word of God and His voice will be easily led astray (Matt. 24:24)!

Those who either reject the church or are neglected by the church will look to fill their hearts with promises from another. Once allegiances are sworn, it is easy for them to do the will of their master, whether it is the love of money, to persecute the church for its "false" beliefs and doctrine, or to even further extend the range of the great deception. Just look at how many now fight daily for ungodly causes. Paul warned us in 2 Thessalonians 2:3 that "a falling away" would happen. We are living that verse right now!

THE SECOND HORSE

If the first rider could perform so much damage on its own, what could be next? Let's look now to the next horse:

> And when he had opened the second seal, I heard the second beast say, Come and see. And there went out another horse that was red: and power was given to him that sat thereon to take peace from the earth, and that they should kill one another: and there was given unto him a great sword.
>
> —REVELATION 6:3–4, KJV

Oh my lands! Does this not sound like what we're witnessing around the world and in our nation right now? It might be early in the Book of Revelation, but this is most certainly where we are.

Our first rider had a useless bow, and now the second rider is an absolute contrast, carrying a powerful and useful weapon of warfare. Let's break this down for a few moments so we can properly understand it.

If the first horse is a conqueror, then the second horse is a thief. Specifically, he has the power to remove peace from the earth. Human history is rife with conflict: crusades, world wars, smaller wars, and so on. But there is more to this translation than meets the eye. The word *peace* is the Greek word εἰρήνη, or *eiréné*, and emphasizes a wholeness of well-being, an individual's or a nation's ability to prosper.[2] In essence this horse is here to remove peace, prosperity, and every bit of security from the earth. In their absence the earth's inhabitants will turn on one another and kill one another.

The second horse, therefore, brings both war and terrorism to the world. As I told the congregation on December 31, 2019, "This is war in the streets."[3] It is no longer the type of war and open conflict we've once known. Gone are the days of world wars and an armed conflict between nations, at least in exclusivity. Let's look to the Word of God for clarification:

> For nation shall rise against nation, and kingdom against
> kingdom.
> —Matthew 24:7, kjv

Nations and kingdoms? The repetition in this scripture isn't intentional; in fact, it doesn't even exist. What we're reading here is nothing more than a poor translation. The word *nation* in the original Greek is ἔθνος, or *ethnos*, and is defined as ethnic groups.[4] A proper translation of Matthew 24:7 then is "For *ethnic* group shall rise against *ethnic* group, and kingdom against kingdom."

Racism shall rise, and it has already risen. We saw in 2020 an immeasurable rise in racism, fueled by terrible tragedies that resulted in the deaths of many innocent people. Individuals have been slain just for the color of their skin. Police officers were slain not for their actions but just for wearing the uniform. Protests haven't erupted only in the streets of America; they've sprung up in nations around the world too.

These actions on their own are appalling. But when coupled with the white horse and those it has deceived and manipulated, this erupts in further violence and bloodshed. Not every riot in 2020 was violent, and not every protest was destructive. Still, innocent lives were lost and others destroyed by those blinded by this War on Words and racial actions. And yes, this movement was hijacked by agencies looking to advance their agendas. In doing so, those who have been previously hurt are pressed deeper into their deceptions and misunderstandings. If the church cannot answer this terrible cry, the Antichrist will gladly use this to his advantage, take the stage, and implement his agenda. Even now many overarching political and public actions are racially driven, and many continue to harm the very same groups they are trying to help.

As we continue into this next decade, I believe that not only will the war in our streets intensify, but it will be lauded from the sidelines by those with the ability to influence and deceive. As proof I point to social media posts from Hollywood and political elites, which have called for canceling and destroying those who advocate for the church and conservative groups, as well as duly appointed members of the Supreme Court and the forty-fifth president of the United States—not to mention many former Founding Fathers and leaders of America![5]

THE THIRD HORSE

If the first two horses were connected to the many riots that are shaking America and the world, what could the third horse be? More importantly, how is it affecting us now? Let's take a look:

> And when he had opened the third seal, I heard the third beast say, Come and see. And I beheld, and lo a black horse; and he that sat on him had a pair of balances in his hand. And I heard a voice in the midst of the four beasts say, A measure of wheat for a penny, and three measures of barley for a penny; and see thou hurt not the oil and the wine.
>
> —REVELATION 6:5–6, KJV

I have often taught that this verse is connected to inflation and famine. In fact, I usually teach this passage through another translation for better clarity. Here it is in the New International Version (emphasis added):

> Then I heard what sounded like a voice among the four living creatures, saying, "Two pounds of wheat for *a day's wages*, and six pounds of barley for *a day's wages*, and do not damage the oil and the wine!"

A day's wages? Revelation is warning us that the third, black horse will ramp up inflation metrics so much that a day's pay will only buy one or two ingredients. Is this because the currency has become so devalued, or is it because food itself has become so scarce that an individual can access only certain food items? Recently both our economy and our ability to produce and distribute food have been flipped upside down.

In the years leading up to 2021, the Food and Agriculture Organization of the United Nations reported that 653 million people did not have enough food to eat in 2017. Just one year later that number rose to almost 678 million and then in 2019 to almost 688 million, nearly 9 percent of the world's population.[6] Matthew 24:7 foretells that "there will be famines," which is more than just people not getting enough food. It's a complete lack of food. The New Century Version of the same scripture says that "there will be...no food for people to eat."

In April 2020 the World Food Programme executive director, David Beasley, warned the UN Security Council that the world would "be facing multiple famines of biblical proportions." He informed it that of the hundreds of millions of people who currently go to bed hungry each night, 135 million are facing crisis levels of hunger, with that number expected to increase to 265 million by the end of 2020 because of the COVID pandemic.[7] Already a plague of locusts—the worst in recent history—had ravaged multiple farms in Africa, and other farms across the world saw massive amounts of crops die due to drastically changing weather patterns.[8]

Natural disasters are not the only cause of the lack of food throughout the world. In April 2020, America saw a record-high unemployment rate of 14.7 percent as businesses laid off employees or even shuttered their doors due to COVID-19 and governmental directives.[9] Food quickly disappeared from grocery store shelves, leaving vital staples such as meat and produce in short supply. Many families lamented that they could not source enough food to feed their families, much less pay for it.

Famine may be on the rise, but I honestly believe that there is more to this rider than meets the eye. Let's take a closer look at Revelation 6:5 and the tool the rider is carrying. Our first rider had a powerless bow, and our second rider a powerful sword. Our third rider has a pair of scales. The Greek word here is interesting. It is ζυγός, or *zygos*.[10] While it is translated here as a pair of scales, it also has a different usage. This word appears five other times in the New Testament, two of them in a commonly quoted Scripture passage. I once commissioned the great Joseph Wallace King to immortalize this passage in a painting:

> Come unto me, all ye that labour and are heavy laden, and I will give you rest. Take my yoke upon you, and learn of me; for I am meek and lowly in heart: and ye shall find rest unto your souls. For my yoke is easy, and my burden is light.
>
> —MATTHEW 11:28–30, KJV

I can hear what you're saying: "Matthew 11 and Revelation 6 have no possible connection. I don't see anything about scales or balance!" This is why I always urge you to dig deep into the Word using the many tools scholars have provided to us over the centuries. You must always "study to show yourself approved" (2 Tim. 2:15)! The Greek word for "pair of balances" and "yoke" is the same. Paul uses *zygos* in both Galatians 5:1 and 1 Timothy 6:1 to describe being in slavery, the yoke of bondage. Revelation 6:5 is the only time *zygos* is used to describe a pair of scales.

Therefore, the third horse has the power to take what the white horse has conquered and place them into bondage. We in America don't have to look far to see a modern example of this. For example, in the early years of coal mining, companies would establish entire towns around a mine. Its employees were often not paid in regular currency but rather in scrips, which could be redeemed in stores owned by the employer for goods and services. The company controlled the mine, the stores, and the goods and groceries available to the miners and their families. They even owned the homes the miners lived in. It, therefore, commanded the people. Such acts were practiced as recently as 2008, when the Mexican subsidiary of Walmart was forced to stop paying its employees with vouchers that could only be used in its stores.[11]

What would America look like if the government were the sole provider of income and goods, especially through socialistic models that many politicians campaign for? What if you became wholly dependent on what was in food banks or through what the government would allow stores to sell to their customers? Does this third rider give us more insight into the future mark of the beast? I believe this rider gives us a little insight into what socialism, and possibly even this "great reset" many are pushing upon the world, could bring to America. I also believe that without the prayers of the saints, we are teetering on the edge of a massive economic collapse in America, which could happen in the next few years.

THE FOURTH HORSE

Three horses are riding, each using their charges to twist our culture and society to prepare for the next stage of Revelation. There is still yet one horse, and its rider brings a major power to the table:

> And when he had opened the fourth seal, I heard the voice of the fourth beast say, Come and see. And I looked, and behold a pale horse: and his name that sat on him was Death, and Hell followed with him. And power was given unto them over the fourth part of the earth, to kill with sword, and with hunger, and with death, and with the beasts of the earth.
>
> —REVELATION 6:7–8, KJV

Our final rider has a name. The Greek word here is θάνατος, *thanatos*, and it is aptly translated as Death.[12] There is no mystery with this horse and its rider. There is no need for speculation or inference. Where this horse rides, death will follow in its wake. Most importantly, one-quarter of the world is given to this horse, unlike the unspecified realms granted to the other horsemen. Death will come by warfare (much like the rider on the red horse), by famine (much like the rider on the black horse), and by Death himself.

The Greek word for *death* here is also translated elsewhere as "plague" or "pestilence."[13] This is absolutely in line with Matthew 24:7, as it follows the order of how these horsemen are released. There, Jesus also confirmed to His disciples that there would be pestilences.

I have always pondered, however, how this rider would use the beasts of the earth. This small portion of Scripture brought mystery to this straightforward verse. As I began to study and look at world events, I began to understand the connection between death, disease, and the earth's beasts.

Many diseases, such as cancer and autoimmune syndromes, can be linked to chemicals used to produce and cultivate the air, food, and drink we ingest throughout our lives. Others have come from improper, unorthodox, and often unknowing interactions with animals. HIV, for example, has been connected to monkeys.[14] Ebola virus, bovine spongiform encephalopathy (mad cow disease), H5N1 and H1N1 (avian and swine influenzas), and even SARS have all originated from animals.

Can a disease truly wreak such havoc? From 1347 to 1351, the bubonic plague (black death) made its way around the known world. The exact death count is still unknown. It's estimated that 30 to 60 percent of Europe's population alone perished under this plague.[15] To this day the plague hasn't been eradicated and occasionally resurfaces throughout the world. Two outbreaks occurred in the 1600s, and another in the 1800s![16] The black death appeared again recently, this time striking Madagascar near the end of 2017, with the World Health Organization reporting over three hundred cases of bubonic plague and close to two thousand cases of other forms of the plague.[17]

Could there be a connection between this rider and now? On December 31, 2019, unbeknownst to me and many others, the World Health Organization was alerted to multiple cases of an unfamiliar pneumonia outbreak in Wuhan, China.[18] At the time, the disease remained managed and contained, or so China thought. China would not lock down Wuhan and the neighboring Hubei province until January 23, 2020.[19] By that time, the disease had already left Wuhan, traveling by person to the major cities, being transmitted to locals and travelers, being carried by plane to other countries, and sprouting new cases of this unfamiliar strain worldwide.

Suffice it to say, this event quickly transformed into a global pandemic. Entire nations closed their borders and their businesses and forced billions to stay at home throughout the crisis. In December 2019 the American economy was the best it had been in a long time, but its fifty-year record-low unemployment rate of 3.5 percent skyrocketed to over 14 percent.[20] Hundreds of food-processing plants across the country were shuttered for months, and the supply lines themselves were disrupted.[21]

The world was stunned by what had transpired, but I was not. Several years ago I discovered what I believe to be one of the greatest books I've ever read: *The Great Influenza* by John M. Barry. This book is an excellent and detailed account of the 1918 Spanish influenza, including the origins of the disease, the fight to corral it, public and military officials' responses, and many excellent lessons for the world to learn.

And some of these lessons have been learned.

When I first read this book, I was dumbfounded with how the nations of the world and their leaders had acted throughout the most devastating pandemic of the industrial age. The Spanish influenza spread like wildfire throughout the world over eighteen months. Many dispute the final death toll, but Barry suggests that the number may have been as high as one hundred million people worldwide. Infection was spread through proximity to one another and person-to-person contact. Even when families locked themselves in their homes, the mailman carried the disease to the mailbox. Public events continued to be held despite the threat of an outbreak. Even when those in attendance started to get sick and die, it took officials weeks, or even months, to decide to postpone or even cancel public gatherings.[22]

For more than a decade I frequently warned my viewers that the only way to avoid a coming plague was to be prepared to lock themselves in their homes and avoid human contact with those who did not live under their roofs. Several who watched my program and heard me say this began to ridicule me for recommending such extreme measures. I was accused of instilling fear into my viewers!

But when COVID-19 struck, governments worldwide, including the United States, told their citizens to do exactly what I had been recommending for more than a decade! Individuals and families were urged, and some even forced, to stay home. Businesses deemed nonessential were closed. Those who could transition their employees into telecommuting solutions managed to stay afloat; those who couldn't were forced to shut down. Many wound up filing for bankruptcy. Unemployment didn't just rise; it shot up faster than a Saturn V rocket.

UNITED THEY RIDE

I stood in front of my congregation members on the night of December 31, 2019, and declared to them, "The four horsemen are a worldwide event."[23] I added, "God's judgment is coming, and it's coming around the world."[24] Not since the last world war have we seen as major an event as the COVID-19 pandemic that has swept our world in such a disruptive manner. Under its banner all four horsemen are galloping, rampaging throughout the earth without interference. Even now they continue to rampage, destroying whole industries and crippling governments, all while laying the foundation for the final stage of Revelation.

This pandemic, brought on by the pale horse, confined millions, if not billions, of people to their homes for months on end. As I pen this chapter, several million people still refuse or are unable to leave their homes. Many millions are still unemployed, unable to find work due to bankrupted industries. As 2020 progressed, many Americans had nowhere to go and all the time in the world to stare at televisions and social media and be subjected to the deception wrought by the white horse. The War on Words was ignited and inflamed, directly targeting religious and conservative groups alike, including President Trump, ultimately resulting in the eviction and banning of our president and other groups from these platforms.

Under the white horse's deception and with nowhere to go, tensions flared and desperation grew. The red horse stepped in, feeding these tensions until they sparked real-life warfare and threw opposing ideologies at each other, resulting in violence, bloodshed, and destruction. Mental health problems, drug abuse, and domestic violence quickly rose to new levels.[25]

Thanks to the black horse, supply lines were disrupted, jobs were lost, and many individuals and businesses depended on the government to survive. Food itself became scarce. In some cases, food and supplies became unaffordable or even unavailable. Millions drove to food banks in their nice minivans, SUVs, and sports cars to get food to feed themselves and their families.[26]

The four horsemen are riding together, acting in complete unity and cooperation. Although they continue to dominate the landscape, they are only the opening scene in this final act.

I delivered several more words from the Lord that night. There was so much to unpack and share from that New Year's Eve night that we could be here for several more chapters. I will be presenting these words to you, along with updates on each of them from what happened during 2020. But first, we are about to go on a journey through the valley of the shadow of death.

That night, December 31, 2019, after I had shared my message and Lance Wallnau had delivered his urgent warning to the church to rise and act, we prayed for guidance in 2020, and we repented for America and its departure from its foundation. I returned home and collapsed in my bed. While I hoped rest and relief were near, I had no idea that 2020 was about to take off like a roller coaster with wild highs, steep lows, and a turbulent track.

I wish I could say that I was talking about the world in general, but the personal cost I would soon bear would be the last thing I expected.

CHAPTER 3

THE CELEBRATION BEFORE THE STORM

THE YEAR 2020 had begun just like any year, with little fanfare besides the celebrations around the world. Even though I had delivered several words of warning, as instructed by God, I had a good reason for a moment of celebration before 2020 would show us what it planned to do. On January 2, I would be turning eighty years old.

I felt as though I had lived multiple lifetimes in a short window. Many people are lucky to have one or two careers in their life; I have lost count of how many I have had. I grew up in an Assemblies of God church where my family was always involved. I went to college and then on the road as a traveling evangelist. For eight years I planted my feet in Portsmouth, Virginia, to stand alongside CBN and help found Christian television. I then returned to the road to help other ministries, such as TBN, plant their networks before landing in Charlotte, North Carolina, to launch the PTL Television Network and Heritage USA.

After more than two decades of fruitful living and building one of the largest television ministries in the world, I lived through the seven most difficult years of my life, when I watched my dreams, my ministry, and even my family get snatched away from me. After prison I wandered in a lonely wilderness until God began to restore me like Job, bringing me my wife, Lori, at the LA Dream Center and many wonderful children after our move to Camp of Hope in Florida. And finally, He allowed me to be restored in my calling back to television after moving to Branson,

Missouri, and then to our seven-hundred-acre campus of Morningside USA.

Though I have lived a turbulent life, I find myself extremely thankful. I learned in prison that my God is not just the God on the mountaintop but also the God of the deepest valleys. The Bible declares that God is with us even in "the valley of the shadow of death" (Ps. 23:4). I have often asked God how He can continue to use a man such as me. His answer has always been a simple one. "It's because you keep saying yes to Me." This is why I believed I could celebrate turning eighty. And my family absolutely agreed.

No matter how tired I was, I was absolutely looking forward to this day. Much of my journey after prison had been a lonely one. Even though I enjoyed traveling the world again to share the gospel and the sobering messages I had been given by the Lord, I could not escape my loneliness. While I was in prison, my eldest children had begun lives of their own, and it was not my place to join them in their new journeys. The family members God brought to me didn't just sustain me; they all reenergized me in ways I never thought possible. This is why my eight-ieth birthday was not just a celebration for me; it was a way for us all to collectively rejoice in what the Lord had done in our lives.

I intended to enjoy the day as much as I could. My excitement had reached peak levels, and I wanted to be careful not to burn myself out. It was hard to believe that just two nights before, Morningside had hosted a powerful prophetic night on New Year's Eve with sobering words, intense prayer, and personal ministry. You couldn't tell just from looking at our staff and volunteers. Everyone was excited, and that excitement was infectious. I could only hope I had the strength to see the day through.

Little did I know at the time that this celebration would be a moment of calm before the gigantic storms 2020 would soon bring upon our ministry and the world. Each member of our family would play a part not just in standing beside the ministry through the crisis to come but in saving my own life.

IT'S A CELEBRATION

Hosting the day's festivities was my longtime friend and adopted son, Mondo De La Vega. Before Mondo and I met at the Los Angeles Dream Center, he'd been a legal immigrant from Central America who had fallen into the wrong crowd by joining the infamous 18th Street Gang. And like many gang members, Mondo found himself in jail. Mondo eventually was confronted with a major life decision. Either he would continue in the gangster life and face certain violent death, or he could leave it all behind for something greater.

Saved by grace, Mondo began to travel the world, sharing what Jesus had done for him. When he was home, he plugged in to the Los Angeles Dream Center, eager to serve in whatever capacity Pastors Tommy and Matthew Barnett needed him. One day he was assigned to pick someone up from the airport, and that someone just happened to be a certain Jim Bakker. I had been in LA at the time for a speaking engagement, and I fell in love with the Dream Center. At this point in my life, I was as close to being a recluse as I would ever get, and I was prepared to spend the rest of my life in the background of the Dream Center, just serving the people.

Mondo was the first person to try to befriend me. He was also one of the first people to see me as I was, a broken man in need of restoration. Mondo made it his mission not to let me get lost in the shuffle or wallow in self-pity. For all this and more I am eternally grateful that the Lord brought Mondo into my life. Words cannot express my thankfulness. Mondo's faithfulness and resourcefulness throughout our days in Los Angeles prompted me to award him with the most endearing name that I learned in prison, Road Dawg. A road dawg is someone who is the most trusted on the road, even closer than a best friend.

My road dawg, Mondo, has stood by my side through it all, from my marriage to Lori to multiple moves around the country, and he is still with me in Branson at Morningside. The Lord has rewarded his faithfulness as well, through marriage to Beth and through their wonderful twins, Mila and Mateo. Mondo now serves as cohost of *The Jim Bakker Show* and executive in charge of television production.

Sharing hosting duties alongside Mondo was my beautiful wife, Lori.

Our story did not actually begin in that back alley at the Los Angeles Dream Center that we always talk about. In fact, it began three years before that famous back-alley meeting. It was in 1995 at Phoenix First Assembly during what became one of the most historic nights in church history. That night, Pastor Tommy Barnett was hosting the church's annual Pastor's School to honor all the different ministries the church supported. Pastor Barnett would have people give testimony after testimony about how Jesus transformed their lives, thanks to these ministries. I was there that night to hear my son Jamie Charles give his testimony. Shortly before I heard my son, I saw Lori Graham. She was onstage with a postabortion ministry, and she shared her love for Jesus and how He had worked in her life. For me, it was love at first sight. But we would not officially meet until 1998.

Once we met, we married within seven weeks. The full story is too great to try to condense, so I encourage you to read her book, *More Than I Could Ever Ask*. We both say we never had a honeymoon since we immediately entered a joint circuit, traveling the globe, going from pulpit to pulpit. We both would share our testimonies of love and restoration wherever we went. But years before we met, Lori was already unknowingly laying the groundwork for our future together.

While Lori attended Phoenix First Assembly, she got herself involved in every ministry she could, including a ministry school called Master's Commission. Lori became known as the Church Lady among those in Phoenix's inner city, doing her best to bring anyone and everyone to church. She grew close with a woman named Margie, a single mother on welfare with many children. Lori had such a profound impact on Margie and her life, especially during a particularly rough pregnancy. When Margie went into labor, she wanted only one person in the delivery room with her. "Get me the Church Lady!" she told everyone. Lori was quickly brought to Margie's side, and soon Margie had a beautiful baby girl in her arms. Lori quickly told Margie how lovely her daughter was and asked Margie what she planned to name her. Margie answered, "I want to name her Lori. I don't ever want to forget what you've done for me and my family."[1]

Their close relationship continued after Lori and I were married. It was strong enough that Lori convinced Margie and her family to join us across the country at Camp of Hope in Florida. The waters were first tested with two of Margie's daughters, Lori (whom we now call Little Lori, or Lil' for short) and her older sister, Maricela.

Maricela, then eleven, and Lil' Lori, ten, were flown from Phoenix to Florida shortly before Christmas. Neither girl knew what to expect. A grand time began as Lori and I, along with Lori's mother, Char Graham, treated the girls to a perfect Christmas. We took them to the nearby beach, where Maricela and Lori got their first glimpse of an ocean. Maricela's nickname is Nena, so we had a meal at a place named Nena's Seafood Restaurant. We showered the girls with gifts, bought them new outfits, and shared our favorite Christmas traditions. Shortly after Christmas, we would send both girls back to Phoenix.

A few months later, Margie and several of her children joined us in Camp of Hope, arriving from Phoenix via a bus. Lori and I welcomed them with open arms, got them settled into the camp, and then hit the road to travel to a few different churches. When we returned, Margie had her hands full and was looking to ease the load somewhere. She called and asked if Lori could take her granddaughter Marie for a couple of nights. The alternative was to send her back to Phoenix, which Lori and I didn't want. Lori immediately picked up Marie and brought her over to spend the night. Marie never left and would become the first of several children we'd adopt from Phoenix.

Meanwhile, it was Margie and the children's first real plunge into the ministry. Not only did my wife and I have a schedule to keep at Camp of Hope, but there was also a lot of fixing up to do at the run-down camp. When we weren't traveling or making repairs, we held Bible studies. This was too much for Margie, but she knew it was the life she wanted for her children. Margie talked with Lori and me, and overnight we found ourselves in our new role as parents to many children.

Some would come and go while we were in Florida. Others stayed with us until they were ready to begin adult lives of their own. We worked hard to find everyone a home, even after we moved from Camp of Hope to our new home in Branson, Missouri. Every child who came through our door was able to find a home and start a new life.

Maricela followed in Lori's footsteps and became the first of our children to attend ministry school, a chapter of Master's Commission in Fort Myers under the leadership of my dear friend Pastor Dan Betzer. After two years there, she graduated and moved back home to help start our media training program and work as a producer on my show. I learned quite quickly that she had a mind for business, able to see the big picture and how to get us there one step at a time. Maricela is now the chief operating officer of our ministry, overseeing the ministry's business operations. She and her husband, John, have two wonderful children, Jackson and Natalie.

Lil' Lori also continues to stand by Lori and me at Morningside. She spent time as a producer of the show, learning the ins and outs of television before being appointed into executive management. Lil' Lori is incredibly gifted, able to think of things that we need before Lori, I, or any other member of the team can, even down to the smallest detail. She and her husband, Jasper, have two beautiful daughters, Olivia and Kate.

Marie has helped us with several different aspects of the ministry, from producing the show to helping behind the scenes and even cohosting various programs. She and her husband, Orion, have a lively son, Grayson.

Maricela, Lil' Lori, and Marie were all on hand, along with their children, standing beside Mondo, Lori, and me onstage for my eightieth birthday celebration. We had a wonderful time, but there were still a few surprises in store for me.

MORE AND MORE

In the days before my birthday Mondo had asked me whom I wanted to see at my party the most. I didn't hesitate and immediately answered, "Vestal Goodman." This answer showed my family my longing for simpler, happier times. Vestal and her husband, Howard, were always by my side throughout our days at Heritage. She would always help take care of Tammy Sue and Jamie Charles, even going so far as to protect them from the paparazzi and reporters when our world fell apart.

I knew having Vestal at my celebration was an impossible request, as she had graduated to heaven in 2003. So you can imagine my surprise when Mondo introduced Vestal Goodman as the opening act at my eightieth birthday celebration! At first, I didn't know what to think, and I suppose I expected some footage of her to roll on the monitors. But when I heard the voice coming from the staircase behind me, I couldn't stop the large smile that appeared on my face as I saw Tammy Sue, dressed exactly like my old friend, walking down the stairs and performing a medley of Vestal's songs. Even Tammy Sue's hair was on point, mirroring Vestal's iconic look!

My heart was thrilled to see my eldest daughter doing what she loved. Tammy Sue's voice continues to be incredible every day. There isn't a day that goes by that I can't hear my daughter sing an uplifting hymn or powerful song in my head.

In 2012 my daughter Tammy Sue was just coming out of a period of sadness. She hadn't performed much in public since her mother passed away in 2007, and Tammy Sue was ready to return to what she loved most, and that was singing. Most importantly, she wanted it to be a surprise. She put a plan in motion with several members of our staff and family so she could secretly fly out to Morningside. Her return performance was planned very carefully, bringing just enough staff members in on the surprise. Being unaware of this grand surprise, I had been taping for more than two hours with another guest and not giving the show a single chance to go to music. After multiple cues from our producer, I finally relented and went to a song, only to be shocked and amazed when I heard her voice singing from backstage. I'd honestly thought I would never share the stage with her again. The experience brought me to tears, and I wept throughout her entire performance. Without a doubt, it was one of the highlights of my life to have her singing by my side once more. Tammy Sue stayed with us at Morningside all that week. Shortly after, she decided to move from North Carolina to be near us at Morningside.

On my birthday Tammy Sue was joined by her two children, James and Jonathan. I have always had a special relationship with both of my eldest grandchildren. James was born shortly before I began my time in prison. I had few possessions throughout my five years behind bars, but the most precious of them all was a photo of my grandson James. He was one of the first students in our media training school when we first launched it in 2009. He soon graduated into a staff role as one of our top cameramen before ultimately moving back to North Carolina to be with his immediate family.

Jonathan had married Christy, whom I was now getting to meet for the first time. Their birthday present to me would be one I would never forget. Christy was visibly pregnant with their son, Jett, who would be my very first great-grandchild! This was such an exciting announcement that I could not help myself from shouting in front of the cameras.

Several beloved family members could not attend the day of celebration and restoration, including my eldest son, Jamie Charles. Jamie never gave up on me while I was in prison, even though most of the church had given up on both of us. He struggled with it all, seeing his family torn apart and his childhood stolen from him. Though Jamie's and my beliefs do not fully overlap, we still share a tremendous relationship, and we never pass up the chance to talk to each other. Although Jamie could not attend my birthday party, he and his children did surprise me just a few days before, on Christmas, when he walked into my home for the holidays. It is always a joy to embrace my son.

My youngest son, Ricky, wasn't able to attend my birthday either. Ricky was one of our family's last additions after we moved to Florida and Camp of Hope. Lori had flown to Phoenix to get some paperwork for our other adopted children. After arriving, she was greeted on the doorstep by four-year-old Ricky and his younger sister, Jenny, who was just a year old. While Lori was collecting what she needed in Phoenix, she was asked if she could take two more kids with her, Ricky and Jenny. Lori's heart was to say yes, but she wouldn't do it without talking to me first over the phone. I too declared, "Yes!" A few short hours later, I met Lori at a Florida airport with two more children.

It was a joy to watch Ricky grow into a man and develop an unquenchable hunger for the Lord. I still believe the Lord is preparing Ricky for a key position at Morningside. He graduated from Christ for the Nations Institute about a year before answering the call to enlist in the US Army. As tough as it was to accept this decision, I knew Ricky was following the Lord, and I am grateful to see the man he has become while in the service.

Ricky's baby sister, Jenny, now a fully grown woman and mother, was able to come to my birthday celebration too. When Lori first returned from Phoenix with Ricky and Jenny, she was severely dehydrated. Our family doctor, Dr. Dawn Frost, helped nurse my wife back to health and became introduced to our rapidly growing family as a result. In fact, she became part of our family.

One day, as Dawn connected a dehydrated Lori to an IV, she couldn't help but notice young Jenny in the crib with a headful of lice. The rest of the kids and I were leading an outreach at Camp of Hope, and Lori was in no condition to take care of a young baby alone. With permission, Dawn took Jenny to her home for the evening and began to care for her. All the while, Dawn's heart was broken. Previously, Dawn had given birth to a little girl, who was born without kidneys. She did not survive for long. Caring for Jenny brought a flood of emotions to Dawn, who was now experiencing motherhood for the first time. We soon discovered that Jenny had been born on the exact day and year Dawn's daughter had passed away. In short, Dawn and her husband decided to adopt Jenny. Lori and I became like second parents to Jenny, even though she calls us Uncle Jim and Aunt Lori.

I was overwhelmed with all the love from Lori and my sister, cousins, children, and grandchildren that day. The Book of Proverbs declares that "grandchildren are the crown of old men, and the glory of children are their fathers" (17:6). I count myself blessed beyond measure for my family. I do not see a distinction between natural and adopted children; I only see love. The Lord had grafted us all together as a testimony and witness to His perfect will. As I stood on that stage with my family, I rejoiced unto the Lord, thanking Him for every memory and for restoring my soul.

What we would soon find, however, was that our collective faith was about to be put to the ultimate test.

CHAPTER 4

THE CRISIS BEGINS

THE YEAR 2020 began with a roaring start. Not only had I shared one of the most sobering messages with the local congregation and national television audience, but we also brought in 2020 with a bang. We held a midnight prayer service in our newly constructed Prayer Mountain Chapel, where we lifted our nation, our leaders, and one another in prayer and repentance. I also celebrated my eightieth birthday with much of my family and friends, including people I had not been able to see for several years. In my moments of weakness I found these events had brought me a breath of fresh air, even if it was just for a moment. The world, however, kept moving all around us.

By early January 2020 the eyes of the world had not yet turned their full attention to China. When our research team members came into the office on Monday, January 20, an Associated Press headline flashed on their screens: "China Reports 2nd Death From Virus Behind Pneumonia Outbreak."[1] At this point our team began to research and follow the developing outbreak. Our television broadcasts, however, would not yet report on this virus. While we maintain a calling to share world news on our broadcast and connect it to Revelation events, we also wanted to give the story a couple of days to develop to see if this event was worth reporting to our viewers. We did, however, start to report this on our website.

The afternoon of January 21, I began to review the material and facts the research team was collecting on this outbreak, and I also noticed that reports were now popping up on major television networks. It was not the first time I had seen a situation like this develop during the winter. The common cold and the flu had already been spreading around the country, as they had in years past. But there was something about this strange pneumonia from China that didn't seem right at the time.

On January 21 our news wire reported China's death toll at six people.[2] The first report we received on January 22 was that the death toll was at nine.[3] By the afternoon, it was at seventeen![4] I had never seen a virus launch so fatally, at least not with my own eyes. However, my memory began to draw parallels between this outbreak and a book I had become familiar with: John M. Barry's *The Great Influenza* and its account of the 1918 Spanish influenza, which he believed claimed the lives of as many as one hundred million people worldwide.[5] I knew I had to get on the air and start reporting on this virus, but I could not.

I previously shared with you how I didn't feel well the day I was supposed to deliver my prophetic word on December 31, 2019. That day, I felt the strength and anointing so strongly that the Lord enabled me to preach for over an hour and a half that evening. But my feelings and my health hadn't changed, and I believe I had gotten worse as January went on. I had been moving nonstop between birthday celebrations, time with long-absent family members, and the taping of extra shows in preparation of our annual sabbatical at the start of the year.

By the end of the month, I didn't have any motivation to leave. It wasn't that I didn't want to. I was just in so much pain that all I wanted to do was lie down, not move, and rest. Unfortunately, we had decided to postpone our sabbatical for a variety of reasons, including the very fact that it just didn't seem right. The prophetic words were weighing heavy on my heart, and I didn't feel the assurance from the Lord that it was appropriate to step away at that time. And I was still exhausted and barely able to continue.

Our usual taping schedule meant that we would tape two days a week for at least two to three hours per day. These tapings would then be divided by our editing department and molded into one-hour shows to be broadcast nationwide through a variety of satellite and cable channels and select local markets that we call our "stations." These stations require our episodes to be delivered several days in advance. In most cases, therefore, when you are watching *The Jim Bakker Show* on television, you are watching something that was taped at least five days beforehand, sometimes longer. That is why our news sometimes feels outdated by the time our programs finally air. Our taping schedule gives us enough material to cover a five-day week. But by January 23 we had enough material to last us on the air until February 11, which was more than two weeks away. Lori and I, along with our staff, agreed that it was time to take a short break.

My children and the team did one more show on January 29, which was live-streamed on our website to share some of the news we hadn't been able to share in the last week or so, including updates on this outbreak, now identified as a coronavirus. This broadcast marked the first occasion we had talked about the novel coronavirus on the air. At that point, China had locked down the Wuhan province and other locations. I believe their efforts were too late, as the CDC had already confirmed the first case within the United States' borders, and other countries, such as Germany, Japan, Vietnam, and Taiwan, were seeing the virus in their hospitals as well. The World Health Organization would finally declare a Public Health Emergency of International Concern on January 30, 2020.[6]

The more I studied this coronavirus and the news reports, the more I realized I was starting to see that this event was connected to what God had shown me in preparation of 2020. This novel coronavirus, still unnamed at that time, was part of the four horsemen's work and the worldwide judgment that was coming. I knew then that we had to make reporting this on the show a priority. And soon the world would be shaken.

PREPARING THE FIRST REPORT

January was coming to a close quickly, and while I was resting, I was working with our producers to prepare our next series of shows. We hadn't booked many guests yet for February, save for a couple of prominent figures coming to promote their new books. They were not prepared to discuss or comment on these worldwide events. It was all still very new to many of us, and we were scrambling just to get on top of the reports.

I've always valued our research staff, but I knew they needed help to dig into the story properly. We reached out to my former head of research and former cohost of seven years, Zach Drew. Zach was one of the first students in our media program at Morningside. The first time I met and spoke with him, I knew the call of God was strong on his life. I was impressed by the hunger Zach had for truth, prophecy, and the Word of God. When he was still a member of our staff, I had given him a copy of my raw Revelation teaching notes, and it was a joy to watch him dig further into the Word and expand on the foundation he had received. As much as I wanted Zach to remain with us at Morningside, God had other plans for him. He had recently started a television ministry of his own in Illinois, and he'd started reporting on the coronavirus outbreak on his show. I needed his help as we started to tackle this coverage, and he graciously agreed to join us at Morningside for a full week of tapings.

But Zach was not a disease expert, much less a virus expert. The one trouble with our studio being located in the middle of the Ozarks is that it is sometimes difficult to find a local expert on short notice. Finding someone with the knowledge to help us understand what the larger medical community is dealing with is an even harder challenge. A staff member mentioned Derek and Sharon Gilbert, our dear friends who live just a few miles away from our studio. We had come to value their professionalism and their innate ability to comment on news and events as they were happening. Sharon, especially, had studied molecular biology at Indiana University before marrying Derek and joining the SkyWatch team as its science and geopolitics adviser. Both Derek and Sharon agreed to join us for a full week at Morningside to study and analyze news reports, which were still coming in.

SILVER SOLUTION

In a previous chapter, I shared that I didn't want to spend time on our broadcasts raising funds when we first returned to television in 2003. We quickly realized that we could not sustain our calling and ministry on television without devoting time and energy to fundraising. I did not want to turn to the same methods that I had practiced back at Heritage. We instead focused on what our calling was: to sound the alarm and help people prepare for the days ahead. Every product we brought to our broadcast was strategically selected as we felt God was leading us. And each product had to align with our mission. We started to offer products such as Bibles, books, CDs, and DVDs to equip our viewers with the spiritual tools they would need to prepare for the last days. Over the next few years, we would expand these efforts to include items for physical preparedness, such as backpacks, flashlights, radios, generators, and food. Our mission expanded to include teaching people how to be healthy in mind, body, soul, and spirit, knowing that our bodies are temples for the Holy Spirit and must be treated accordingly (1 Cor. 6:19–20). To accomplish this, we began to bring health supplements, materials, and teachers to our program.

All fundraising efforts would be balanced with ministry and biblical teaching in the forefront. Because we have a daily need to meet our budget, we have to consider what we will do for fundraising in every program. If we have an author, our featured product that day will be that author's latest book. Sometimes we will mention other products, and those decisions are based on various factors, including the season, situation, or topic. This was February, and it was during the annual cold-and-flu season, which began back in mid-fall when the temperatures started to drop. And just as in all seasons throughout the year, we have a particular set of products that we rely on for fundraising. The first quarter of each year, especially, we tend to focus on products that can help our viewers live healthy lives.

Over the years, we had partnered with multiple organizations to bring some of the best and most innovative health supplements available to our broadcast. Many of these products have become highly valued by our television audience, as well as our family and staff. Among these products was something we had considered to be one of our staples: Silver Solution, which contains the patented SilverSol.

Our journey with Silver Solution began when one of our primary suppliers introduced us to this revolutionary product. They brought to us several studies and fact sheets, including documentation provided by the manufacturer that demonstrated the abilities and range of Silver Solution's effectiveness. Each study I read on SilverSol was equally astounding. These studies on the product had a wide variety of applications and helped treat various diseases and conditions.[7] Labs at universities such as Penn State,[8] Brigham Young University,[9] and the University of Utah[10] completed some of the research, while other studies were conducted abroad in India[11] and Ghana.[12] Studies were also conducted by organizations such as the National Institute of Allergy and Infectious Diseases.[13]

I remember being shocked when I read a report published in *The Indian Practitioner: A Monthly Journal Devoted to Medicine, Surgery and Public Health* that detailed several studies conducted in Africa involving over fifty patients in Ghana who were all treated for malaria. This study stated that all of them, after receiving treatments with SilverSol, showed no sign of the disease after several days.[14]

On April 26, 2005, the president and CEO of American Biotech Labs (ABL), the manufacturer of Silver Solution, testified before the 109th Congress as to the effectiveness of its product in malaria treatment overseas.[15] The transcript of this report is a matter of public record and can be retrieved from Congress' website.

Just two years prior, in 2003, Lieutenant General Paul K. Carlton Jr., the director of the Integrative Center for Homeland Security, petitioned Tom Ridge, then secretary of Homeland Security, to add silver products to the National Push Pack stockpile:

> The ABL Antimicrobial [Silver Solution] has undergone rigorous testing and has been found to kill Anthrax, Bubonic Plague, Hospital Staph and SARS....
>
> In addition, the ABL product is non-toxic to humans, EPA Approved (Hospital Staph and Bubonic Plague), and currently awaiting Sec 18 approval (Anthrax).
>
> ABL's solution has shown to be a proven wide-spectrum anti-microbial/bio-decontaminant—that can be used to increase the safety and functionality of healthcare facilities

in the event of a bio-terror attack or infectious disease outbreak such as SARS.[16]

I was so impressed and amazed with the information we had been given that we began to offer this product on the air. Were it not for the countless studies by multiple organizations, the recommendations and reviews of government officials, and the proven results, I never would have offered this product.

Silver Solution became a hit and one of our top products—not just with our partners but with our family as well. Some of our testimonies and firsthand experiences include using the silver gel on cuts and scrapes or my daughters using the gel on diaper rash with their babies. Our singers would use the lozenges before and after every performance to help their throats and vocal cords deal with the intense strain. One of our employees had been badly burned by a greasy skillet, and the silver gel decreased his healing time by weeks, impressing his doctors. We would even use the liquid in conjunction with over-the-counter or prescribed medications to help recover from the common cold or flu.

We have offered this product throughout the last decade, pulling back only when the season had come to an end or when the product itself became unavailable due to manufacturing or packaging delays. We were also connected, through our suppliers, to several experts who could help us properly inform our partners about the products on the air. We have used the same silver products on our broadcasts for the last decade. We've always featured a starter kit and paired it alongside various bundles, which our partners have loved immensely. We often had special packages that we used in conjunction with ministry anniversaries and in honor of birthday celebrations, where the giving would always go back to support the ministry.

Because February was still in the cold-and-flu season, we carried on with our annual plan to feature Silver Solution in the early months of 2020. We did not have anything new regarding Silver Solution to introduce in this particular February 4 taping. In fact, we relied on a small grouping of packages that we had been using since the season began in October 2019. It's also important to note that we had decided to book an expert, who had been recommended to us by the manufacturer, weeks in advance of this taping, long before we had made the decision to report on the new coronavirus on the air.

When promoting these items on the broadcast, we would refer to the expert provided to us to represent Silver Solution. Our team planned to promote it as we always had, a wellness tool to help support one's immune system throughout the winter season's usual wear and tear, especially as we braced for the arrival of spring and the rise of allergy season.

THE SHOW SEEN ROUND THE WORLD

On February 4, 2020, we stepped onto the set on Grace Street to tape the show. We began by welcoming all our guests back to the show, and we quickly dug into the situation in China. For more than half an hour, we discussed the headlines, what they meant, and even dissected what we knew of the timeline thus far. We shared with our audience the parallels we'd drawn with Barry's *The Great Influenza*, along with some other knowledge we'd gained through other means. We again reminded our audience of the pale horse (Rev. 6:7–8) and its role in Revelation events, especially with what was still yet to unfold on earth. Time was quickly slipping away from us in the first hour, and that meant that we had to shift from our news and commentary into our fundraising avenues.

We briefly shared the different food bundles we had available and moved into discussing SilverSol with an expert recommended by the manufacturer. Just as she had countless times before on the program, she shared the results from various tests and peer-reviewed studies and informed us about the product's effectiveness. As she spoke, I felt that we needed to be clear regarding SilverSol and the novel coronavirus. I looked across the set to the expert, and I asked, "This influenza that is now circling the globe, you are saying that Silver Solution would be effective?"

She answered, "It hasn't been tested on *this strain* of the coronavirus. But it's been tested on other strains of the coronavirus, and has been able to eliminate it within twelve hours" (emphasis added).

Remember, COVID-19 hadn't yet received its name. It was still just simply *a* coronavirus. Studies on Silver Solution's effectiveness had been conducted throughout the last couple of decades, including a 2003 study on the Severe Acute Respiratory Syndrome (SARS).[17] Studies such as these were among those I first reviewed before offering Silver Solution to our partners.

We continued to tape the show, sharing further news articles and studies and analyzing what we could see happening. When the taping concluded, we determined that we had enough to produce three episodes, so our editorial staff went to work breaking the material down accordingly. The first hour would then air on our stations on Wednesday, February 12.

For years, several websites and organizations have closely watched our program and extracted clips from it. These clips are then shared out of context and twisted, making it seem as if my guests or I said something that they or I hadn't said or meant.

On February 12 these same organizations extracted my question about Silver Solution and the expert's answer. This clip was then twisted as these organizations claimed that we were presenting Silver Solution as a cure for the coronavirus. Neither the expert nor I ever said that Silver Solution was a cure for this disease.

The War on Words that I prophesied would sweep the nation and globe was only just beginning. The white horseman galloped around the nation, fueling this fire. Within days this clip and the twisted accusations went viral, appearing in prominent news organizations around the world. Nation after nation, including America, was just declaring a public health emergency. Everyone was taking the coronavirus situation seriously, and rightfully so, but they were not doing the proper research on what we had said. Every organization played the same clip of this question and answer, and every single one drew an incorrect conclusion. Our website, email accounts, call center, and social media accounts were bombarded with media inquiries, hate mail, and other profane messages. There was so much to process and deal with in this bombardment that it became difficult to stay current with all the correspondence.

The entire ordeal bothered me, no matter how much I tried not to let it faze me. I kept having flashbacks to the late 1980s when I'd been forced to let go of Heritage USA. I recalled the harsh treatment I'd received at the hands of the media throughout the entire process. It was difficult to endure then, and these new reports only served to dredge up that unpleasant feeling.

Lori and I believed that this onslaught would just be a temporary matter. On February 15, even though I was still not well, we flew to one of our survival product manufacturers to tour its facilities and inspect a revolutionary new product that we were hoping to introduce on our broadcasts in the coming weeks. While we were there, the media attention intensified. I asked my staff to make available on our website the many studies about Silver Solution over the last decade in their raw, untouched form so that our partners and viewers could see the information for themselves. I felt that this information would give us the edge we needed to overcome these hundreds, if not thousands, of negative reports. Unfortunately, I did not know the worst was yet to come. The perception, it seemed, had already become the truth.

THE NEXT WAVE

Thursday, March 5, started like any other day. The teams responsible for responding to partner emails and social media messages were working overtime to contain all the pushback from the negative news reports and attention. Late that afternoon, a staff member noticed something different in one of the stories posted on one of our social media accounts. It was not another replay of the viral clip or a commentary thereof. Our staff member had found a press release from the attorney general of the state of New York titled "Attorney General James Takes Action Against Coronavirus Health Scams, Issues Guidance to New Yorkers."[18]

The press release title and content did not use my name or our ministry's name but contained a link. Once clicked, the link revealed a scanned copy of a cease and desist letter addressed to me. In this letter we were advised to stop making claims regarding Silver Solution's effectiveness against the coronavirus. This letter had been dated March 3, 2020, and it was stated that the letter had been sent both electronically and via US mail, but we had not received a copy of it.[19] Our partner services team was so overwhelmed by the onslaught of emails and messages that we hadn't yet seen the correspondence from the New York attorney general.

The following morning, Friday, March 6, our staff had a conference call with our suppliers and call center. We discussed an action plan, including our responses to partners who were overwhelming our order line with concerns about national media reports. We ended that meeting and began to implement some changes to the show's final edits to clear up anything that could be misconstrued by viewers. Our website was reviewed and updated to ensure every Silver Solution product had the required US Food and Drug Administration (FDA) disclaimer, "These statements have not been evaluated by the Food and Drug Administration. This product is not intended to diagnose, treat, cure, or prevent any disease." We also reviewed the product labels themselves and were reassured when each item already carried the FDA disclaimer, as well as all the previous labels we had distributed over the prior decade. Until we could be sure that this would calm the storm, we also decided not to tape any more shows with the Silver Solution product.

Late that same afternoon, the first big blow arrived. Our partner services and website teams both received an email, a joint communication between the FDA and the Federal Trade Commission (FTC) requiring us to "correct the violations" they'd cited in their letter and investigate ourselves as to whether there were other violations that needed correction.[20] Our team spent some time reviewing the letter and creating a plan and quickly went into action, as a response was required within forty-eight hours. Some of our staff members had left for the day, and they were instantly recalled to address the FDA/FTC's concerns.

Our stations were already closed, with the schedule set for Monday, so that airing could not be changed. Members of our editorial staff worked throughout the weekend to update the show scheduled to air on Tuesday, March 10. They removed anything that could be construed as a connection between the coronavirus and Silver Solution. Even though they could not edit the show that would play nationwide on Monday, March 9, they edited the episode that would be in our daily internet livestream and video on demand. The FDA disclaimer was also added throughout the show whenever Silver Solution was presented. Our team spent the weekend drafting a response to the FDA/FTC and submitted it on Sunday morning, just under their required forty-eight-hour deadline.

We exhaled as we awaited their response to our actions. While it did not quiet down, we kept busy answering partner requests and beginning to draft a response to the New York attorney general. Little did we know it was a temporary calm before the storm.

On Tuesday, March 10, I felt as if I had entered the twilight zone. Once again, we would find out about a major action against us by the government through a news outlet. One of our staff members found an article from our local news on our social media accounts, "Missouri AG Files Suit Against Jim Bakker Show, Says Stop Selling Coronavirus 'Cure.'"[21] Accompanying this lawsuit was a petition for the Missouri courts to issue a restraining order against our ministry to prevent us from offering Silver Solution entirely. Whereas other organizations had already told us to no longer "mislead" our audience, the state did not want us to continue offering Silver Solution in any capacity. Again, we learned of this through the news itself. No agent had yet come knocking on our door to serve us papers. But we certainly knew that the worst was now upon us.

Whereas we were planning to phase out Silver Solution over the next few days, we now needed to take more urgent action. We immediately instructed our order line to no longer take orders for Silver Solution. Every silver product was listed out of stock on our website and then taken down. We reached out to our stations and pulled the already carefully edited programs (with the added FDA disclaimers) off the schedule and rushed reruns of older episodes without any coronavirus mentions or Silver Solution to be aired for the next couple of days while we figured out what to do moving forward. We even decided to go above and beyond in this situation by disabling every episode in our website's video on demand going back to the February 12 airing that had Silver Solution among its products.

This action hurt us deeply. Not only had we just lost one of our primary fundraising pillars, but also we had removed nearly three weeks of programming from our website. Our message, our brand, had been adversely affected and silenced. To this day we have not been able to restore these programs to our website, even in an edited form with all mentions of Silver Solution removed. And to this day we have not been able to offer Silver Solution in any capacity. As the days progressed, we would reach further within our website, taking down episodes containing Silver Solution all the way back to 2010 so we would not appear to be resisting legal action. This affected hundreds of wonderful episodes with incredible teachings and messages from our guests. Our older content continues to be viewed weekly, and we want to make sure that our audience can still enjoy these programs and messages, as we believe God continually speaks through them.

The only positive part about taking these actions is that it appeared to satisfy the attorney general, who decided not to pursue his request for an immediate restraining order at that time. This temporary relief allowed us to focus on the continuing onslaught. Before March had ended, we received letters from Health Canada, the City of Los Angeles, and the Arkansas attorney general.

Our concern began as our legal team started to dive into all these requests and letters and the lawsuit. Among the countless requests was a common theme: the names of our partners, the amounts of their donations, the information we were given about Silver Solution and used on our show, and a list of our guests and their qualifications. This was when we realized that this was not just about a product; this was about our platform and our message.

The entire reason I am back on the air is to act as a watchman. First Corinthians 13:9 states that "we know in part, and we prophesy in part." Amos 3:7 even declares that God won't do anything on earth without "revealing His purpose to His servants the prophets." We all have a piece of the message God wants us to hear, and part of my role as a watchman is to bring other teachers, ministers, prophets, and watchmen to the show to share what God is speaking to them on a daily basis. The Lord knows when His people need encouragement, and He knows when they need warning or chastisement. Our freedom of speech was now being infringed on because of what others were twisting from our messages.

Little did we know that these states and organizations were just a few of the groups about to target our platform during this War on Words. Our crisis was just beginning.

CHAPTER 5

THE UNRELENTING BARRAGE

T HE SUDDEN BURST of legal action was only the beginning of our problems. Our country, and the world itself, had already been teetering on the precipice of change due to COVID-19. In 2009, when we first weathered the H1N1 outbreak, my staff and I came across John M. Barry's *The Great Influenza*, which I consider the perfect summary of the 1918 pandemic. Inspired by that book and history, I shared with my studio audience for years that the best way to handle a massive outbreak is to isolate themselves or their families in their homes until the pandemic passes.

When COVID began to rear its head and demonstrate its strength, I instructed our production team to set up television equipment in my office at home. I had long desired to have a camera in my office so that I could go live with our television audience to deliver breaking news. It seemed that I would now need that camera sooner rather than later.

In the meantime, we continued to use our Grace Street studio. By March 17 air travel was no longer an option, so we began to Skype our guests into the program. This process was not without its challenges, especially since much of the broadcast world was quickly transitioning to video conferencing platforms such as this as well. We began to transition as much of the staff as possible to a working-from-home environment. We also have a lot of staff members who reside on our seven-hundred-acre Morningside campus in their own private homes. This enabled them to continue working in our facilities to maintain our infrastructure and ensure our tapings could still be edited and distributed.

By the time we had worked out some of these challenges, word had come from Missouri's government that the state would soon be locked down. Businesses around the state—and nation—were quickly shut down, and millions of employees were either laid off or furloughed. Our ministry had to furlough several members of our staff as well, many of whom we have not been able to rehire since.

On March 24, just a few days before the state lockdown would be officially implemented, Lori and I entered my office, which now doubled as a temporary television studio, and taped our first episode from home. We had two members of the crew with us in our home to operate the television equipment. I have to admit, it was the strangest experience of my life. However, it was not my first small studio. It reminded me of my early years at CBN and starting the kids show. That old studio was almost as big as my office is now (about the size of a large bedroom), and we only were using a small corner.

"My lands," I told my staff. "We've set television back fifty years."

The word *surreal* could not adequately describe what I was experiencing. Had it not been for the mounting legal issues, I probably would have been fine. But now I felt as though I had stepped into a time machine and traveled back to 1987, when my world first fell apart. My office, where I had been hearing from God, assembling sermons, and more, now felt like a prison cell. I felt as if I was once again being cast out and having to fight to stay alive. I asked God, "Is this really happening all over again?"

My crew members did everything they could to bring some sense of normalcy back to our routine. They brought out additional cameras and other items from our regular studio. The Lord gave them all witty ideas and inventions and found new ways for them to work and tie us into our regular facility, all while allowing us to fulfill the government order. Our studio sat silently at Morningside, and it would sit this way for many months.

I was heartbroken, and it was about to get worse.

THE FIGHT TO STAY ON THE AIR

In the weeks after the barrage of legal notices, our social media staff continued to combat hundreds of negative comments, photographs, and more. Some of these messages were so vulgar that my staff members did all they could to keep me from seeing them. This was an easy task, considering that I had stopped looking at these platforms long ago. Too many people were trying not to let me forget my past, including major news outlets that shared the same stories about me and my ministry every day for weeks. I cannot thank my staff enough for wading through every one of these posts and articles just to be aware of what was being said about us. In fact, this was how we learned of an attack far greater than anything we had been experiencing so far.

Our social media staff investigates every article that is posted and catalogs it for review. One day a staff member was surprised when a link led to Faithful America, a website that featured many petitions aimed at changing multiple Christian and conservative organizations. One particular petition opened with this statement:

> Dangerous and offensive, but true. Right-wing televangelist Jim Bakker tried to sell liquid silver as $125 coronavirus cure (it isn't).[1]

The page went on to say:

> Thankfully, state attorneys general and federal regulators stopped his sales, but it's only a matter of time before he tries something like this again.[2]

A few lines later was a call to action, encouraging the reader to sign a petition to be delivered to Roku, DIRECTV, and every single television station that our show was airing on. There was only one goal in mind: to forcibly remove Jim Bakker from the air and never allow him to return.

Thousands of people had already signed the petition, and more were signing it every hour. This petition was the first of many to appear in what America would call in 2020 Cancel Culture. This website was attempting to cancel me, *The Jim Bakker Show*, and all we hoped to accomplish.

I'm not a fighter, but I've never been afraid to take a stand for anything that I absolutely believe in. I've stood firm for my God, I've stood firm for multiple presidents of the United States, I've stood against abortion, but I've rarely stood up for myself. I had a chance back in 1987 to strike back against those who struck me, but I believed that was not the Christian thing to do. The negative press resumed the moment I returned to the air in 2003, but I've done my best to leave it alone and ignore it. I was convinced that some people just couldn't let go of the past.

The Bible tells us countless times to forgive. Matthew 6:14–15 says:

> For if you forgive men for their sins, your heavenly Father will also forgive you. But if you do not forgive men for their sins, neither will your Father forgive your sins.

And I equally clung to Matthew 18:21–22:

> Then Peter came to Him and said, "Lord, how often shall I forgive my brother who sins against me? Up to seven times?"
> Jesus said to him, "I do not say to you up to seven times, but up to seventy times seven."

In that verse, Jesus was telling us that we must walk in endless forgiveness, which is hard for many to understand. I knew that many people could not forgive at all, including those involved with news outlets and petitions such as these. I could follow Jesus' commands and continually forgive them for their actions and their obsession with smearing my name. But I could not stand by and allow any of these attacks to prosper.

God reminded me not to let what is good be spoken of as evil (Rom. 14:16). But how could this be done? There was only one option: to fight back. This wasn't about defending my name. The Bible tells us to die to our flesh daily (1 Cor. 15:31), but I knew I couldn't let my calling, establishing a platform for the prophets and performing my duties as a watchman, be removed by others. I could not be like the ungrateful servant who hid in the ground what his master had entrusted to him (Matt. 25:14–30). The platform had to be protected so that its purpose and future could be guaranteed. I was reminded of what the Lord told me back in 1976, that there was security in the body of Christ. The church needed to band and rally together and no longer stay silent.

I've always told my partners the truth of what's happening, and I knew I would need them to stand with us now. We went on air and informed our partners of this attack. Our partners had to help us in the fight against this petition and persuade those they loved not to sign this. Almost immediately, we started receiving a lot of positive responses from our partners.

One of the biggest responses came from a long-standing friend of the ministry, Stephen E. Strang, CEO of Charisma Media. Steve, a journalist by trade, and I first met in 1983 at Heritage USA. At the time, he came to interview me for *Charisma* magazine and prominently feature the work we were doing at Heritage USA. When our paths crossed again in 2012, his company had expanded to printing books and Bibles. Thanks to Steve and Charisma, we have featured many top preachers, teachers, and inspirational speakers on our program, including Rabbi Jonathan Cahn. Steve had flown to Morningside on multiple occasions now, finding himself more and more impressed with what our little ministry could do.

Steve wrote a fantastic op-ed for the Charisma News website, "Why I Believe Jim Bakker Is Being Unfairly Attacked Online," where he came to our defense. He wrote:

> I believe the truth needs to be told. Jim Bakker is a good man who has spent a lifetime trying to help people and preach the gospel and support his ministry....
>
> The Jim Bakker I know loves people. He has spent a long time helping people, spreading the gospel, and ministering to those who need to know Jesus and the power of His love. Some of his critics don't understand his Pentecostal

fervor....But is that any reason to destroy Bakker or other ministries that believe like him?...

When people know the facts, I believe Bakker's name will be cleared. Then he can get back to preaching the gospel and doing what he believes God has called him to do. That may not satisfy his critics. They didn't like him before—or other ministries like his—and they won't like him after this pandemic is in the history books. But Jim doesn't answer to his critics. They are not his jury or judge. There is a judge Jim will stand before one day—just as every person on earth will.[3]

More of our guests and close friends circulated Steve's article and some investigative reporting by CBN on the group that started the petition,[4] and even some of their own thoughts. I was amazed to see that even people who hadn't supported me or the ministry for years rose and took a stand for us and what we were being dragged through.

Faithful America's petition to remove our show from the air, however, could not be stopped. Just a few days later, with over fifteen thousand signatures, it was delivered to several of our stations. One Christian station that had carried my show for more than a decade to millions of homes through satellite was the first to react. Our contract was immediately canceled, and our show disappeared instantly from their network. We reached out to them right away, pleading that the reasons behind the petition were unjustified. Their response was simple: they didn't want to risk their whole network for just one show. We also were airing on a station in our local area. The petition reached their doorstep, and they quickly pulled us from the airwaves as well.

We had a call from a third station, another national Christian network that we had had a long relationship with. We had even helped each other for several years, providing training and equipment to each other. They had also decided that they could not support our ministry any longer, fearing that they would wind up losing their entire network because of the perceived actions that had occurred on our show. Our ministry, it seemed, was beginning to unravel. I could see it falling apart. The stress of these attacks was déjà vu, almost a mirror of how

Heritage USA and our television network were torn down one pillar at a time.

I remembered once more what I've said many times since I was released from prison. Just as I learned in the 1980s, I was starting once again to see who my real friends were. I was reminded of this truth in Scripture:

> A friend loves at all times, and a brother is born for adversity.
>
> —PROVERBS 17:17

People I thought were my friends now showed me what they were prepared—or *not* prepared—to do. Rather than take a stand for a fellow believer, some allowed those who had aligned with antichrist values to determine what they could and could not do with their platform. The anguish for my fellow believers at this time ached as much as it did when I first tried to take the Revelation teaching around the world.

Just when I thought I couldn't take any more, I got a call from Bob D'Andrea, founder of Christian Television Network (CTN), based out of Florida. When I first returned to television in 2003, Bob was the first person to take a chance on me, the first person to allow God to work His restoration power. Bob had continued to stand with me through the mountaintops and valleys we experienced as a ministry, going so far as to erase a large debt we had owed CTN in the early years of our ministry. He knew I had a continual word from the Lord, and he was determined to help keep me on the air to deliver it.

When my phone rang and I saw that it was Bob, I didn't know what he was going to tell me. My heart sank. I thought, "Oh God! This is the final blow, isn't it?"

Not one person had called to give me good news, so I had expected this call to go alongside them as well. I answered the phone, and Bob told me that he had received the petition and what it had said. I told him what we had done since the start of the litigation and what we intended to do despite all the negative press. That's when Bob said something profound.

"CTN will stand with Jim Bakker," Bob declared. "We will get through this valley together."

I cried tears of joy that day, recognizing another true friend amid the storm. God's reminder that security was in the body of Christ echoed in my spirit once more, bringing a measure of comfort to combat the darkness.

Bob was not the only one to stand with us. Most of our other prominent stations took the same actions Bob did. One of our major stations called us. "Please!" they said. "Our call centers are flooded. Please reassure your viewers that we are not taking you off the air!" At that moment, we truly realized the strength of the full body of Christ.

Only three of our stations chose to take us off the air. Our potential audience shrank ever so slightly, but our viewership did not change. The damage, however, had been done. The anguish sat heavily upon my spirit, alongside the continuing damage from the press and the lawsuits. And just when I thought it couldn't get any worse...

CREDIT CARDS

Due to all the outstanding litigation and threats of further litigation from other organizations, we had been forced to suspend offering any Silver Solution products until we had further guidance and direction from state and federal agencies. This included the consumable items and the instructional and informational materials, such as the books and DVDs. It took multiple passes alone on all our platforms to ensure that anything that appeared to advertise or provide an ability to order Silver Solution was removed, including past broadcasts where we simply said, "Don't forget to order your Silver Solution!" Some of the most amazing guests, uplifting and edifying messages, and even some of the most serious words I'd ever given were now off our website. It was disheartening, to say the least. These were all words that needed to be said, words that someone needed to hear or reference, and now they would be unavailable for a still unspecified amount of time.

But this was the least of our problems.

Our ministry has always collected the funds for orders before shipments as we require the cash flow to keep the order line moving. Several of our suppliers and fulfillment centers require payment up front. As a result, we have to collect those funds at the start of the ordering process and deliver them to our centers so that our partners' orders will be shipped. And because we had been forced to suspend offering SilverSol, we could now no longer fulfill many of the orders that had been placed before the start of the litigation. We now felt the need to refund the donations back to the partners as soon as we could.

Our already dire situation was about to get worse. We reached out to our credit card processor, with whom we had always had a positive relationship. We'd previously been able to work through any issue that arose with ease and professionalism. This was about to change.

On March 16 we informed our processor of our intent to return our partners' donations using the same means by which our partners had donated, via credit cards. Our team made contact and stated our intentions, as well as what we planned to do. This was a standard procedure for our team, and we made no deviation from the established protocol. As the day closed, our team started the arduous process of collecting the information needed to process credit card refunds. No problems were indicated that day by the processor, but our team realized that we hadn't received our daily deposit of partner donations that the processor collected on our behalf each day. The absence of the deposit was unexpected, but it was too late in the day to get an explanation from our processor.

The next morning, March 17, we would get one. Our processor informed us that due to "public negative news" about our ministry, a hold was being placed on our account. This was to establish a security reserve, in what we believed was an exceptionally high amount, to protect the processor from "potential" fines from Visa and Mastercard. Visa had already flagged our accounts, and we were now at risk of being flagged by Mastercard as well. Any donations that they were collecting from our partners were being funneled directly into this reserve. Once the reserve had been met, any other amount that was collected from our partners would be deposited into our accounts. But for now they would be holding every penny of our partners' donations. According to the processor's terms of service, the security reserve would be kept for a minimum of nine months before even a penny could be released to us. To make matters worse, the processor informed us that our accounts would be closed on March 31, which was two weeks away. This action would leave us unable to collect donations using credit cards.

We now were caught in a major crisis, as we could no longer receive funds to keep our daily operations in motion. Even though March was not over, we made the decision to shut down all order processing through our call center and website because we did not want more of our partners' donations to be withheld and not released to the ministry. Our team started to work on a backup plan, hoping to find a solution quickly.

Before we knew it, two weeks had passed us by and we hadn't come across a solution. Our belt was tightening, and our available funds continued to be depleted as we kept paying our staff, our airtime bills, and other basic operational expenses. We needed a lifeline and fast!

Hope was not lost, as our team already had several different leads. One of those leads indeed became a solution. Within days we had merchant accounts established, and our team connected the new processing company to our systems. On Friday, April 3, we switched on our new system and reactivated our call center and website. Our faithful partners were happy to start ordering and supporting us again. I, for one, breathed a sigh of relief.

On Monday, April 6, we were preparing to tape shows with Lance Wallnau. He would be Skyping to us, as all our guests were now doing, from his home in Texas. I was on the phone that afternoon with our producers, which was customary as we prepared the material and questions for the taping. As we discussed which material and topics we would cover on the taping, I switched over to the monitors I had for the call center and the website, only to notice that the daily income reporting had stopped. Usually there are periods throughout the day when giving is lower than others, but I'd never seen it stop for hours at a time, especially in the middle of the afternoon, when several of our stations were airing our broadcast.

I got off the phone with the producers and called my daughter Maricela. She had just gotten off the phone with our call center, as they too noticed the problem and were just starting to investigate. Every single order that our partners were trying to place was failing. They would not go through. This was a very serious issue, and it usually meant that we had a severe technical problem. I let Maricela go so she could get the information we all were seeking.

My phone rang a few minutes later, and Maricela gave me the terrible news. Our ministry had been put on the MATCH list by our former processor. (MATCH stands for Member Alert to Control High-Risk Merchants.) We had essentially been blacklisted. At that moment, I realized the ability to accept donations through credit cards was now gone. My heart fell as our call center and website once again shut down. This blow was more devastating than all the litigation combined.

DRASTIC TIMES

I knew March had been a devastating month. April was getting off to an even worse start with our two greatest income sources being officially cut off. This had gone on for too long, and I had to let the partners know. It had long been my policy to tell the partners everything, no matter how good or bad. On Thursday, April 9, I asked Maricela to meet with the accountants and determine where we stood. We had been operating for almost a month without income, and I needed to know how much flour was left in our bin (1 Kings 17:8–16). Television airtime was always one of our highest expenses every year, and I knew that this would quickly drain us. Unless we had a miracle, I knew we wouldn't be able to continue moving forward for too much longer.

Maricela reported back to me later that afternoon. "Dad, if we don't receive anything from our partners, and if we use absolutely everything in our accounts, we have exactly two weeks' worth of our budget." This news was given to me on the day before Good Friday, the day our Lord and Savior was crucified. With the weekend and holy days upon us, there was nothing we could do.

"Maricela, I need to know something," I said to my daughter.

"Of course, Dad. What is it?"

"I really want to know if you are losing hope."

Maricela had to think about this. She knew I was asking more than what I was saying. But Maricela remembered the childhood years she had spent with Lori and me. Those years, she had learned firsthand that we never lived by the natural; instead, we lived by the supernatural. This had always been the case for our ministry, and it was becoming a reality once more.

She finally answered me, "Absolutely not. I would never lose hope."

I had lost everything once before, so I could easily visualize the road ahead of me now. I knew our battles were in the spiritual realm, even though we could also see them physically. Even so, I hadn't lost hope. I had faith that God wasn't through using me. The words of the prophets echoed in my soul, telling me I was like Moses, who began his ministry at eighty. This year was to be a year of new beginnings. The road ahead looked to be a dead end, and I knew it was false. We knew our God, and we had faith that He would see us through.

"We will find a solution," I told my daughter. "God will give us one." I think, at the time, I was trying to encourage myself more than I was trying to reassure my daughter.

Maricela, meanwhile, gathered the executive management team members and gave them the bitter news. "We have a very long road ahead of us," she told them as she revealed where the ministry was financially. Maricela believed—as I did—that the ministry was needed on the air now more than ever. No matter what, we had to continue producing the show. The executives unanimously agreed, and they were willing to continue with the ministry even if their paychecks stopped coming. Everyone chose to believe that God was still in this. After all, if He wasn't in this, then there was no way we would have made it this far.

But we did have to take some drastic steps. We'd already furloughed dozens of employees, and we had no choice but to do a second round. My daughter Lil' Lori was assigned to call several valuable employees and deliver the news. One employee in particular, when given the news, said that she understood. "But can I still help? Can I still do my job?" this employee asked. "I know you can't pay, but I still want to help wherever I can!"

This employee's act of faith brought Lil' Lori to tears. It wasn't just the executives who were surrounding me to lift my arms like Moses

(Exod. 17:12), but now many members of our team were fully on board with us as well.

I prayed all evening and night, and God confirmed everything. I was reminded of my time in the Arizona desert shortly before I left CBN to start a television ministry of my own for the first time. At that time, back in the 1970s, I had learned of my brother's death, and it had shaken me to my core. I withdrew to a desert area, free from all distractions, to seek the Lord and try to make sense of it all. Just as He did back in the '70s, the Lord brought me back to this scripture:

> See, I will do a new thing, now it shall spring forth; shall you not be aware of it? I will even make a way in the wilderness, and rivers in the desert.
>
> —Isaiah 43:19

Right behind it was Hebrews 13:5. "I will never forsake you, Jim," God reminded me. Thanks to Him, we had a plan. It might have been Easter weekend, but we rallied the crew on a Saturday morning. I asked Maricela to join Lori, Mondo, and me for a show taping because she knew our financial situation better than I did. Together the four of us presented our status and our problem to our viewing audience. I told them that credit cards would no longer be an option but we needed them to donate via check. For an hour we shared our plight and declared our intent and faith to stay and keep doing what we had been called to do, which was to bring forth the Voice of the Prophets to their homes, and the world, every day.

The cameras were turned off, and the files were delivered to the editing team so they could do what they did best. The show would air later that week on a Wednesday, and since the mail can usually be slow, we had no choice but to wait. Donations via mail had accounted for less than 10 percent of the ministry's annual income for the last few years, but at least it was something. Even if that trickle remained, it could extend the ministry's lifeline for a week or two.

A BEACON OF HOPE

On the evening of April 9, my son Mondo had gone home. He could not stop thinking about what he had learned that day, with the ministry having only two weeks of finances left. He prayed all day, asking God for an answer to help the ministry navigate the storm. God whispered the name of a friend. It was now well into the evening, and the hour was late. Mondo was hesitant to call, but he knew he needed to be obedient to the Lord.

Mondo called his friend and shared what the ministry was going through. "We need help," he said. "And we need it now."

His friend soon replied, "Mondo, I know just what to do."

Elsewhere, Maricela had just put her kids to bed. Normally she would go to sleep after they did, but tonight she was in serious need of some self-care. Her husband, John, worked elsewhere in the home and kept close to the kids while Maricela took time for herself. She was trying to do anything for just a brief escape from all she had been dealing with for the ministry. Suddenly, Maricela's phone rang. She rarely used it after hours, save for an emergency, and she never used it after the kids went to bed. One glance at the caller ID revealed that it was Mondo calling. Mondo, like the rest of the family, was well aware of Maricela's nighttime habits. This left Maricela to assume there was a new crisis, something that couldn't wait until morning. She reluctantly answered the phone.

"Maricela," Mondo greeted, "I have a friend of ours on the other line right now. I called him, and he says he has a financial option for us."

She paused before responding. Maricela didn't know what to say or think about this situation, but she could feel the Holy Spirit nudging her. If nothing else, she could at least hear out their friend and see how viable the option was. Maricela withdrew to her car outside so that she could talk freely without waking her children.

Their friend wasted no time. "Maricela, I know someone in charge of a processing company. I spoke to him today, and God told him that He was about to use this company to help someone. If it's OK, I'd like to connect this gentleman on this call right now."

Again, Maricela knew she had little to lose. She gave permission, and soon there was a fourth person on the phone call. The newcomer introduced himself and quickly explained that he had just finished a Nehemiah fast and the Lord had impressed on his heart that he needed to help someone very important. That someone, it turned out, was Jim Bakker.

Given the nudge again by the Holy Spirit, Maricela quickly explained the ministry's situation, from the lawsuits to the conflict with the processor, including being placed on the MATCH list. He wasn't sure he could do anything with the card brands, but he did have another option. "What about electronic banking?" he asked. She was intrigued by the option, and they discussed various scenarios. The gentleman even added one of his key staff members to the call to hear Maricela explaining how the ministry operated from the call center and the website and how orders were processed. Before any of them knew it, it was well into the night. As Maricela signed off on the call, she felt peace in her spirit. She prayed in her car, asking for God's confirmation and blessing on what had just happened. The ministry would need to move fast to implement this solution, and she could only pray that it would be a better experience than what they'd just gone through with credit cards.

The next day, Maricela assembled the staff for a conference call with this new company. All the options were laid out on the table, and solutions were presented for every one of our ministry's financial workflows. These solutions were quickly integrated into our systems, and the week after Easter, our call center was back in action, now able to accept checks by phone. Our website also came back online a couple of days later.

The news overjoyed me. Not only could we see in real time how our partners were responding to our shows again, but seeing how the Lord brought the right people into our path at the right time brought a wealth of encouragement to my spirit.

For all the blessings, we were still moving forward with arrows sticking out from every side. At best we were only limping along. There's only so far a wounded man can walk.

CHAPTER 6

OVERWHELMED

Lawsuits. Subpoenas. Losing critical stations. Negative press. Angry petitions. Major financial hemorrhaging. Unconventional taping methods. My health was already suffering before we started, and there was no way I could get the rest I so desperately needed. My nights were sleepless, and I kept asking God what was going on. It was all happening so fast. I found myself living what I'd been preaching from the first verse of Revelation, so many events happening so quickly, one right after another in quick succession.

By mid-April my strength was starting to wane. My children were quick to notice that I was becoming a shell of myself. Sitting in my home office, taping *The Jim Bakker Show*, and listening to our guests talking over Skype, I would often lose focus and struggle to keep up. The words on the producing outlines would blur together, and there were times that I just couldn't read them. My mind continued to wander every second, and it took all my strength each day to focus. The ministry was under continual attack, and we were determined to keep going. I don't believe that God ever left my side, but my mind would continually float the words of Job to the surface. I remembered when the Lord had allowed the enemy to assault Job and strip him of his success, family, livelihood, and more. I thought I had lived through this same situation decades ago, and the similarities now were heartbreaking.

I seriously did not think I had the strength to endure it all again. But my decision was absolute. I wasn't going to give up, and I had to push through. Many friends had already come to my aid, my family and staff

73

had locked arms around me, and we had all decided to keep going, no matter what. That was the calling God had given us, and He continued to remind me that I was not to give up.

Yet my weariness continued to grow. We would tape an episode for the day, and then I would retreat to my bed. My family would come over to see me and bring the grandchildren. I would spend some time with them, smiling when I could, and then I would retreat again to the bedroom while they were still in my home. I was exhausted and could not find rest. For all the aid, I still felt the burdens and the attacks. When I closed my eyes, I relived the past. I remembered everything that I had tried to forget for the last thirty years: the trial, the persecution, the prison, and the wandering. I didn't want to go back. I couldn't go back! Every day felt like the day before it. I honestly did not know how much more I could take.

When we'd first started taping our shows from our home during the quarantine, Mondo had decided to stay in his own home and Skype in. His wife, Beth, had had lupus for several years now, and his kids had had some serious health issues of their own. Mondo rightfully decided to limit his contact with the outside world for their sake. I had long respected this decision, and I was equally pleased that he and his wife had been wisely preparing for this moment through the last few years.

But I was so used to having a cohost beside me for decades. In the early years, Uncle Henry Harrison filled this role that Mondo had now inherited. Both Henry and Mondo could anticipate what I intended to say and provide me that word or name I was struggling to look for. Without him by my side, I was struggling more than ever with my words and my thoughts. I called Mondo and told him that I needed him by my side in my home when we taped the show. Mondo consulted with his wife, they prayed, and he agreed. We were family, after all, and since we'd all been living in quarantine for several weeks, we all felt it was medically safe. Mondo sitting by my side again brought some comfort and relief, but there wasn't a single person on this earth who could feel what I was feeling. It was only a matter of time before I reached my breaking point.

MOUNTING PRESSURE

On Monday, April 27, Mondo and I were preparing to tape an episode of the show. We didn't have a guest scheduled for that day because I planned to teach my audience more about the four horsemen and their role throughout this new pandemic. Lori was unable to join us because she had a few errands to run for the family. Mondo and I, along with a couple of crew members, entered my office studio and prepared to tape. I hadn't yet gotten dressed for the show. My focus was strictly on my sermon notes from my black Revelation binder. I knew this binder intimately, as it contained more than twenty-five years of study. Every time I preached from it, I would add new notes with fresh revelation from the Lord. Mondo sat next to me and was ready to tape. I applaud him for being patient with me and preparing our usual documents for that day's taping.

But as I sat there reviewing my notes, everything was a blur. The different-colored highlights, the years of handwriting in different-colored inks, and even the printed type from the original computer print-outs...I couldn't decipher a single word. For hours Mondo and the crew patiently waited as I attempted to pull myself together. Occasionally, I would look up to see their faces, as well as my disheveled look in the monitor. My hair was unkempt, and I hadn't shaved. My eyes, normally full of life, were blank and empty. I could see that the crew was being patient, which only proved that my problem was an inability to concentrate. How could I concentrate? Could I even pull myself together? I finally got up and went upstairs. The crew surely believed I finally went to get cleaned up and ready to tape, but I hadn't said anything to them. Mondo followed me a few minutes later, and he found me lying in my bed. I told him that I simply couldn't do the show. Mondo released the crew for that day, and he instructed me to rest. We had a guest scheduled for the next day, and Mondo knew having someone else to talk to would give me the energy I needed to make it through the show.

Lori arrived home and came into our room shortly after, and we tried to have a conversation. I was so weak and tired at the moment that sentences were incomplete and my voice was weak. The moment was concerning, and Lori thought the best thing to do was just let me sleep. It wouldn't be until the next day that she would learn what was really happening at that moment.

Later that evening, at around 6:00, my phone rang. I was still in bed. Lori happened to be passing through the bedroom at the time. She watched me as I reached for my phone. "It's Cindy Jacobs," I said softly. The last time Lori and I had seen or talked to Cindy and her husband, Mike, was at my eightieth birthday party, nearly four months prior. I was too tired to talk to anyone, but Lori urged me to take Cindy's call.

"Jim!" Cindy exclaimed over the phone. "The enemy is trying to take you out physically." She immediately launched into prayer on my behalf, taking authority as a believer in Christ. Lori stayed with me and joined in. Cindy prayed for several minutes, speaking against the various attacks against the ministry and the warfare we now fought. "This attack is about more than you thought," Cindy told me. "This is about the new network you're starting for the prophets and that new studio. The prophets are not welcome in a lot of places, and where they are welcome, their time is limited. The enemy does not want a place for the prophets to come and share the Word of the Lord freely." Cindy did her best to encourage me during the brief call. I, unfortunately, could not stay awake. I went back to sleep the moment the call ended.

Tuesday came, and I didn't feel any better. The crew arrived on time, but I didn't move. Lori and Mondo came in and out of the bedroom, preparing for the show and getting clothes ready for me when I got out of bed. I finally had to tell them that I couldn't do the show. I knew we had a guest, and I knew he was on a tight schedule. I also knew that, in my condition, there was no way I could pull myself together to tape the show. Both Lori and Mondo understood. They got me comfortable, refilled my glass of water from the nearby pitcher, and went downstairs to tape.

While I was proud of my family for coming through in this dark hour, I felt guilty. I knew that my place was behind that desk, looking into the camera lens and performing my duties as a watchman. I'd been in worse predicaments before—or so I thought—and I always managed to pull it together for the sake of God's call. My remorse continued to grow. I finally managed to get out of bed. The show was still being taped, so I went outside, found a lawn chair on my patio, and just soaked in the sun.

I was so upset with myself that I couldn't bring myself to get in front of the cameras that day. I felt helpless and sorry at the same time, and I told the Lord so. But He started to remind me of everything I had done and everything I'd gone through. "It wasn't for nothing, Jim," He told me. "Don't give up. I'm not through using you."

Mondo and Lori finished taping the show and, with our two dogs in tow, came outside and found me there. Since we were under quarantine and going to the dog groomers was most certainly not an option, Lori had purchased a pair of hair clippers online. She asked Mondo to give the dogs a haircut before returning to his home. Mondo laughed, thinking of all the crazy and wild tasks he'd been asked to do over the years. He declared, "Never did I ever think I'd be asked to give a dog a haircut!" The three of us laughed together and exchanged our favorite stories from our decades of adventure together. Lori even put her mother, Char, on speakerphone, and she gladly joined in, hoping her calming voice could help encourage me.

Together the four of us shared many stories. Everything I was now remembering was a place where the Lord rebuilt and strengthened my faith. Without those moments where He shepherded me, taught me, and rebuilt my soul, I know without a shadow of a doubt that I would not have made it this far today.

"You're not alone, Jim," the Lord told me. "You never were."

I smiled. Mondo finished with the dogs and left, and I went back inside. My confidence had been restored, but I was still tired. "Maybe," I thought, "just maybe I can make it." Though we shared only the happy memories and accolades that made us laugh, I continued to revisit my regrets and disappointments, and they weighed particularly heavily on me.

THE STORM

The sun that day soon disappeared behind dark storm clouds. Lightning flashed within them, and echoes of thunder rolled across the Ozark

Mountains. The weatherman began to warn us all that this would not be a usual storm. Something severe was developing.

Lori was in the living room, on the phone with Lynn, her longtime assistant and confidant. Lynn and her late husband, Wayne, had been pillars in our lives for nearly two decades, always ready to help us with whatever we needed. By this point Lynn was a full-fledged member of our family. Lori looked up from the couch to see me coming out of the bedroom.

"Lori," I said in an urgent and worried tone, "I am dying."

My wife didn't believe me at first. While she knew I had been having many difficulties lately, she didn't want to accept that something much more serious was lurking behind my tired face. "No, you are not, honey," she told me. "You are going to be OK."

I said it again, this time with a tone more serious than before. "I am dying!"

That statement was the last thing I remember saying or doing from this fateful day. All that happened next has been told to me by my family, just as they will now share it with you as it happened.

*****

Lori, having just heard me say that I was dying, looked at my face carefully. The Spirit whispered to her and confirmed the statement. She instantly realized that the storm wasn't just brewing outside; it was also forming inside our home. "Lynn, I have to go." Lori hung up and dialed a new number.

Maricela was leaving the ministry's main office at Morningside after another grueling day meeting with the legal team and handling our responses to the multitude of matters that had befallen our ministry. She'd just gotten into her car and turned the ignition when her phone rang. Maricela glanced at the caller ID, saw that it was her mother, Lori, and answered it.

"Nena," Lori said, urgency and uncertainty fueling her tone while she used Maricela's nickname, "I need you to get here now. Something's wrong with Dad. He says he's dying." In the background Maricela could hear me, but my speech was not making any sense. Some words were clear, but the rest were gibberish. The more she heard me speak, the less she could understand. She'd been hearing me through different phone calls and in visits the last few days, but this time something was different. Something was seriously wrong.

Maricela put her car in gear and left the parking lot. "Mom, call Doctor Luke!" she urged. "Tell him what's going on, and put him on speaker. Let him hear Dad for himself. I'm on my way." All the way to the parsonage, Maricela did her best to stay calm. The storm continued to grow outside her car, but the rain had not yet fallen. A different kind of storm grew with it, and Maricela recognized it immediately. The mounting crisis had taken a new turn, and the war had emerged in the physical. She knew my life was now at stake.

As her car raced to the parsonage, Maricela entered the courts of heaven with her prayer language. Every second, she kept speaking life over me—the one who had adopted her and helped her see that her destiny didn't have to be resigned to never knowing God loved her and had a plan for her. She cried out, "God, there's no way that this is going to be how it ends." All she knew to do was remind God of who I was, who I had been, what I'd done for the Lord, and the unfulfilled promises that were still on my life.

It was the fastest drive in Maricela's life. When she arrived inside the parsonage, she saw me sitting upright in bed. Lori was standing there next to me, with her phone in her hand. It was on speaker, and Doctor Luke was listening to my attempt to speak. Maricela saw the worried expression on Lori's face. I was attempting to talk, but nothing but gibberish was coming out. I was excited that Maricela had come home, but there was some frustration in my tone when I couldn't figure out why Maricela couldn't understand me.

Maricela reached for Lori's phone. "Doctor Luke? What should we do?"

Doctor Luke had been the family physician for more than a decade. He was a friend, a confidant, a member of Morningside's board of directors, and the one person who truly knew what was now at stake. "You need to get him to the emergency room as soon as possible! I don't care what it takes; get him there now." At that moment, Lori didn't find herself panicking. Calm commanded her senses now as she realized that it would be up to both women to make sure I got the help I needed. Time was of the essence.

But I couldn't understand what was going on. My demeanor was slightly frustrated now, combined with fragmented speech and an inability to move. Both Lori and Maricela worked together to get me dressed. I kept trying to talk to both of them, but nothing was coherent, and I still couldn't move. "Dad," Maricela told me, "if you don't start moving now, I will pick you up and carry you to the car myself." Of course, Maricela didn't know how she would pull that off. She is a few inches shorter than me, but she would have relied on her matriarchal strength if she had to. They finally got me into the car, placing me into the front passenger seat. Lori jumped in the back with a few things she had quickly put together. Maricela jumped into the driver's seat and started the journey to the Branson emergency room, which was more than thirty minutes away.

Winds had kicked up outside. The thunder rolled louder now, but the rain still hadn't started. For all her calm, Maricela felt incredibly insecure behind the wheel of her mother's car. My life was in the balance. There was no time to wait for an ambulance to take me, and she didn't know if she could make it to the hospital in time. She asked the Holy Spirit to help keep her calm. They were determined to make sure that I got the help I now desperately needed, and they could only do it if they didn't give in to their growing fears. I kept trying to carry on a conversation throughout the car ride, as my scattered gibberish and thoughts effectively kept both calm and uncertainty alive. One moment I was trying to talk about the show. In another I tried to talk about a friend. And in another I tried to praise God.

I even picked up my phone to call Mondo because I had grown frustrated that Lori and Maricela could not understand me, even though they kept trying to encourage me past my frustrations. Mondo, who had just left our home only a few hours prior, was shocked to hear his father and friend incoherent. He also picked up that Lori and Maricela were trying to keep me calm, and he joined in all the way to the hospital.

It seemed as if an eternity had passed by the time we finally arrived at the hospital. Maricela parked the car outside the emergency room entrance. Leaving Lori and me in the car, Maricela entered the building. It had been difficult getting me into the car, and she believed that any time spent trying to get me into the hospital on my own power would further endanger my life. She was able to secure a wheelchair, which she took outside immediately. As the storm grew, Maricela and Lori helped me out of the car and into the wheelchair. Lori stayed at the car to gather what she thought they would need in the hospital while Maricela pushed me through the hospital entrance. Having taken note of the new arrivals, the hospital staff met Maricela and me at the door before we could enter.

"I'm sorry," a staff member said and reached for the handles of the chair. "You can't come in with him." Like the rest of the country, the hospital was now operating under COVID-19 restrictions. Patients were not allowed any visitors under any circumstances.

"You have to let us in!" Maricela protested. "He can't speak. We believe my dad is having a stroke. He won't be able to answer any of your questions for himself. We have to go in!"

The staff looked at the receptionist, who had heard the entire exchange. The receptionist picked up the phone, called the doctor on duty, and explained the situation. For Maricela, this moment was horrifying, not because of the policies but because of the thought of me, her dad, being taken away without the ability to speak for myself. She knew I could not be alone at this moment. Maricela looked down at me. My hyper demeanor was now fading. I had realized where I was and knew I was in serious trouble.

Seconds felt like hours. Maricela's calm was challenged with every heartbeat. Finally, the receptionist set down the phone and looked across her desk at Maricela. Lori, having just parked the car, was now standing beside us.

"You can't go in with him," she told them. "But you can come to this next checkpoint to answer questions for the doctor."

Lori considered herself—and me—fortunate. The staff met her at the checkpoint, which was just inside the door. Maricela began the paperwork as the nursing staff started to ask Lori questions about me. By now

I had almost stopped talking and all comprehension was totally lost. The staff swelled in urgency, whisking me away for immediate brain scans to confirm my condition. Lori and Maricela were not allowed to follow. Maricela did, however, make sure that I had my phone. After all, there needed to be some way for me or the staff to give Lori updates as they progressed.

Lori stood still in the lobby. Her heart stopped while her eyes fixated on the sterile doors in front of her. For several moments her senses grew numb to her surroundings. She fought to keep tears from welling up in her eyes and wondered if this were the last moment she would see me alive.

"Lord," she silently prayed, "I don't know if I'll get to see Jim again, but I trust You. Remember who Jim Bakker is."

"Ma'am?"

Sound rushed into Lori's ears, a cascade of air-conditioning, computer fans, keyboard clicks, and the rattling of the glass entrance due to the storm winds behind her. Lori turned to face a nurse who had been fighting to gain her attention for the last few moments.

"I'm sorry. But you can't stay inside the hospital. You have to wait outside."

Both Lori and Maricela felt defeated. They had done all they could, and now there was nothing left to do but wait. What felt like hours had been less than a minute. Both women exited the lobby to where their ears traded the familiar whirring of air pumps circulating chilled air for the loud wails of rushing winds. Lori's phone blasted an emergency alert that was echoed instantly from Maricela's phone. These were not regular notifications. Maricela pulled out her phone from her pocket. Sitting on top of countless text messages was a National Weather Service notice. "Mom, Branson's under a tornado watch."

The tornadic winds were picking up, tossing trash and small rocks across the parking lot. Even the wind threatened to rip their masks from their faces. Lori and Maricela got back into their car and moved it into the nearby parking garage for safety. As soon as the car was safely parked, both women prayed together, committing me fully into the

Lord's hands. It was up to the doctors and the heavenly forces to fight the war now.

Neither of them knew what to expect next. While they waited, both Maricela and Lori began to call members of the family. Within minutes family members had been notified, briefed quickly on what was transpiring, and instructed to pray. Several others were notified that night as well, but calls and information were now primarily limited to family members.

Just as they finished, a thought struck Lori. "Maricela, call Cindy." It was time to get as many people praying as possible. Maricela searched her mother's phone for Cindy's contact card and tapped the call button.

Cindy answered immediately. Just the day before, God had told her that the enemy was trying to take me out, and now Cindy confirmed that this was what she had seen. Cindy prayed with Lori and Maricela, launching a battle cry of her own in the spiritual realm on my behalf. The prayer finished, and Cindy began to encourage both women, knowing that the night would entail a long and uncertain road for them both.

By now at least half an hour had transpired since they'd entered the parking garage. The prayer and conversation with Cindy Jacobs had masked the passage of time. Cindy was still connected when a second call came to Lori's phone.

The call was coming from my phone.

Lori quickly said goodbye to Cindy and took the call. Her thumb tapped a button, and the caller was now on speaker. "Honey?" she asked, her voice trembling. She didn't know what to expect. When I was wheeled away from her inside the hospital lobby, I looked the worst Lori had ever seen me. She wondered if she would now hear more of my fragmented speech or something else entirely.

"Lori Bakker?" asked a voice that she didn't recognize.

"Yes?" Lori answered.

The caller, Jim's doctor, asked, "Are you still here? Are you near the hospital?"

"Yes. We're in the garage."

Without missing a beat, the doctor said, "I need to see you immediately."

Lori's mind immediately assumed the worst. "Is Jim dead?" she thought. "Is he paralyzed? What fates are worse than death?" There was no time to speculate. The doctor had summoned them, and they had to move quickly. Lori and Maricela both exited the vehicle and ran over to the emergency room entrance. They both struggled to put on their masks, which the wind threatened to yank off with every quick gust. Though Lori had been the one called and requested to come, Maricela was determined to stand by her mother and help her through this dire situation as best she could.

The security staff was equally determined to keep both women outside. A moment later, as security kept Lori and Maricela from entering the lobby, the doctor arrived. "Let her in!" he told security. "I called her inside."

Security obeyed, allowing Lori to pass but not Maricela. Lori refused to enter without her daughter, and she begged the doctor to give permission. Lori did not want to handle this situation alone.

The doctor looked at the staff, then to Maricela and Lori. He held his hands up to the security guards and ordered, "OK. Let them both in."

Lori and Maricela, grateful for the moment of favor, followed the doctor down the long hallway. The physician wasted no time and began updating them immediately. "Mrs. Bakker, I do want you to know that Jim, your husband, has experienced a stroke."

Lori's worst fear had suddenly been confirmed. Questions and uncertainties swirled in her head, filling it with worst-case scenarios about my life and the ministry's future. "Would he lose mobility? Would he still be able to talk or think? Did I already lose more of Jim than I thought?"

The doctor gave those uncertainties little time to gain traction. "Our scans show a sizable blood clot in his brain. It needs to be broken up quickly if there is any hope for him to live. But we cannot treat him here. The treatment he requires must be performed at our facility in Springfield, which is close to an hour away."

As soon as he finished speaking, they turned a corner and met an open doorway. There I was, right in front of them. My eyes were not fully closed, and what they could see was hollow. Gone was the stammering man from an hour ago, and absent was the light and love that they had always seen radiating from my face. In its place was fear and uncertainty. My chest was bare, and my lower half covered. Various wires connected me to monitors to allow the medical staff to maintain watch over my vitals.

Lori quickly entered the room, her fear for the future now replaced with a fear of me being alone. She did not respond to the doctor and instead stood next to me. She placed her hand on my forehead. After a second, she started to stroke my head, as she would often do when we were close together in bed or with family. Instantly my fearful look evaporated. My eyes closed, and my frown vanished. The comfort and love between husband and wife melted the stress, panic, and uncertainty, even if only for a moment. I knew that Lori was with me and I was safe.

"Mrs. Bakker?" the doctor repeated while the nurses continued to move in and out of the room freely. "We need you to make a decision. We believe the best course to save your husband is to administer the tPA." He quickly explained what the tPA would do and how it could break the clot. However, the procedure would be dangerous. Either the treatment would be successful, or hemorrhaging would start in the brain and I could die. The chances of success were fifty-fifty.

The doctor echoed the worst part of the news, knowing that Lori and Maricela were still in shock from the initial report and seeing my condition for themselves. "We do not have what we need to administer the full treatment here, and it can only be finished at our Springfield hospital. If we are to have any success, we must leave now. But we can only do this if we have your permission."

Lori was internally distraught. For a moment, my fate was in her hands. She looked at me and took in the peace on my face as she weighed the options. If she refused the treatment, then this would be the end of my story. She remembered the prayer with Cindy Jacobs and the many prophecies over my life. The battle was not destined to end today. There was only one thing to do. Cool and collected, Lori signed the authorization forms without further hesitation. A few minutes earlier she had committed me into the Lord's hands. This signature would now be a physical embodiment of that surrender.

I was quickly wheeled to a waiting ambulance, escorted by the doctor to the vehicle. Lori followed and tried to join me in the ambulance, but she was swiftly blocked. Lori pleaded with the EMTs, "My husband needs me. I must ride with you."

The lead EMT shook his head and refused. "I'm sorry. COVID restrictions prevent us from allowing ride-alongs."

There was no time to argue, but Lori continued to plead for my sake. She knew I needed her now as much as she needed me.

"Ma'am, I'm sorry. The Springfield hospital won't let you in. There is a tornado watch, and you will be stranded outside. Ethically we cannot do that to you."

Lori didn't get a chance for a rebuttal. The doctor spoke up and warned the EMT, "Every minute it takes you to get to Springfield increases the chance for brain loss." In all respects the doctor was correct. For the tPA to have any chance of success, it had to be administered within the first three hours of the stroke. It would take close to an hour to get to Springfield, and by Lori's estimation, two hours had already passed since the stroke began.

The argument was settled. Lori did not like it, but she had to step aside. Both she and Maricela jumped into her car, and they followed the rushing ambulance with its lights flashing and sirens blaring. In the tornadic weather, it was nearly impossible to hear the sirens in front of them. Wind gusts were now up to seventy miles per hour around them, threatening to push both ambulance and car off the highway. The road between Branson and Springfield was known for its multiple high peaks and low valleys, to which the high winds tried to exploit every advantage. Lightning struck in the distance, yet the rumbles were lost in the winds. The skies were dark, even though the sun had not officially set. Weather alerts blared from the phones, announcing a tornado warning had been issued for the county the ambulance was now passing through.

Panic set into Maricela. "This is it," she thought. "This is how it's all going to end. Dad, Mom, and I will be swept up into heaven by a tornado." Maricela struggled to keep the car straight, fighting panic, fear, mountain roads, and wind gusts. Lori demanded that Maricela pull the car over. Nothing was going to keep her from getting to me. Maricela instead refocused, fighting through the fear. There was no way she could pull the car over, not now, and certainly not with the storm raging outside. Both she and Lori moved into their prayer languages, interceding in the courts of heaven for my life.

The storm raged on as the ambulance arrived at the Springfield hospital, with Maricela pulling in not far behind. Lori leaped out of the car, planning to rush inside with the paramedics alongside me. As she had been warned in Branson, the medical staff would not permit her entry. Lori was forced to remain outside while the doors closed in front of her. She watched, frustrated and afraid, as I disappeared from her sight into the belly of the hospital whale. There was nothing more she could do but wait and pray, along with the countless prayer warriors who had already stormed the courts of heaven.

There was nowhere safe to park, especially with the warning still in effect. Nor did either of them know how long it would take before they received an update. Nothing in the medical world was instant, nor could she expect a quick update from the doctors. Maricela found a hotel nearby and took her mother there. Its location was perfect, close to the hospital. It was a miracle that it was open because of the pandemic and the storm, but they did not have any trouble securing a room.

Maricela had nothing with her except for her purse and phone, but not Lori. Since Hurricane Katrina in 2005, Lori was determined that she would never be caught off guard. Her trunk was always full, usually carrying copies of books they'd offered on the program as well as a few emergency items. Lori pulled out from the backseat the items she had grabbed from her home before going to the hospital, including her grab-and-go bag. She had maintained this bag since the hurricane, always keeping it stocked and up-to-date. She pulled out food. She pulled out clothes. She pulled out toiletries. She pulled out a small power generator to recharge their cell phones.

"Mom!" Maricela exclaimed, watching her mother pull out these items as if she were Mary Poppins withdrawing a multitude of items from her bottomless bag. "You really do practice what we preach!"

Both women shared a laugh as Lori opened their food pouches, a meal that only needed to have water added. All the restaurants had closed due to the weather, so they would have gone hungry without these pouches.

Alas, hour after hour passed by, and there was still no update from the hospital. The lack of momentum stopped the flow of adrenaline, and now both women were starting to fade. Maricela urged her mother to sleep for a little while. After all, neither one of them knew how much longer this would take, and once the news came, they would need energy to keep going.

Lori, however, refused. "I'll sleep when I know he's OK," she told Maricela. As her daughter fell asleep, Lori remained upright. She continued to pray, hanging on to the many promises she knew the Lord had given to us, including the many that were still unfulfilled. Lori knew without a shadow of a doubt that the Lord wasn't done with me. The hour continued to grow late, and there was still no notice from the hospital.

Outside, the storm had subsided. No longer could she hear the wailing wind rattle the windows and the trees outside, and the room filled with silence. The only sounds now came from the air conditioner and her sleeping daughter. Lori fought to stay awake, even forcing herself to move around the room to keep the blood flowing. The task was proving more and more difficult with each passing minute.

A staccato tune broke the silence as a ringtone blared from Lori's phone. She reached for it and looked at the screen. My face was there, the photo she had long connected to my number. Lori's heart skipped a beat. The last time she saw my face and name, someone else had been on the other side.

This was it. No matter what happened, she would learn the results of the decision she had to make for her husband. There were only two possible reasons for this call, and she feared the worst.

Lori didn't allow herself to linger on the possibilities and quickly swiped the electronic latch from left to right and answered the call. "Hello?" she gasped.

"Mrs. Bakker?" came a female voice.

"Here we go," thought Lori. She listened to the voice of the woman, who introduced herself as my nurse. Lori's senses went numb immediately. Her sight locked onto the brilliant phone screen in front of her, and her ears filtered out all other noise as she mentally locked into what was about to be said.

"Mrs. Bakker, I wanted you to know that we have successfully administered the tPA to your husband. Jim's body has handled it very well. The clots are still breaking up, but we are happy to report that he made it."

Lori's lips began to quiver while tears formed in her eyes. A glance to her side told her that Maricela had been woken up by the ringtone, and she was on the edge of the bed listening as well. Tears also formed in Maricela's eyes as both women realized the final storm had passed. Both their hearts were filled with gratitude and thankfulness for their Lord and Savior, knowing that I was going to make it. God indeed wasn't through using His servant.

Neither woman, however, was expecting what would happen next. "Do you want to talk to Jim?" the nurse asked.

Lori did indeed. "Yes! Absolutely!"

There was a muffling as the phone was passed to me. "Lori?" I asked, my voice weak, hollow, and tired. Most importantly, I was coherent. Lori did her best to explain what I had just gone through, but she avoided the details. There would be time to explore those later. But what mattered now was that I was going to be OK. She did her best to reassure me. The nurse stepped in, insisting that I needed to get some rest, and the phone call ended.

As a mother, Lori wanted to reassure her children. Her fingers went to work, tapping away at her phone until each member of the family had been told their father would be OK. She heaved a sigh of relief, even though she knew that while one storm had passed, it was still too dark to know how extensive the damage would be. Lori climbed into bed and swiftly fell asleep.

Little did she, or anyone else, know how long and difficult the road to recovery would be.

CHAPTER 7

THE SHOW MUST GO ON

THE NEXT MORNING, reality began to set in.

I do not remember that first night in the hospital, nor do I fully recall the day of the stroke or the days leading up to it. What I do remember is the first morning in the hospital was one of the most disorienting days of my life. Lying in the bed half-asleep, I would get flashes, glimpses of memories. I remembered feeling nothing but cold steel and cold air, along with being jolted from side to side. I could see two dark figures, barely silhouetted against a dark sky. There were dim lights above me, just enough to see but not enough to make things clear. I would later be told that this was my ambulance ride through the tornadic storm.

Those memories were chilling, but nowhere as depressing as the sterile room I now occupied. My body was still in shock, and my mind foggy and dazed. Though the medication was working, I was still not in full control of my senses. I could, however, sense one horrible reality. I was alone. My trembling fingers found the button that would call a nurse. When she came, I asked where Lori was. I did not understand why my wife could not be at my side.

The nurse gently explained what had happened to me and that I was in an intensive care unit in the Springfield hospital. And due to restrictions recently implemented to prevent the spread of COVID-19 throughout the hospital staff and patients, there was a strict "No Visitors, No Exceptions" policy. She did let me know that I had my phone, and sure enough, it was there on the bedside table, fully charged. I picked it up, my hands still trembling from the trauma my body had suffered. Because my mind was foggy, it took me a bit to find Lori's number and make a phone call.

Lori and Maricela had been awake for a while in their hotel room. Calm, clear, and sunny skies had replaced the violent storm from the night before. Yet the room was anything but calm and clear. Lori had contacted the hospital staff, trying to figure out the next steps we would have to take. According to the hospital, I would remain under observation for a couple of days to ensure that there wouldn't be a second episode and that there wouldn't be any side effects from my treatment.

For over one hundred ministry employees and volunteers, the day had begun just as it had any other, as they were completely unaware of the jeopardy from the night before. While many of our staff were eating breakfast, reading their daily devotionals, and preparing themselves for another day at Morningside, my family was left with a multitude of unanswered questions. Only my family knew the dangerous precipice on which we now sat.

I not only felt their uncertainty from my hospital bed; I had plenty of my own. I could feel it in every inch of my body. The sterile walls of my small room felt worse than a prison cell, and I could only hope that I would not have to stay longer than needed. The worst part was that I lacked both energy and the will to move forward. I knew what needed to be done, but I knew I could not do it myself.

I relayed the marching orders to Lori and Maricela. I told them that no matter what, the show must go on.

In recent years, I'd begun to hate the word *show* in the context of Christian television. We weren't meant to entertain. To me, *show* implied that something was fake or staged. My God was not a theatrical God even though He loves to demonstrate His mighty power. More importantly, I've long felt that Christian television needs to return to its roots, to convey the real miracle-working power of our Lord.

Despite all my feelings, the tried adage still applied. The doctors were already telling me what to expect from my body for the next few months, not to mention the damage the stroke had done to my morale, body, and energy. I was ordered to rest and to get plenty of it. Brother

Halverson's warning to me when I was nineteen years old replayed once again in my head. He'd warned me not to get overtired, as the enemy would use my exhaustion against me. And here I now was. I had pushed myself past the point of total exhaustion, and I would now pay the price again.

I had no choice but to turn over the hosting duties of my television program to my family. I also knew that we would not want to hide this incident from our faithful ministry partners. Word would leak out eventually if we tried to keep it under wraps. Therefore, I instructed Lori to make sure she told our television audience what had happened to me. After all, per the doctor's instructions, I would not be able to appear on the air for several months. Our partners would undoubtedly figure out something was amiss if we didn't say anything.

Lori and Maricela checked out of their hotel room and started the journey back home. While one drove, the other texted key family and production team members and had them assemble in a single room for a conference call. Until this moment, the only two people with all the details about my stroke were Lori and Maricela. And now the only two people with my marching orders were an hour away from Morningside. Maricela turned up the speaker on her phone, allowing both her and her mother to speak with Mondo, my daughter Lil' Lori, and Andrew, our executive vice president of broadcasting. There was much to do, and there was little time to do it in. Before Lori and Maricela returned home, they set a plan in motion to inform our partners of what had transpired, as well as when and how to continue taping *The Jim Bakker Show*. My wife would fill my usual role as host. Mondo would continue to serve as cohost, reporting the news and recalling the significant moments and prophetic words I had delivered over the last few years. Maricela would permanently join the panel as a backup to both Lori and Mondo. Lil' Lori would be on standby to jump in whenever her mother would need to take me to doctors or if something else came up.

News of the stroke needed to come out as part of a unified effort. Because we tape our episodes well before they are scheduled to air, we had to contain the news of the stroke until the episode itself aired, lest any rumors become too big and spun out of control by the media before we had a chance to respond. If the news broke prematurely, then too many people would be looking to our broadcast for news and updates well before we could properly share it. We, therefore, told select members of our staff in stages (based on who would be coming into possession of the information due to their job duties, such as our production staff on the day of taping), asking them each time to keep the news to themselves until the day of the broadcast.

On Friday, May 8, we released the episode with the first news that I had had a stroke on our website and through all our stations. A statement on all our social media accounts immediately followed. Many of our friends, guests of the show, and partners quickly rallied around us, sharing wonderful messages of support and joining with us in prayer. These encouraging words brought some of the first real light in our dark tunnel. That Friday, the light was so bright we'd almost forgotten about all our dark spots.

LONG ROAD TO RECOVERY

As I was in the hospital, my anxiety was on high alert. I couldn't have visitors. I still didn't know everything that was going on. The fog in my mind persisted. As the shock finally wore off, I could feel pain in every inch of my body. This pain was insignificant compared with what I was feeling under my skull. It felt as if a bomb had detonated in my head. There were important things that I could not remember. My speech was slow, and my ability to think was sluggish. A few things came quickly to the surface, especially when I would talk to my loved ones. In those brief moments, I could feel warmth. Every time my phone disconnected from Lori, the cold rushed back in. I don't think any blanket could have kept me warm.

Monitors surrounded me, and on occasion I would be taken for new scans. However, I was frightened by the MRI machine. Lying on the bed and being stuck inside this machine felt worse than solitary confinement back at prison. At least in solitary I could move, but here I was confined to my bed. I couldn't turn; I couldn't shift. I couldn't even slide back out. I had to lie still and listen to all these strange noises. Loud metallic clunks and echoes and pulses and jitters echoed throughout the chamber. For a moment I felt as if I were having another stroke, but this thankfully was only a feeling. Only one thing was on my mind. I wanted out!

"Lori!" I gasped the next time I spoke to her. "You have to get me out of here!" For a few moments I was working on an escape plan.

"I'll come get you," Lori assured me over the phone. "But if I do, I know they'll arrest me. I won't be able to take care of you once you get home."

That truth cut us both deeply. Was I now an invalid? "God," I thought, "why did this happen to me? Will I be able to recover from this? Will I ever be able to get back to my calling?"

As much as I could, I kept my phone on and connected to Lori. I was equally panicked and exhausted. Only in my bursts of energy could I talk to anyone, including the nurses and doctors, but hearing Lori share about everyday life at home and with the family brought me just enough peace. Just the ability to have my phone on all the time was the only thing that made this ICU stay more bearable than prison.

A more sensitive issue was developing, however. The constant pressure that I had felt in my head for months had relocated to my gut. Among the memories I didn't have was a recollection of the last time I had gone to the bathroom. My eyes scanned the room. There were two doors. One was the entrance, and the other was unmarked. This had to be the bathroom, or so I thought. I mustered what little strength I could and started to sit up. An alarm immediately sounded. On the one hand, I figured that alarm would prevent any escape attempt I might have been bold enough to try, but on the other hand, it genuinely startled me. What on earth could that alarm have been for?

One of the nurses rushed into the room and witnessed my feeble attempt at getting off the bed. "Mr. Bakker?" the nurse asked. "Is something wrong?"

"I need to use the bathroom," I replied, my tone matter-of-fact.

"I'm sorry, Mr. Bakker, but you can't get out of bed. Hospital rules." The nurse called for an assistant and reached for a metal bedpan that was nearby. "However, we can help you take care of that."

My eyes locked onto the bedpan. I'd seen them used plenty of times in movies and on television shows, so I knew precisely what they were for. "No, no, no," I muttered, horrified at what its presence meant.

"It's OK," the nurse said. "This is part of our job, Mr. Bakker." Her tone was absolutely sincere, but it did little to assuage my fears. I had no choice but to allow them to help me with my growing problem. In the next few moments, as I filled that pan to the brim, I felt every ounce of my dignity evaporate as if it were being forced out of my body along with my refuse. Without any question, I was absolutely embarrassed, perhaps the most embarrassed I had ever been in my life. There are few memories I never wish to revisit more than necessary, and this is on that very short list.

Despite my embarrassment, I am thankful for the nursing staff, the doctors, and others who looked after me during my forty-eight-hour stay in the hospital. I later found out that many who helped me during this time were Christians and had been praying for me every step of the way. Every person, without a doubt, helped me through the two most difficult days of my life.

But I would soon find that the days ahead would be even more intense.

HOME AGAIN

There was only one destination in my mind as soon as I got home, and that was my bed. The entire experience had drained me emotionally, physically, and spiritually. I couldn't talk to anyone, and the new medication drained any energy I could hope to build. I slept continually as home health care professionals slipped in and out for the next couple of weeks, monitoring my vital signs. When I was awake, I found myself nauseated, a feeling that continues even to this day. I could not sit up. I could not stand. Every time I tried, the room and the floor would spin. The doctors assured me that the best thing I could do was rest. My body had suffered massive physical trauma, and I had to be patient with myself and my body as it worked in the background to repair the damage.

My family would slip into the bedroom every day before and after the show tapings. Occasionally, I would wake up and speak to them for a short while in quiet tones, and other times I would just lie there and listen to their voices and prayers.

I wanted to cry. Every waking moment, my weakness and failings were all I could think about. I felt as though I'd been violated, injured, humiliated, and most of all, beaten down. The worst part of it all was that I didn't want to get back up. I had plenty of time, and each minute brought all my mistakes and sin and regrets back to the surface. My mind replayed many regrets—my hasty decision that led to the loss of Heritage USA and my ministry, the heartbreak as I watched my son, Jamie Charles, sob in the visitor's room in prison, the lonely cold nights in the prison cell, and multitudes more.

"Jim."

The voice nearly startled me. I was alone in my room, and the family was downstairs taping another episode of the show.

"Jim."

This voice was familiar, but I hadn't heard it in years. I had to concentrate, push past all the mental fog and bad memories. An image slowly materialized in my mind, belonging to the great E. V. Hill. Pastor Hill had been the senior pastor of Mount Zion Missionary Baptist Church in Los Angeles, California, for decades. He had joined me several times out at Heritage USA as a guest on my show. When I had lost everything, E. V. had called me before the trials began. It was the memory of him speaking to me that filled my mind now, thanks to the Holy Spirit plucking a shining light out of my murky past.

"Jim, you're coming back."

E. V. Hill had prophesied that to me as I was just beginning the darkest days of my life in the 1980s. Despite all my shortcomings, God used this memory of an old friend to remind me that I wasn't done yet. A scripture floated to the surface of my mind as well. I couldn't see the Word clearly, so I sat up and looked around the room. I found one of my oldest friends, the Bible that had lasted with me throughout prison. For the last few years, I had to be careful in using it, as the spine had completely worn out. Entire books of the Bible had been reduced to individual pages that took effort to keep in order. My friend Steve Strang, having seen this Bible with me on the show one day, offered to have it repaired and rebound for me. This wonderful act of kindness yielded the full return of my closest friend, and it was ready to show me the Word the Lord now had for me.

> And I heard a loud voice saying in heaven, Now is come salvation, and strength, and the kingdom of our God, and the power of his Christ: for the accuser of our brethren is cast down, which accused them before our God day and night.
>
> —REVELATION 12:10, KJV

"Salvation and strength," I thought. "Lord, I welcome it!" The accuser of the brethren had been standing before the Lord, reminding Him and me of all my sins. Just as He will in the final days, the Lord was going to help me look past my shortcomings and bring me back to where I belonged. Another scripture drifted into my mind, this time Proverbs 24:16, reminding me that the "just man falls seven times and rises up again." My turn to rise again was coming.

I soon fell asleep, comfortably resting in the Lord's promises. Lil' Lori entered my bedroom shortly after and saw me sleeping next to my open Bible. After weeks of uncertainty, she was filled with hope for the future, a hope that would sustain her for the next few months. This same hope sustained us all.

ON THE RISE

The road to recovery would soon prove to be the most challenging days of my life, making my worst day in prison look like child's play. Day after day I was able to be awake more and more, but my strength was still limited. I was not allowed to leave home unless it was to go to the doctor and back. Boy, did I see a lot of doctors! To this day, I still endure countless doctor visits, checks on vital signs, and various treatments and therapy. But constant travel is exhausting, especially since we were so far away from our doctors. Adding to this exhaustion were several uncertainties that can accompany those who have suffered strokes.

Did I lose some of my mobility? How damaged was my speech center? Would I have to suffer in this mental fog forever?

I found myself thankful when a therapist was cleared to come to our home. This thankfulness was quickly tried, however. The therapist's job was to evaluate and help me redevelop my speech and cognitive faculties. I would have to be tested on my current abilities every time she was in my home. The accuser of the brethren came back into full play, reminding me of my days in elementary school. I still remember my first day in gym class. The other kids loved to run and play, but I did not. I couldn't throw or kick a ball. I couldn't run for very long. I was one of the last people picked to be on a team. Report cards in the 1940s were still handwritten, and the letter grade for gym still echoes in my soul.

F. Jim Bakker is an F.

I did not do well on my first tests, and with each failure, the accuser would not let me forget my past. Suzanne, however, looked past my difficulties and frustrations. She helped me to overcome them. She even joined with my family to cheer me on throughout my recovery process. Suzanne, too, was a Christian. I know without a doubt that God used her to restore and heal me quicker than I could have thought possible.

Healing was more than just cognitive tests. The stroke had forced a new label on me in the hospital: Fall Risk. This was the reason the alarm had been activated on my ICU bed. Even now on my own, I still would fall several times. Just a couple months after the stroke, I was in our pool with Lori trying to get some exercise. I held the railing tightly as I was getting out of the pool, but I still fell and cut my leg badly. I could hear the accuser prey upon my weakness, but I was determined to stand on God's promises. I also knew that, as James says, faith without works is dead (2:17).

Most of my home is on the same level, except for my downstairs office, which we had converted into the television studio. It was also the way to get to the pool and backyard. So, in my determination that I would not let the accuser get the best of me, I decided to institute new rules for myself. The first rule was that I must always use the railings when I use the stairs. Our stairs feature two railings, and using them both would ensure that I would not fall. The second rule was that the light must be on, day or night.

These may seem like silly rules. I attest that there is much more here than preventing a fall down the stairs. First, thanks to Matthew 7, we know that the way ahead is narrow, and few there be that find it. The broad path may seem the obvious way, but it leads only to destruction. And second, the light overhead is a guiding light, enabling us to see what dangers lie ahead so that we can avoid and overcome them. These simple rules for navigating stairs are the most straightforward metaphor for our journey with our Lord and Savior. By leaning on the railings, I am relying on Jesus to guide me through a challenging road ahead, knowing that nothing but victory awaits on the other side. I'm happy to report I've not fallen down the stairs since I implemented these rules.

THE POWER OF LOVE

As the weeks went by, I continued to struggle with the challenges presented to me. Every day was different. On one day, I could feel as if I'd never experienced a stroke. I'd be happy, fully alert, and coherent. I could sit with my children and share stories and the love of God for hours on end. But the next day, I could not muster enough strength to climb out of my bed. It seemed I had as many bad days as I had good days.

But I had constants to gird my soul. I saw my children every day, and not just because they had come to tape the show. It didn't matter if Mondo was in a suit and tie, a t-shirt, or a hoodie. "Come on, Dad!" he would say when he came into the room. He'd help me out of bed and take me to my exercise bike for a few minutes. Mondo had made my physical therapy his personal mission. And because COVID had shuttered all the barbers, Mondo would cut my hair and trim my beard.

Lil' Lori, and her daughter, Olivia, age eight, would come by at least once a week. Olivia would help fill my water cup and sometimes would even help me put on a collared shirt. Both would sit next to me on the bed as Lil' Lori would read entire Scripture passages and share the things that the Lord had shown her. I'd always been proud of my children, but I had never been prouder of my daughter before this moment.

Maricela would share with me regular updates of what was going on with the ministry. In many cases, she spared me the discouraging details, which would be based on how I felt on a particular day. Throughout my process, I entrusted the ministry's operations to her care. While she always asked for my blessing on the plans she'd created (often with God's help), I allowed her to operate however she felt was necessary. She would just come in and pray, reminding the Lord of all the promises and messages He had given to me throughout my life. Some days I felt as though my past self was ministering to my present self, with each word charged by the Holy Spirit.

My children and grandchildren brought a new joy to me in my valley walking. They put several plaques on the wall throughout my home that declared "My Story Isn't Over Yet." The family would come over for every birthday, and I would sit on the couch or by the pool just watching in awe as my grandkids laughed and played. Not a single one of them wanted to leave my side either. Three-year-old Grayson's smiles were infectious. Jackson, five, would always bring me a little toy car or plane so I could play with him. The hugs and love from Mila and Mateo, ten, lifted my heavy soul. Even little Kate and Natalie, both three, the youngest of the bunch, found ways to make me laugh. My son Ricky couldn't make it because of his commitment to the army, but his wife flew to see us with their newborn daughter, Jacqueline. Even Lucky and Snowball, our two dogs, never left my side, no matter what!

Lori, my wife, stood by me at every step. Sure, she had a few appointments of her own, and she was now the primary host of our show, but she made sure I wasn't alone. Most importantly, she never allowed me to give up. She helped me through every rough moment, including ones that completely humbled me. If it wasn't for Lori, I never would have made it through this valley.

The road was not easy for her either. Overnight she had become more than my wife; she was now my caregiver. She insisted that she take me to every appointment, including a full physical at Dr. Don Colbert's practice. We deeply love Dr. Don and his wife, Mary, for many reasons, including the incredible lessons they'd provided to us over the years to live healthier lives. I believe if I hadn't heeded these lessons, my body would not have been in a position to recover from the stroke.

Upon our visit with Dr. Don, he observed a few things about Lori that he had felt the need to look into further. After a few tests, he revealed to Lori that she had suffered a mild heart attack not long ago. It was a miracle that she hadn't required immediate medical attention or that it didn't stop her when it happened, but she now needed some additional care of her own.

A few weeks later, while taking out the garbage, another incident occurred. Living in the middle of the Ozarks and in a rural area, we've been able to observe all kinds of wildlife. We've seen turkeys, bobcats, deer, and all manner of birds and critters. I've always loved sitting on my deck with a pair of binoculars, just watching God's creatures operate in their habitats. On the downside, some of these creatures scavenge for food from our trash cans. We quickly grew tired of cleaning up their mess, so we had a metal cover installed over our trash cans years ago. But this day, when Lori was taking out the garbage, the rain had made the cover too slick. It slipped and fell on Lori's head, slicing her forehead open. I tried to help her, but neither of us could stop the blood from flowing. I called Lil' Lori, hoping that she was close by. She and her husband, Jasper, dropped what they were doing and rushed to our aid. Within a few hours, Lori was released from the hospital, all bandaged up. The first time I saw her with her bandages wrapped around her forehead atop two black eyes, I called her a wounded warrior. She and I shared a laugh, recognizing the double meaning in the name.

Lori and I were most certainly wounded, and we were equally warriors of the faith. Her appearance now was a physical manifestation of what we had suffered for our calling. And no matter what we had suffered, our calling still remained. All throughout my recovery, I kept my eye on the news. I watched riots erupting in our streets, the burning of whole city blocks, and all manner of civil unrest and natural disasters sweeping our country as never before. I kept seeing the light in our country grow darker and darker. My thoughts would drift back every time to the messages God had given me throughout my life, specifically during my time with Him in prison. The final time clock, He told me years ago, was ticking. Even though a stroke had placed me on the bench, my time there was coming to an end. Much was happening in the world now, and it was time my voice returned to where it needed to be.

I called Andrew and asked him to come to my home. Though packed with important information, my mind was still challenging to navigate, and I knew I couldn't trust it on the air. I shared with Andrew what I wanted to say. Andrew had come to the ministry as a cameraman and editor in 2007 shortly before we moved from Branson to Morningside. For the last thirteen years, his job has been to watch me closely and edit what we tape into shows for national airing. If anyone knew how to help me communicate what I needed to say, it was him. Andrew took what I shared and created a simple script for me.

On June 30, 2020, I entered our temporary studio in my downstairs office for the first time in two months and sat at the desk. To my left were Mondo and Maricela, and to my right was Lori. I had planned to record something that was just ten minutes long. I wound up recording for eighty minutes.

That day was remarkable, and as I closed the taping with my trademark statement, "God loves you, He really does," my family and the crew offered a standing ovation. I had been through the valley of the shadow of death, and though I was not fully, or even halfway healed, I could feel the love all around me and the touch from my Father above. It was at this moment that I wondered, "Could I dare to believe that I would be fully restored?"

MOUNTAIN MOVERS

It wasn't one word that sustained me through this difficult season, but four. I have received many messages from the Lord throughout my ministry. A few of them have been timeless, meant to serve as a constant reminder of how I, or any Christian, for that matter, should always walk forward in faith. Among those few is a small passage of Scripture from Psalm 37 that has sustained and enriched my family daily since 1969. I used to call it the "Big Three" Mountain Movers, but I've since added the fourth.

1. Trust.

> Trust in the LORD, and do good; so shalt thou dwell in the
> land, and verily thou shalt be fed.
>
> —PSALM 37:3, KJV

To trust in the Lord requires you to confide fully in Him so that you may be secure and without fear. In the darkest of storms, it is difficult to trust your own eyesight because it is hard to see through the darkness and past the clouds that obscure the sky. Yet even though that storm may be whipping you about with winds and pouring rain, the sun is still shining above the clouds, as are the moon and the stars. The heavens remain untouched by the storms, and God can still see all. These trials are not unexpected, and in fact, He designs them. He's not trying to ruin your life. These storms are used to remind you of His glory, lest we take credit for what He is trying to do. We should only ever boast in the glory of the cross (Gal. 6:14). When you trust in Him, you can count on Him to guide you, provide for you, and use this experience to enrich your faith for the next phase of your life.

2. Delight.

> Delight thyself also in the LORD: and he shall give thee the
> desires of thine heart.
>
> —PSALM 37:4, KJV

Just because we delight in the Lord does not mean that He will immediately grant the desires of our hearts. Not every one of our desires is godly. Much of our pain comes from the struggle between flesh and salvation. This is why we are told in Scripture to "die daily" (1 Cor. 15:31) and to "take up [our] cross daily" (Luke 9:23). When we delight in the Lord and learn to praise Him at every moment, including the strongest and weakest, we discover one of the most incredible abilities we have as Christians. Nehemiah 8:10 reminds us that "The joy of the LORD is your strength." When we delight in our Lord and Savior, we tap into a supernatural strength that sustains our soul. When we do this, our desires will align with His desires for our life. The most beautiful part about praising and delighting in the Lord is that this is a choice. Take the Israelites who wandered in the wilderness, for example. The Lord was leading them to the Promised Land, but they complained all throughout the journey. Because they complained, they remained. An entire generation was forbidden to enter the Promised Land. Only those who praised God and found delight in Him throughout the wilderness were able to endure the forty years and enter His promises. The principle is the same for you. Delight in the Lord, and He will take you into His promises.

3. Commit.

> Commit thy way unto the LORD; trust also in him; and he shall bring it to pass. And he shall bring forth thy righteousness as the light, and thy judgment as the noonday.
> —PSALM 37:5–6, KJV

When we commit ourselves to the Lord, we are doing more than trusting and delighting. We are surrendering every part of ourselves, our flesh, and our desires unto Him. Every victory in my own life would not happen until I committed every single aspect to God. In the flesh, it always seems impossible, and God knows this! Jesus told us in Matthew 19:26 that "with God all things are possible." He encourages us in Matthew 11:28–30 and 1 Peter 5:7 to come to Jesus and surrender our cares and woes because He cares for us. A friend of mine once said, "Let go and let God," meaning that once you let go, God is free to do what He does best. Just step back and watch Him work! When we think we are alone, we believe a lie. God will never leave us or forsake us (Heb. 13:5), and His Son Jesus is standing in the gap for us as our Advocate who will ensure our vindication from sin and unrighteousness (1 John 2:1). But again, this only happens upon our full surrender.

4. Rest.

> Rest in the LORD, and wait patiently for him: fret not thy-
> self because of him who prospereth in his way, because of
> the man who bringeth wicked devices to pass.
>
> —PSALM 37:7, KJV

Finally, we must rest in the Lord. Every single event and circum-stance on earth happens only within His timing. God has a plan, and it will always be far, far greater than anything we can ever imagine. But there are times when our flesh wants an immediate resolution. We want our sons and daughters who walked away from the Lord to return immediately. We want our financial situation to be remedied immedi-ately. We want our persecution to end immediately. I, for one, wanted my body to be healed instantly. But the truth is, the suffering I have endured is now a testimony to you of what God can do. It is also proof that our steps are ordered by the Lord (Ps. 37:23) and that my journey on this earth isn't yet complete. There are things I must still yet do for the kingdom. And as you read this book, there are things you must still do as well.

When you and I commit to trusting, delighting, and resting in the Lord, healing and restoration begin. The accuser of the brethren will be cast down, and God will act on both my behalf and yours. Choose today to trust, delight, commit, and rest. When you fully adopt these four mountain movers, just sit back and be amazed at how God will move.

Morningside USA, located outside Branson, Missouri, spans over seven hundred acres. At the heart of the campus is the Grace Street building, with over one hundred condominium units, a restaurant, a general store, and more. It is also the current home of *The Jim Bakker Show*. In the middle of Grace Street stands *The Resurrected Christ* statue, which weighs more than twelve tons.

Our Prayer Mountain Chapel was built using the framework of a 120-year-old building. From this chapel residents and visitors alike continue to intercede for the future of our nation and for God's will to be done throughout the world.

Lori's House is a place for hope and healing for pregnant women and a place of safety during the first months of the baby's life.

Pastor Jim and Lori pray for and meet several of the new babies born at Lori's House.

Thanks to Bishop Ron Webb and the Farmers to Families Food Box Program under the Trump Administration, each week, month after month, Morningside was able to deliver thousands of boxes of fresh produce and dairy and meat products to the local community and surrounding churches.

Pastor Joe Campbell's grandson delivers food.

Grace Street was packed to capacity on New Year's Eve 2019, with so many people eager to hear from Pastor Jim Bakker what God had in store for the coming year.

Though he was very sick, Jim stood behind the pulpit on the Grace Street stage for nearly two hours and delivered one of his most sobering messages to the local congregation on December 31, 2019.

The night may have been long, but Mondo, Jim, and Lance Wallnau were still smiling in amazement at 3 a.m. The Lord had moved mightily among the congregation that night.

Shortly after midnight Jim, Mondo, and Lance Wallnau led a prayer service at our Prayer Mountain Chapel as 2020 began.

Jim stands out among the audience as he delivers the many prophetic words, including the warning that the four horsemen would usher in a worldwide event.

Grace Street was packed with family, friends, and loved ones from all around the world, all of whom had come out to celebrate Jim's eightieth birthday on January 2, 2020.

After eight long hours the party kept on going! Jim loved every minute of it! Pictured with Jim (left to right) is Olivia, Lil' Lori, Lori, and Maricela.

Jim applauds as Tammy Sue, dressed as Vestal Goodman, performs a medley of Happy Goodman songs.

(left) Cindy Jacobs prophesies a birthday blessing over Jim Bakker.

(below) Jim speaks with Bob D'Andrea of the Christian Television Network. Bob was one of many who'd come from around the country to celebrate Jim's birthday.

(above) Jim interviews Joni and Marcus Lamb, founders of the Daystar Television Network.

As the pandemic began to sweep the nation, *The Jim Bakker Show* was relocated from its Grace Street stage to Jim's basement office. Where he would normally craft his sermons and hear from God had been transformed overnight into a full-blown television production studio.

The small crew prepares to tape a broadcast in the home studio.

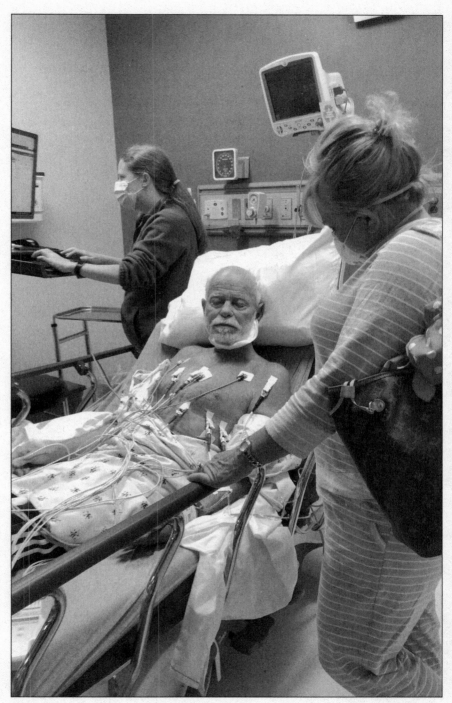

Jim, pictured during his stroke, lies in an emergency room bed. Lori stands beside him, having just been told that her husband has a fifty-fifty chance of living. This would be the last time Lori would see Jim before he is released from the hospital three days later.

During the early phase of Jim's recovery, Mondo, Maricela, and Lil' Lori hold one of their many breakfast meetings with their parents before going downstairs to tape an episode of *The Jim Bakker Show*.

Mondo, Maricela, and Lil' Lori pray for their father.

Lil' Lori, Marie, and Maricela honor their dad during Father's Day 2020.

Many members of the Bakker family gather around for Lori's sixty-third birthday. Life continued to move forward during Jim's recovery, and the family would celebrate every birthday and milestone.

Bishop Ron Webb, Morningside's world outreach director, visits with Jim while he is in recovery.

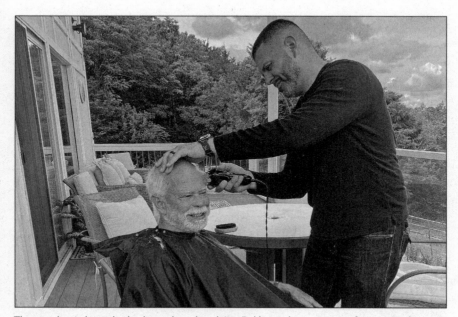

The pandemic kept the barbers closed and Jim Bakker at home except for essential doctor's visits. To keep Jim looking good, Mondo practiced his barber skills and cut Jim's hair!

Jim and Lori enjoy a day of fun with some of their grandchildren in their pool, while Jim obeys his doctor's order to exercise.

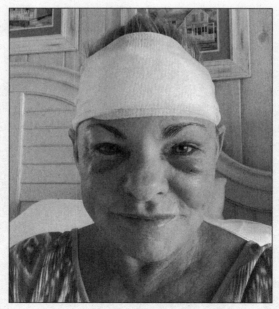

While Lori was taking out the trash, a metal grate fell on her head, slicing her forehead open and giving her two black eyes. This is one of the first photos taken after she came home from the hospital. It was at this moment that Jim called her a "wounded soldier."

Visiting Jim in his sickbed, Lil' Lori and her daughter, Olivia, read to him and Snowball many of the get-well-soon cards from our partners.

Jim reads one of the thousands of get-well-soon cards sent to him by the faithful partners of *The Jim Bakker Show*.

Two months after his stroke, Jim gets in front of the cameras for the very first time. He planned to tape just a ten-minute message for his partners but wound up recording an entire hour-long episode instead. He would not return to the air full time for several more weeks.

On his eighty-first birthday, January 2, 2021, Jim and Lori, along with family, the board of directors, and several staff members and volunteers, broke ground on the new Hall of the Prophets Studio!

A couple of days after breaking ground, Lil' Lori, Lori, Jim, Maricela, and Mondo tape new episodes of *The Jim Bakker Show*, reminding their television audience of the dreams, visions, and promises the Lord will soon fulfill.

The annual Bakker family portrait taken for Christmas 2020. Not all family members could make it.
Left to right, back row: Mondo, Beth, Mateo, Brooke, Jacqueline, Ricky, Natalie, John, Maricela, Tammy Sue, Lil' Lori, and Jasper;
front row: Mila, Donna, Snowball, Jim, Lucky, Lori, Char, Jackson, Kate, and Olivia

CHAPTER 8

TAKING A STAND

ONE OF MONDO's favorite sayings is, "Whenever you have a setback, don't take a step back, but get ready for your comeback!" As a ministry and family, we had endured much for the gospel and my call as a watchman. Our battles were in the physical realm with lawsuits, petitions, and a stroke. They were also in the spiritual realm with the sheer fight to remain on the air and not compromise the message. Our first act was to trust the Lord and His process. We then delighted in His ability. We committed our every step and action to His will. And finally, we rested in the Lord's timing.

We did not have to wait long to see the beginning of His master plan. The very first thing God did was to remind us of the very same thing He showed me back in 1976, that the place of security could be found only in the body of Christ. This reminder came through our faithful partners. In March and April, we told our partners the hard truth that we as a ministry were teetering on a cliff. Without them, we would not make it more than a couple of weeks. Our partners responded to our plight and still are responding to this day. We had several surprising donations from unexpected sources that had rarely or never supported our ministry and message before.

Donations were just a piece of the tremendous support we had received. After we had announced that I had a stroke, our ministry mailbox was stuffed for weeks with cards and letters of encouragement. Lori and I were deeply touched by each and every handwritten note. My children and grandchildren would sit on our bed and read many of these cards with Lori and me. Our staff would even collect encouraging messages posted on our social media accounts, print them off, and send them over to us every week. We might have been wounded, still taking shot after shot, but every single note gave us the strength to endure. If it were not for the partners allowing God to move through them, I firmly believe we would never have made it this far.

FULFILLING OUR PURPOSE

No matter how many trials and tribulations we endured as a family, we also had to recognize that part of our ministry's core tenets was rooted within the community at Morningside. I wrote a book in the year 2000, *The Refuge: A Look Into the Future and the Power of Living in a Christian Community*. In other words, security for the future is within the body of Christ. And 2020 proved to the church not just the urgency of this fact but the necessity of the body. Hebrews 10:25 explicitly warns:

> Let us not forsake the assembling of ourselves together, as is the manner of some, but let us exhort one another, especially as you see the Day approaching.

The two operative Greek words in this scripture are *episynagōgēn* (assembling) and *parakalountes* (exhort). The word for *assembling* in Greek defines a gathering together in the name of Christ, much like a church. Likewise, the word *exhort* means to encourage, admonish, comfort, and console. The church is not just where we worship together. It is where we as a body of believers unite for kinship and encouragement, work through our grief and pain, and rejoice in the glory of the Lord. Only when we assemble as the body of Christ can we truly realize the hope that sustains our soul. Christ's body reminds us that we are not alone in this journey with Him. Through our togetherness, our faith is maintained and our eyes remain fixed on the high calling of Christ Jesus. We are easier targets for the enemy when we are divided and removed from one another. The COVID pandemic and lockdowns only demonstrated this point, something that the rider on the white horse was eager to exploit. When we are united, the Lord can use us all collectively for great and mighty things. This is why we, as believers, need to stay involved in our local church fellowship. This is why our churches need to always remain open!

Morningside is not only a city of refuge for the days ahead; it has been charged to be a light for the community around us in addition to carrying the light of Jesus over the airwaves. Over the past decade, our family and ministry have done their best to pour into the community around us. In our early years at Morningside, we brought a Christian rock band to perform in our Grace Street facility. The lead singer traveled to several junior high and high schools in the area, where he shared his testimony and invited them to Morningside. Hundreds of youth came to this incredible concert. God was moving, but not everyone agreed with this outreach. An elderly couple who lived there pulled aside Lori's mom, Char, and told her how much they despised this effort! It didn't matter to them at all that through this Christian rock concert, several dozen teenagers and young adults from the city and area accepted Jesus Christ as their Savior. We did not let people such as this couple discourage our outreaches as we moved forward.

When Haiti was struck by a devastating 7.0 earthquake in 2010, we rallied our partners to send hundreds of Seychelle water filtration bottles to the ravaged island. In 2011, after a series of devastating tornadoes and floods that ravaged the Midwest, we partnered with Bishop Ron Webb to supply building materials, furniture, manpower, food, and more to rebuild the community of Morehouse, Missouri. I visited the town and met those affected the most by the floods. Every single person, including the mayor, was glad that we helped in their darkest hour. The mayor even presented us with the key to the city. In 2017, after Hurricanes Harvey and Irma, we took food to Houston, Texas, and Immokalee, Florida. A Hispanic pastor in Immokalee was thrilled to have something besides hot dogs to eat!

We also strove to make inroads with our local community—not for our sake, but for the sake of the gospel. We opened a food pantry to provide free food to the local area for those who needed it. This pantry provides thousands of meals to hundreds of people every single week.

At Christmastime, we invite the entire local area to Grace Street for a massive breakfast buffet, free Christmas shopping, incredible prizes, Christmas caroling, and even have a visit from Santa Claus. My own children would look forward to this event every year just to have a chance to impact their neighbors the same way they had been impacted when living in Phoenix.

It was no surprise how hard COVID-19 hit our local community. The schools were closed instantly, and many families quickly found their breadwinners unemployed. Our own pantry was doing its best to provide food to the community, but we knew those resources were only going to go so far. I wanted to do even more for our neighbors, and I was not alone in this line of thinking. Bishop Ron Webb, our World Outreach Director, was just as passionate as I was to feed our hurting neighbors. He traveled the nation regularly, and he continued to see the need everywhere he went. I remember speaking to him countless times on the phone, and we both prayed for a solution.

Shortly after I had my stroke, Bishop Webb called me with incredible news. By order of President Trump, a national food distribution system was being constructed. Through this program, Farmers to Families Food Box Program, we had an opportunity to become a local distribution hub. Within days, the first truck arrived and delivered one thousand boxes of fresh produce. Bishop Webb was present at Morningside to lead our team in giving these boxes to anyone who came through. Mondo, Tammy Sue, and Lil' Lori were on hand as well. Everyone, including our volunteers, was gloved and masked according to health department regulations. Hundreds of cars came through that day, the line stretching almost a mile up to Morningside's main entrance at a couple of points. It wasn't just a particular group of people either. COVID was no respecter of persons or positions. Boxes were placed in all kinds of vehicles that day, ranging from rusted and abused to polished and expensive. Bishop and Mondo personally prayed for several people who came through that day, including a woman in a sleek Mercedes who had no idea what to do because COVID had destroyed her ability to make a living. We still receive regular truckloads of produce, along with meat and dairy products, and we'll continue to distribute these to the community as long as the program is available.

This serves as a strong reminder for us all of our calling as Christians. It is not enough to seek Him daily. We must continually shine His light among the world, to be the salt that provides flavor and purpose. No matter who we are, what political party we identify with, where we've been, and what we've done, Jesus is waiting for each and every one of us with open arms. We must demonstrate that love on a daily basis to everyone around us, no matter what.

Our Morningside community stood with us in other ways. Near the end of the year, the Lord impressed a statement of faith on the hearts of both Maricela and Pastor Joe Campbell, the senior pastor of Morningside Church. Pastor Joe was one of the first pastors to greet our family when we moved to the Branson area.

Not only is he one of the greatest men of faith I have ever met, but I have also been impressed by his ability to find things. When we were building Grace Street, our first building at Morningside, he was able to find dozens of beautiful railings that had been discarded in warehouses, along with other fantastic building materials that we incorporated into the building's facade. Then, in 2018, when we could not get the construction moving on our Prayer Mountain Chapel, God told me to bring in Pastor Joe. God used Pastor Joe to get that building finished and open! Pastor Joe's wife, Becky, watches after Lori's House, a center for pregnant women who need a safe place to have their baby as an alternative to abortion. Lori's House continued to operate during the pandemic, seeing seven new births to date!

But what had been impressed on Pastor Joe's and Maricela's hearts now was a massive step of faith. Just as the children of Israel marched around Jericho for seven days, so would our community march around Morningside, believing God would bring down a spiritual wall. For seven days, our community prayed for deliverance from our litigation, release of the funds being withheld from the ministry, renewed health for Lori and me, the continued reach for our television platform, and the manifestation of the promises the Lord had promised for our community.

As the week progressed, more and more of the community came out to join us. Cold weather, rain, and snow didn't stop our congregation from forming and interceding in prayer on behalf of the ministry. Not only was every department visited and prayed for every day, but our congregation began to lift up one another in prayer, standing in agreement, just as Jesus instructed us all in Matthew 18:19–20. Our congregation experienced breakthroughs in many aspects of their lives, from healing to answers to long-awaited prayers. Pastor Joe, Maricela, and other family members experienced a total shift in our way of thinking. The experience reminded us all to trust, delight, commit, and rest in our Lord and Savior. As the world began to accelerate and experience the things we had already been going through for months, the Lord provided a clear vision for our ministry's future.

Even though I was bedridden, recovering from my stroke, the miracles just kept coming. God also began to reveal some of the purposes behind the persecution we had experienced.

LITIGATION

Our struggles with litigation began in early March. We received multiple letters from government officials demanding that we cease and desist using Silver Solution in association with COVID-19 (which we did swiftly). These letters were followed by a lawsuit from the state of Missouri. Several other entities continued to communicate with us, requesting information about our business practices and lists of contact information and financial contributions of our partners and guests.

We brought our board of directors into the developing situation and kept them informed at every turn. On their recommendation, we worked quickly to expand our legal team. Every day we prayed that a resolution would come for all the litigation swirling around us, and God spoke to us through several qualified individuals. I know from experience that this attack would not merely go away, and God often allows us to endure hardship for a reason. I had to endure five years in prison to hear properly from the Lord and receive an infusion of Scripture so that I would be prepared for my next phase in life, which was to build this platform for the prophets.

You have to be willing to recognize, no matter the occasion, that God has a purpose for every little thing that happens. Sometimes, He will use you to impact someone else's life, such as what appears to be a meeting of happenstance outside a store or business. Or sometimes, He wants to use a situation to connect you with others in His kingdom. After all, if security can be found in the body of Christ, we must make efforts to get to know our fellow believers. And sometimes, those connections just go to prove that God is ultimately in control, and His master plan is set to confound the wise.

Because of the wisdom God granted to our board of directors, we were able to network with several fantastic attorneys, including Jay Nixon, the former governor of Missouri. Governor Nixon brought a wealth of information and knowledge to the table and was essential in getting several early victories with the state. Yet these other entities had a growing presence, continuing to send in request after request after request. Each of these requests followed a pattern, asking for the same details, including the names, addresses, and financial contributions of our partners, as well as a list of our guests on the show along with their credentials and qualifications.

We found these requests to be both morally and religiously appalling. We also believed that these requests represented a dangerous attack that would soon be demanded of other religious organizations and believers around the nation. Freedom of speech and freedom to assemble and express what the Lord has placed upon our hearts were at risk—for us and for thousands of Christian pastors across the country. We felt that we had no other choice but to push back against these unlawful requests. To do so, we filed a lawsuit in federal court against multiple government officials from other states who were trying to reach into Missouri and require us to turn over information that we strongly felt was intended by the founders of our great country and the framers of our Constitution to be protected from compelled disclosure. I am a firm believer that the Constitution of the United States protects our rights, and the rights of our partners, to freely practice our religion, to seek God and share what He has impressed on our hearts. As we navigate deeper into 2021 and this new decade, I believe that these freedoms guaranteed by the First Amendment are now more important than ever!

I do have one area of praise to report. As I shared in an earlier chapter, two of the first players in this process were the Food and Drug Administration (FDA) and the Federal Trade Commission (FTC). In a joint letter, they listed several items and demanded that we take action within forty-eight hours, which we absolutely complied with. We did not hear back from them for months, and we wondered what they planned to do next. Our answer finally came on July 8, 2020. The FDA replied, acknowledging that they were satisfied with our actions. In other words, they had considered the matter closed.

As I write this book, most of our litigation is still ongoing. We continue to pray for this situation as a whole. We encourage all Christians throughout the nation and world to pray against the persecution we and now other ministries have suffered due to the stand we have taken for Christian values. We have learned through this ordeal that the enemy will use any agency he can, including governments and courts, to try to stop the message of the cross and the efforts of the church. This is proved even in Scripture when Jesus commissioned His disciples.

> But beware of men, for they will deliver you up to the councils, and they will scourge you in their synagogues. You will be brought before governors and kings for My sake, for a testimony against them and the Gentiles. But when they deliver you up, take no thought of how or what you will speak. For it will be given you at that time what you will speak. For it is not you who speak, but the Spirit of your Father who speaks through you.
>
> —MATTHEW 10:17–20

I believe that I, along with many others, were the forerunners of this new wave of persecution that is now upon us all.

PROTECTING THE PLATFORM

Our platform for the prophets had been threatened in other venues as well. The activist group Faithful America had issued a petition in April

2020 that had cost us two of our long-standing Christian stations. In addition, our local station had also pulled *The Jim Bakker Show* from the air. The rest of our stations had committed to standing with us. We continued to move forward with our program. After all, our calling was, and is, to share the voice of the prophets through *The Jim Bakker Show*. Bringing voices such as these to the nation every day is a solemn responsibility. Every time an extension of our platform is lost, we also lose opportunities for people to hear these messages. Many times in my life have I seen God use a simple television broadcast to transform just one person's life.

Through our struggles, we once again found security within the body of Christ. Several of our frequent show guests had already actively publicized what we were going through, namely Tom Horn, Derek Gilbert, Zach Drew, and Steve Strang. They had quickly recognized our persecution for what it was: an attempt to silence our voice and platform. The role of an end-time watchman is a particularly difficult one. The messages we bring are at times unpopular, seemingly outlandish, and often offensive. This is all because we are sharing a truth that the world does not wish to hear. Those who signed the petition to take us down believed that our intention was to deceive. Our regular and faithful viewers know this isn't true.

But those walking beside us, holding our arms up amid this crisis, had a radical thought: If a petition of over fifteen thousand signatures could affect Jim Bakker this deeply, how much more could a counter-petition do? Several ministry supporters quickly went to work, and an independent petition was launched. Rather than use a popular website designed for petitions, its independence was by design so that the platform itself couldn't be damaged and the petition removed. Tom, Derek, Zach, and Steve started to share this petition online. Steve posted another op-ed on the Charisma website to raise awareness and support. Derek leveraged his own networking skills and appeared on several shows within his circle to raise awareness of the petition.

Within a month, over twenty-seven thousand people signed the petition.

Our local station reevaluated *The Jim Bakker Show*. Thanks to the petition, along with a series of assurances that we were not circumventing any laws and proved that we were not attempting to deceive the viewers, the local station returned *The Jim Bakker Show* to its daily lineup.

We praised God for the victory, but we also knew that this battle wasn't over. Jesus warns us in Matthew 24, Luke 21, and Mark 13 that the future ahead for all believers involves persecution. In those first few months of 2020, we experienced firsthand what this persecution and censoring would look like. From November 2020 to January 2021, many conservative and Christian groups would experience this persecution and censorship firsthand just for presenting views that were counter to the mainstream narrative.

I believe that in the days ahead we will have to fight harder than ever before for our freedoms of speech and religion. Nothing in our nation's history, including the Revolutionary War from 1775–1783, will compare to the struggles we are about to face. Jesus told us that we would be hated by all nations for His name's sake (Matt. 24:9).

This is unavoidable. The need for a secure platform is now more necessary than ever.

CHAPTER 9

THE VOICE OF THE PROPHETS

WHEN JESUS WALKED with the disciples throughout His three
years of ministry, He became known for the many parables that He would tell the crowds, the Pharisees, and His
disciples. These parables served multiple purposes in that day, ranging
from fulfilling Old Testament prophecy (Matt. 13:13–15) to illustrating
the true motives and missions of the kingdom of God. We know from
experience and Scripture that He keeps some matters secret (Dan. 12:4),
that what is in secret or mysterious will one day be revealed and fulfilled (Rev. 10:7), and that the Lord wants to share everything with us
(Amos 3:7).

Scripture itself hasn't been trusted to just one person. Four of Jesus'
disciples wrote the Gospels, Paul wrote much of the New Testament,
and much of the Old Testament was written by prophets and historians.
Even today, there is not a single person on the earth who carries the
complete picture. This is done so that one person can't make a claim
for His glory. There's also a scriptural basis. According to 1 Corinthians
13:9, "We know in part, and we prophesy in part." We are each given a
piece of the puzzle, much like we each have a role to play in the body
of Christ. Some of us have been called to be hands, some the feet, and
others the eyes (1 Cor. 12:12–30).

The office of the prophet is one that has not just been overlooked in
some circles and churches. It has been branded as one that is not welcome. To an extent, this is understandable. After all, it is easy to avoid
false prophecy when you don't listen to any prophecy. On multiple

occasions, Jesus warned us that false prophets would arise and deceive many (Matt. 24:4, 11, 24). Paul witnessed this in his own time, and he wrote against it many times (1 Tim. 6:3–5; Gal. 5:7–12; 2 Cor. 11:1–15). False prophets exist for one reason: it is the enemy's attempt to prevent you from listening to voices that you cannot afford to ignore.

When we force the prophets to remain outside our doors and away from our parishioners and minds, we blatantly ignore what God has designed.

> He gave some to be apostles, *prophets*, evangelists, pastors, and teachers, for the equipping of the saints, for the work of service, and for the building up of the body of Christ, until we all come into the unity of the faith and of the knowledge of the Son of God, into a complete man, to the measure of the stature of the fullness of Christ, so we may no longer be children, tossed here and there by waves and carried about with every wind of doctrine by the trickery of men, by craftiness with deceitful scheming. But, speaking the truth in love, we may grow up in all things into Him, who is the head, Christ Himself, from whom the whole body is joined together and connected by every joint and ligament, as every part effectively does its work and grows, building itself up in love.
> —EPHESIANS 4:11–16, EMPHASIS ADDED

Prophets are a requirement for completeness. You cannot unlock and understand the full Word of God without listening to every portion that He has made available to us. First Corinthians 12 informs us that not only is prophecy a spiritual gift (v. 10), but that it is the second office installed in the church, right between apostles and teachers (v. 28). The role of the prophet, according to 1 Corinthians 14, is to edify the church. *The Oxford Dictionary* defines *edify* as "instruct or improve (someone) morally or intellectually."[1] In other words, prophecy is meant to impart knowledge. This knowledge can bring understanding, direction, or sometimes even comfort. But most importantly, the gift of prophecy is designed to be spoken to one another.

As we venture into this final phase, this last act on the earth, we cannot afford to ignore the office of the prophet. If you have been purposely trying to shut out the prophets, you will soon find that it will become increasingly difficult to do so.

> And it will be that, afterwards, I will pour out My Spirit on
> all flesh; then your sons and your daughters will *prophesy*,
> your old men will dream dreams, and your young men will
> see visions. Even on the menservants and maidservants in
> those days I will pour out My Spirit.
> —JOEL 2:28–29, EMPHASIS ADDED; SEE ALSO ACTS 2:17–18

All across the world, God's children are receiving downloads from God, just as I have received throughout my life. Prophecy is not about "reading someone's mail," nor is that a necessary part of the office. Sometimes, the gift of prophecy is just having a specific word of knowledge for someone else in the church. This can sometimes be a promise or a warning. Because of the importance of the gift, as well as its necessity, the enemy desires to corrupt and disqualify it, cutting you off from a vital part of God's communication network.

But how can you know if a voice, no matter if it is a known or unknown voice, can be trusted? Many people have come to me with a word of knowledge or a message from the Lord. Because I have spent so much time in God's Word, I have been able to determine that many of these words were attempts to deceive me off the path I've been designated to walk. The simple truth is, you cannot trust a singular voice unless it is God Himself speaking directly to you. When you hear a word, you must first seek confirmation in two different ways.

The first is to test the prophetic word on the authority of God's Word. I believe the Bible is filled with patterns and templates that provide the basis for everything that happens on the earth today. For example, we have been provided with instructions for restoring our brothers and sisters who've fallen into sin, templates for prayer, and examples of faith in the darkest valleys. Prophetic messages do not override what is written in Scripture itself. If the Word fails the Scripture test, then you can safely say that it was not of God.

The Bible also provides, in multiple locations, the other method to confirm a prophetic word. This is testing the word with other prophets. First Corinthians 14:32 states plainly that the prophets are subject to the prophets. Meaning, the collective voice of the prophets will be able to confirm or disprove whether or not a word has genuinely come from the Lord. Chapter 14 even requires that when a prophet speaks, at least two or three others must also speak. This template exists in multiple forms. Deuteronomy 19:15 confirms that two or three witnesses are required to confirm every fact. My life verse, Matthew 18:19–20, establishes the power two or three people have when they are united in Christ's name.

But what happens when multiple people who prophesy the same thing turn out to be wrong? All too often, we see many prophets jump onto a spiritual bandwagon because we believe that something has to happen. We believe that a politician will be elected to a certain office because God's hand is on that person. We believe that a spiritual breakthrough will come in a certain area or region because we've been told a great revival is about to come and sweep the nation. And then we get disappointed when these things do not come to pass.

Can prophets get it wrong? Yes. Being wrong once does not invalidate a prophet's entire ministry. But an incorrectly interpreted prophecy can have unfortunate consequences. We must remember that there was only one perfect man in all history, and His name was Jesus Christ. And we must also remember to test every word of prophecy against Scripture. Our prophets and our pastors are fully capable of stumbling. We should not mock them when they stumble, but we should instead come alongside them and follow the scriptural instructions for restoration. The God of the mountain is also the God of the valley, and He will use the time in the valley to further teach and impress His will on those who walk in it.

I have lived through these consequences firsthand, and because of that, I do my best to diligently seek the Lord and do my absolute best to confirm what He gives to me. Each and every word that God gives me to share comes with an important responsibility to get it right. This is why we are instructed to test the message with other prophets and with Scripture. These God-given safeguards will help maintain the office of the prophet and help you identify who is acting as a false prophet, casting deceit over a group of believers. While I am able to test what I've been given most of the time, there are occasions when I just have to trust that the urges I have are the Holy Spirit leading me to say something important.

I remember a day when I was unwittingly testing a word first given by someone else. At the time, I was living at the Dream Center in Los Angeles. A member of the team tracked me down and told me that a very famous professional football player had come to see me. I was extremely nervous because there had been no clear indication of what he wanted, and this person and I had never met before.

When this player and I were alone, he looked at me carefully and said: "You have a word for me."

I paused for a moment and silently prayed. The Holy Spirit whispered to me, and I offered one simple command. There was no one near me to test the word, and I couldn't tell this man I had never met that I needed to rush and check this command with someone else. I had to deliver the message immediately.

"The Lord says don't sell the farm." For a moment, I thought this was ridiculous. Who was I to tell a pro football player to not sell a farm? I didn't even know if he had a farm! Farming and football, after all, were two very different things.

What happened next was something I didn't expect. He whooped and cheered right in front of me as if he had just scored a touchdown. "Jim!" he exclaimed. "You were the third person to tell me that I shouldn't sell my farm. That means I've got to obey it!"

I have tested many other prophetic words in front of other prophets. One of the most accurate prophets I've met in my lifetime is Bob Jones. The night I delivered the first "31 Things" at a MorningStar Conference on December 31, 1999, Bob approached me after my message. I have to admit that I was nervous. It wasn't that I wanted to be wrong or feared that I was wrong. I simply didn't want to lead anyone astray. He not only confirmed to me that he had seen several of the things that I had shared, including major earthquakes in Japan and Los Angeles. He gave me an order in which they would happen.

Other times, I would meet with a group of prophets at a roundtable held every year under Rick Joyner's Heritage International Ministries. We would all share words we had received and test them among one another. To this day I stand amazed at what God has shown His prophets. Many of the words I've heard in that room have come to pass. I remember attending the roundtable in 2018, just a few days after Billy Graham died. Many were asking what Billy's death signified. Some had hinted that this would indicate a sea change, but I knew something else was on the horizon. Just a few hours before, when paying my respects as Billy Graham lay in repose in his childhood home, I had the opportunity to speak with Franklin Graham. He shared with me what he believed his father's death unlocked. His belief didn't shake me to my core; instead, it lit a confirming fire within my soul. I was already thinking what Franklin had told me, and now I was assured it was accurate. "Billy's life was holding everything back," I told the assembled prophets. "With his death, a whole lot of shaking is coming. All of heaven and hell on earth will shake, and everything will change." I poured my heart out to the prophets and shared more and more. As soon as I was done, there was silence in the room, and everyone was just nodding their heads.

Rick Joyner looked at everyone in the room, one by one. A minute later, he asked, "Can anyone top that?" No one could, and everyone agreed that it was correct. Not only that, we are still seeing evidence of this word today.

PROPHETS AND WATCHMEN

Just as the body is made of many parts, the prophetic office is made of many voices communicating the singular message of God. I have received many dreams and visions throughout my life, both in front of and behind the camera. In the early days of Christian broadcasting, God allowed me to see through the camera lens and into the homes of many, calling out certain people with a specific word. Even with this knowledge, I do not claim to be a prophet. My role, along with many others throughout the world, is to be a watchman. I've often been asked what the difference between the two is.

Both roles are absolutely critical to the church's future, and while the positions have some overlap, they are really very different from each other. As shown previously, prophets are for the church's edification, which has multiple purposes—instruction, education, warning, promise, assurance, and comfort. Watchmen, however, are assigned to be looking ahead for specific signs of warning. Let's look to Scripture for clarification.

> Now as for you, son of man: I have set you a watchman to the house of Israel. Therefore you shall hear a word from My mouth and warn them from Me. When I say to the wicked, "O wicked man, you shall surely die," and you do not speak to warn the wicked from his way, that wicked man shall die in his iniquity. But his blood I will require from your hand. Nevertheless, if you on your part warn the wicked to turn from his way and he does not turn from his way, he shall die in his iniquity. But you have delivered your soul.
>
> —Ezekiel 33:7–9

The watchman's call bears an immense responsibility, and it involves actively watching, listening, and conveying what is seen. Most importantly, the watchman takes the complicated and breaks it down for now. When warnings come, there is little time for explanation, and immediate action is required.

I think of back in December 2012 when I was taping a broadcast with Philip Cameron and I suddenly couldn't get the image of Boston out of my mind. I felt great pain and suffering, but I couldn't understand why. Right then and there, I interrupted the conversation and just urged people to pray for Boston. It was the only warning I received before the bombing at the Boston Marathon just four months later, in April 2013. I say this to illustrate that when you hear a word of warning, the responsibility is yours to heed the warning and take appropriate action, whether it be to pray, share it with others, or otherwise prepare for the inevitable fulfillment of God's promise.

THE VOICE MUST BE HEARD NOW

To navigate the days ahead, we must give authority and respect to the offices of prophets and watchmen. We must bring them to our churches, we must bring them to our meetings, and we must listen to them whenever and wherever we can, including through our television sets, computers, and smartphones. After I was released from prison, I had no desire to return to the airwaves. I had been dragged through the wringer, and the last thing I wanted to do was experience it again. Yet God strongly impressed on me to use my knowledge, experience, and skill to build a platform for the prophets.

The return of *The Jim Bakker Show* was only a first step in the fulfillment of that calling. Every prophet I spoke to, no matter how much they knew me or my past, told me that not only would I be coming back, but my latter ministry would eclipse the former. In the early years in Branson, I had no idea how this would be accomplished. The call on our ministry had always been simple:

> And this gospel of the kingdom will be preached throughout
> the world as a testimony to all nations, and then the end
> will come.
> —MATTHEW 24:14

I simply just kept lifting this calling up to the Lord each and every day. Year after year, we would add new stations to make our broadcast available to more people. By 2020, *The Jim Bakker Show* had been expanded to reach up to 1.6 billion people every week. And we are still growing.

As incredible as this is, I knew that the show was only one aspect of this platform. We could only cover so much within an hour-long broadcast, and our reach was totally dependent on other networks. This became abundantly clear in January 2019. Julie Pigg, who represents our show and brokers our airtime arrangements, called me with some unexpected news. One of our longtime, largest, and most responsive networks had made the unfortunate decision to close. Not only was I heartbroken, but I also knew what this meant for us. Our message had to continue going out each and every day, and without the Angel One network millions of faithful viewers would now be losing access to the program.

I asked Julie a simple question, knowing the time had come to be bold: "Can we buy their channel?"

At the time, I don't even think the ministry had the money to purchase a channel on a satellite network. But I knew every vision I could cast in front of the television audience could be caught and funded. The fact that we had done so much in fifteen years had proved that to be true. We researched the possibility and found out that not only was such a purchase unable to happen at that time (some contracts and circumstances were out of our control), but there now seemed to be a clear path ahead of us to establish a network. We had already been building an online network, providing several new hours of content a day through our website, streaming services, and other mobile devices. These efforts brought new partners and viewers to our table, so we could clearly see the demand for a prophetic network.

Months would pass before we would finally be able to prepare our network for a serious, national launch. By the end of 2019 we were in serious discussions with a satellite provider to launch our own channel and return the PTL Television Network to the air after a very long hiatus. This time I cast the vision before my staff and audience. I told them the network would have a singular focus. The tagline for this network would be "The Voice of the Prophets" in recognition of the full platform the Lord had called me to build while I was back in my prison cell and repeated to me multiple times in the next decades. I even nicknamed PTL "Prophets Talking Loud!"

Our partners caught the vision immediately. Thanks to them, we raised enough money to get everything started. On January 9, 2020, my daughter Maricela brought our contract onto the broadcast. As she stood next to Mondo, Lori, and me, Maricela affixed her signature on camera, activating the contract. This was significant, as it was a physical fulfillment of the promise God had made with me that the Voice of the Prophets would have a home. This home would keep running twenty-four hours a day, seven days a week, even after our one-hour broadcast ended for that day.

Everything was moving along just fine until March. In the middle of the cease-and-desist letters, the lawsuits, and all the public backlash, negotiations and preparation with the satellite provider suddenly went silent. We were unable to get any updates for several weeks. When we finally did, we were told that the satellite provider was no longer interested in pursuing the channel, citing all the negative attention we had been receiving. This was absolutely heartbreaking. Very few times had we seen rejection before we even had a chance to get started. But we were in the middle of a crisis, and I figured with everything going on, we needed to focus on the issues before us.

Months later, after I had had my stroke in June 2020, Maricela would receive a phone call from Julie. Back when we had started negotiations with that satellite provider, we had made an agreement with a third party to help us make the connections and carry our signal to the satellite provider. This company had helped several other Christian networks get started, and they were committed to helping us get the PTL Network back off the ground no matter what it took. "Maricela," Julie said, "they've put together some options for us if we're still interested." She explained that though the reach would be about the same as the satellite provider, the network would be built very differently. "I think this is a great opportunity, Maricela. But I won't move forward unless your dad approves it."

We were still in the thick of it all, dealing with the legal issues and trying to just stay on the air. I had already been sidelined by my stroke, and my only priorities were to get rest and focus on recovery. But Maricela knew instantly that God was making a way where there didn't seem to be a path. Maricela made a promise to get this information to me as soon as possible.

The next day, Maricela entered my bedroom with Lori and Mondo to see me before going downstairs to tape an episode of our show. She told me, "Dad, we still have a chance to launch the Voice of the Prophets. What do you think?"

Lori and Mondo were in the room with me. I remember jolting

awake, the news providing a sudden burst of energy. Amid chaos and darkness, God had worked a miracle on our behalf. I looked at Maricela and said two words, "Sign it."

Maricela, Julie, our team, and our connection company went to work immediately. Missing pieces of equipment were ordered, and the network connections were established. By the end of July, the PTL Network began broadcasting on select cable networks around the country. By September, we had added a variety of cable companies throughout the United States. The PTL Network was now available in twenty-five states, the Virgin Islands, and Washington, DC.

I couldn't believe the miracle that was happening. Amid our storm, our chaos, and our darkest hour, God shone one of the brightest lights on us that I'd ever seen. By remaining faithful and not wavering or giving up, He began to fulfill a promise that was first issued back when my world fell apart in the 1980s. The PTL Network continues to grow every month, both in viewership and new and established voices coming to edify our viewers and warn them of things to come.

Here, within these pages, I once again commit this network and its calling to the will of our Lord and Savior. I believe that not only will this platform be the greatest soul-winning vehicle God has allowed me to build, but it will be used mightily by Him in the days, months, and years to come.

CHAPTER 10

THE NEW NORMAL

Y OU'VE JUST BORNE witness to incredible highs and terrible lows that we have experienced as part of the cost of answering the watchman's call. We know, thanks to Scripture, that the road ahead for all of us is narrow, that we will be persecuted for His name's sake, and that we must be willing to lay down our own lives for our Father above so that He may be glorified. Jesus even told us in John 16:33 that we would have trouble, but He has already overcome the world, and we can have peace in our spirits accordingly.

The world ahead of us now is different from the one in July of 1976, on America's bicentennial. It is different from when I was released from prison in 1994, when I first returned to daily television in 2003, and even on January 1, 2020, when we entered into a new decade.

We've been told to stay home, wear masks in public spaces, don't gather in large groups, buy only what you need in stores, and don't hoard food so that it can be spread among more people. On top of that, we must now take extreme measures to maintain higher-than-hospital sanitation levels to keep COVID-19 and autoimmune diseases at bay.

"This is the new normal," or so everyone with a microphone or a platform continues to say day after day. I personally have come to hate this phrase, no matter how applicable it is.

The year 2020 redefined our "normal" more quickly and more vastly than any singular event in this generation. We have seen other changes over time, such as a rapid increase in security at airports after

September 11, 2001. I was too young to remember, but the only comparison I can draw was the economic practices during the second World War. America entered this global event amid a worldwide economic depression, but it quickly revolutionized industry and manufacturing and emerged from the war as an economic force to be reckoned with.

But this is not the type of "new normal" I'm referring to. We're not talking about rationing food or materials. Nor are we talking about masks and public health and safety.

What we are talking about is a massive cultural shift. When the church is unable to act as a check and balance to society, civilization will act as directed by the evil one. The apostle Paul is the perfect example. He was a devout Jew, trained under one of the most notable rabbis at the time. He was so attached to his beliefs that he went to extremes in his persecution of Christian believers, going so far as to participate in Stephen's stoning (Acts 7:58). He'd pursued the "evil Christians" with zeal, and because the Lord knew the full extent of his passion, He personally saw to Saul's conversion. Our Father in heaven knew all too well that it would take a radical event to transform a radical life.

You can read Paul's passion in his multiple letters to different believers and churches. Because of his rabbinical training, he had expert knowledge of the Old Testament. His walk with Christ helped bridge the gap between generations and became the foundation for the New Testament. This expert training gave Paul great insight into what would soon come upon the earth. He writes in his second letter to Timothy:

> This know also, that in the last days perilous times shall come. For men shall be lovers of their own selves, covetous, boasters, proud, blasphemers, disobedient to parents, unthankful, unholy, without natural affection, trucebreakers, false accusers, incontinent, fierce, despisers of those that are good, traitors, heady, highminded, lovers of pleasures more than lovers of God; having a form of godliness, but denying the power thereof: from such turn away. For of this sort are they which creep into houses, and lead captive silly women laden with sins, led away with divers

lusts, ever learning, and never able to come to the knowledge of the truth.

—2 TIMOTHY 3:1–7, KJV

Jesus gave us all sorts of mile markers and signs for the last days, and many of them were rooted in disasters and global conflict that resonate with the passage above.

Then shall they deliver you up to be afflicted, and shall kill you: and ye shall be hated of all nations for my name's sake. And then shall many be offended, and shall betray one another, and shall hate one another. And many false prophets shall rise, and shall deceive many. And because iniquity shall abound, the love of many shall wax cold.

—MATTHEW 24:9–12, KJV

Notice the parallels? We saw rampant persecution of the early Christian church in the Book of Acts because God's chosen people refused to accept that Jesus is the Messiah. Because they could not believe this, about forty years after Jesus was crucified, the second temple was destroyed, and the Jewish people were cast out of their land for centuries. The people of Israel had become just as immoral as their ancestors, forcing God to pronounce judgment on them as He had done hundreds of years before. Despite having seen and delivered this persecution firsthand, Paul knew that, eventually, Jesus would be accepted by the world, and revival would come. He also knew that this revival would be temporary, and it would be soon followed by apostasy.

And Paul was absolutely right! He'd noticed Israel's patterns, just as Jesus had. He acknowledged at least twenty-three specific behaviors that would identify the final generation at the end of days, each behavior exhibited by Israel throughout the Old Testament. This massive description in 2 Timothy 3 describes everything opposite of a Christian walk.

Many believe that in Matthew 24, Jesus was describing the destruction of the temple, but I can't accept this! There are too many signs in that passage of Scripture that did not appear in the first century. Even though Christians were largely persecuted and killed for their beliefs, the conflict was mainly between three parties: Christians, the Jewish people, and the Roman Empire. These are not the "many nations" that Jesus refers to, nor are they the betrayal or even the false prophets that He speaks of. Not to mention there weren't any signs in the sun, moon, and stars.

Since the fall of Jerusalem and Israel, Christianity has risen to a place of prominence. Christianity is very much part of the world's history and is even involved in many critical historical moments. This vast history contains tremendous and terrible events, not to mention the massive infighting that has caused church divisions. Jesus warned us that a house divided could not stand (Matt. 12:25).

Though we have been called to be a light to the world for Christ, many generations gaze upon the church's fractures and blemishes. They see only our imperfections and not the love of the Father. Generation upon generation continues to rise, seeking only to flee our Father. As a result, they unwittingly fulfill Paul's warning. Unlike those in the disciples' time, it is now all humanity that is building up those unwanted characteristics and using them as the basis for their morality—that is, if you assume one can call it morality.

Are you able to recognize these characteristics from 2 Timothy 3? We see narcissists aplenty, jealousy, pride, blasphemers, people who feed on the negative, accusations without proof, betrayals, self-righteousness, and so on. We see people carry these attributes not just in America, but all across the world. How many cultures and comedians make a mockery of God and the church? How many people pursue wealth and fleshly treasures rather than heavenly ones? How many betrayals have we seen in our government and among our leaders? The list of examples is practically endless!

In 2012, the Lord gave me five stages for the days ahead. Each of these stages is something our nation and the world will have to go through to reach the tribulation and realize the full kingdom of God. Almost a full decade has passed since I was given these, and based on the events that have transpired, I believe we are now halfway through.

STAGE 1: CONFUSION

In Ezekiel 7 the word of the Lord came to Ezekiel, warning that the day of the Lord's wrath was soon to come.

> Disaster has come for you who live in the land! The time has come; the day of *confusion* is near. There will be no happy shouting on the mountains.
> —EZEKIEL 7:7, NCV, EMPHASIS ADDED

The entire passage is a preview of what Jesus shares about the end in the Gospels and the judgments in Revelation. But the word choice in this translation is interesting. Other translations, such as the Modern English Version and King James Version, call this "the day of trouble." The Amplified and others call it a day of "tumult." The New International Version calls it "panic."

The Hebrew word here is מְהוּמָה, or *mehumah*, and does mean both tumult and confusion.[1] Its Greek New Testament counterpart shows up for the first time in Luke's version of the Olivet Discourse. Whereas Matthew 24:6 warns us that we will see "wars and rumors of war," Luke 21:9 tells us we will see "wars and commotions." The Greek word used for *commotion* is ἀκαταστασία, or *akatastasia*. The full definition of the word is instability, disorder, and confusion.[2]

So, in the greatest sense, we are not talking about a state of confusion, where one is trying to think clearly; we are talking about a time of unrest. Clearly, we have seen a massive time of unrest sweep America that shows no sign of stopping.

A deeper study of the word *confusion* expands its reach: bewilderment, perplexity, uncertainty, misunderstanding, disorder, disarray, instability, turmoil, tumult, upheaval, commotion, muddle, mayhem, bedlam, mess, and unrest. Doesn't this look like today's America to you?

Yes!

Just before Moses died, he addressed the Israelites in one massive message, encouraging them to remain with the Lord and follow His commands. In Deuteronomy 28, he gives a template for blessings and does so in fourteen quick verses. And in those fourteen verses, he says four times that those who want God's blessings must follow His commandments. (See Deuteronomy 28:1–14.) When you were a child, how many times did your parents repeat to you the necessity to do good or follow instructions before you finally got it?

Opposite those fourteen verses in chapter 28 is not another fourteen but, in fact, *fifty-four* verses that issue curses for disobedience. I have never seen anything like it. For the sake of brevity, let's go directly to verse 20:

> The LORD will send cursing, *vexation*, and rebuke on you in all that you set your hand to do, until you are destroyed and until you perish quickly because of the wickedness of your doings, by which you have forsaken Me.
> —DEUTERONOMY 28:20, EMPHASIS ADDED

The Hebrew word for *vexation* in this scripture is the same word used in Ezekiel 7: *mehumah*. Confusion and all its counterparts are the results of turning away from God and the disobedience that follows. God has warned that reprobate activities will sweep mankind! Is this not what we're seeing now?

Have we not seen an outcry against our police? Between races? Have we not seen riots turn violent and businesses and lives destroyed because a small group of people saw a short-term gain? Have we not also seen attacks on the concept of family? Fathers are unwelcome and unwanted, babies are aborted because they "inconvenience" a mother's life, and children are abducted from their lawns and sold into sex slavery. And yet we ask why.

The answer is simple! The church stood on the sidelines when prayer was removed from our schools. We've seen the Ten Commandments removed from courthouses. We've seen mass murder in abortion clinics with over sixty million American babies lost since 1973's *Roe v. Wade*.[3] We've seen crosses removed from chaplains' tents on army bases. We've seen churches vandalized, statues destroyed, and Bibles burned. We have seen Paul's warning to Timothy slowly realized over the last several decades in our country. We have seen biblical principles replaced one by one with secular planks.

Some of these secular planks have come with good intentions. For instance, we have seen many powerful and influential individuals from high positions in the television and movie industry, corporations, and even seats of government removed from their office because of their sexual immorality. While we can celebrate the fight against this immorality, we also have to pray for those who have sinned. Jesus came to save us all (John 3:16), and it does little good to remove people like this from authority and not fill the void with God and His commandments. Without Jesus Christ in our hearts, without a life seeking after Him, we will be like the house swept clean of a demon, only for that demon to return sevenfold. Jesus says in Matthew 12:45 that if this happens, "the last state of that man is worse than the first. So shall it be also with this evil generation."

This confusion, this unrest, is what has set the stage for the four horsemen. The church has been lulled to sleep and has not kept its watchful eye on society as a result. I applaud those who continue to stand for godly principles, no matter the cost. But the more our parishioners fall away from the faith or continue to sleep and cast a blind eye to what is happening around them, it will become increasingly difficult to evangelize and sound the watchman's trumpet.

STAGE 2: EXPLOSIONS

Merriam-Webster's second definition of the word *explosion* is "a large-scale, rapid, or spectacular expansion or bursting out or forth."[4] It's very easy to associate explosions with weapons of warfare or even fireworks displays on the Fourth of July. I've often associated this word with the red horseman and the nuclear bomb the Lord told me is connected to him.

But in 2012, the Lord told me these explosions were the second part of the confusion. We've already learned that confusion is the same as instability and disorder, both of which are already gripping the nation today. Explosions, therefore, refer to the rapid expansion of this confusion. Before 2016, confusion was slowly doing its work. In several decades prior, it had slowly touched each biblical principle one by one. First was prayer in schools in 1962. Second was *Roe v. Wade* in 1973.

The Jesus Movement in the 1970s did slow these advances, but as David Wilkerson frequently noted in his books, the enemy still continued forward.

> For the time will come when they will not endure sound doctrine; but after their own lusts shall they heap to themselves teachers, having itching ears; and they shall turn away their ears from the truth, and shall be turned unto fables.
>
> —2 Timothy 4:3–4, KJV

Heap is an interesting word choice used here in the King James Version. Other translations use *gather* or *accumulate*, but the word *heap* means to accumulate additionally. We often use heap to describe a great abundance of something. Here we see an immoral generation collecting and amassing immorality because they strongly lust after it. James' letter confirms the results of these lusts.

> Then, when lust has conceived, it brings forth sin; and when sin is finished, it brings forth death.
>
> —James 1:15

A phrase has been popularized among the younger generations in recent years: "You only live once," or YOLO, as they abbreviate. Because you only live once, this generation is encouraged to live for the moment and only pursue what brings them pleasure. We in Christ know that this statement is the furthest thing from the truth. Our security is in Christ, and we are storing up treasures in heaven (Matt. 6:19–20)! Our future is guaranteed when we place our faith and trust in Him and accept Him into our hearts as forgiveness for our sins. Paul writes in 2 Corinthians 4:18 that we are to look after the eternal things, not the temporal.

But this is not what a corrupt generation wants to hear. Because of the church's inaction, corruption, and perversion, this generation views the church as an unreliable enemy, an opposition to their lives of indulgence.

> Because iniquity will abound, the love of many will grow
> cold.
>
> —MATTHEW 24:12

Iniquity, again, in the Greek means lawlessness and an utter disregard for God's law.[5]

This is where we see the persecution we've been warned about in Matthew 24, Luke 21, and Mark 13 come into play. This is the ultimate issue with what I call "Happy Church" and the false gospel. As Christians, we cannot expect our lives to be smooth and without incident. Jesus says that we will "be hated by all nations for My name's sake" (Matt. 24:9; Luke 21:17; Mark 13:13). In China, the church has been forced underground yet again, with Christian pastors imprisoned and often facing death. Christian missionaries are often captured in Africa and put to death. In 2014, the terrorist group Boko Haram kidnapped 276 girls from a Nigerian school, most of whom were Christian. To this day, the whereabouts of 112 of them are still unknown.[6] At its height, ISIS published several videos online with their followers brutally beheading Christians in captivity.

American churches have seen unprecedented persecution rising in recent years. In 2020 alone, many states forced churches to close their doors throughout the pandemic. Not every church complied with these orders, believing that the church was, and still is, an essential service to the community. Pastors in many cities, no matter how obscure or prominent they were, faced charges for continuing to hold in-person services. St. John's Episcopal Church in Washington, DC, was set ablaze during a protest in June 2020. Many have decried that statues of Jesus are a symbol of white supremacy and must be torn down.[7] Even well-known scholar and pastor John MacArthur has been facing legal battles and time in prison in the state of California for continuing to hold services. Franklin Graham was targeted by Faithful America (the same group that petitioned our stations to take us off the air). They launched a petition to remove him from both Samaritan's Purse and the Billy Graham Evangelistic Association (his father's ministry!) for standing beside President Trump and conservative groups.[8]

This onslaught has yet to end. While I applaud churches for reaching out to social media to broadcast the gospel live each Sunday (just as we do each week), thereby participating in Jesus' commandment to reach the entire world, there is no replacement for gathering as one body. God has confirmed to me many times that there is security in the body of Christ, especially as we near the end (Heb. 10:25). If the body is not allowed to gather, how can there be security?

Persecution is only amplified when those performing the persecuting grow worse, determined with their policies and actions. God told me on December 31, 2019, that while many of these evil leaders will continue to excel and expand their influence, several others will drop dead to slow the attacks. This will keep the church from overwhelming adversity and give time for those who must still receive their salvation.

This was the most sobering of all the words I was given for 2020 for one key reason. The Lord did not say that the attacks would stop; He said that they would *slow down*. Persecution will not end. But there is hope! Jesus says that "he that shall endure unto the end, the same shall be saved" (Matt. 24:13, KJV).

Revelation 7 tells a great story of God's mercy and love. All seven seals have been opened, and the four horsemen of the apocalypse have finished riding. It begins with four angels in the four corners of the earth, each preparing for the next wave of judgment. God instructs them to hold back, giving those a chance to seal the servants of God in their forehead (Rev. 7:1–3). John then outlines the 144,000 that would be saved from the twelve tribes of Israel. What follows next is a beautiful sight.

> Then I looked. And there was a great multitude which no one could count, from all nations and tribes and peoples and tongues, standing before the throne and before the Lamb, clothed with white robes, with palm branches in their hands....
>
> Then one of the elders asked me, "Who are these clothed in white robes, and where did they come from?"
>
> I said to him, "Sir, you know."
>
> He said to me, "These are those who came out of great tribulation and washed their robes and made them white

in the blood of the Lamb. Therefore, they are before the throne of God, and serve Him day and night in His temple. And He who sits on the throne will dwell among them. 'They shall neither hunger any more, nor shall they thirst any more; the sun shall not strike them,' nor any scorching heat; for the Lamb who is in the midst of the throne will shepherd them and 'He will lead them to springs of living water.' 'And God will wipe away every tear from their eyes.'"

—REVELATION 7:9, 13–17

This beautiful sight is next for all believers. We are the Revelation Generation! Eternity awaits those who endure and also those who are taken up early. I know many who have lost family members and friends throughout this pandemic, whether it was the result of the novel coronavirus or other causes. Among those the Lord has taken home recently are incredible evangelists and teachers such as Bishop Harry Jackson Jr., Dr. Irvin Baxter, and Reinhard Bonnke. Many others continue to struggle physically, and I am led to wonder who God will heal and who He will call home.

STAGE 3: DECEPTION

Make no mistake. This is where we are today. Earlier in this book, I proved that the white horseman is riding throughout the world today. This rider has taken advantage of the confusion gripping the world and has used the opportunity to reshape truth to further its goals. His partner, the red horseman, has exploited this deception, bringing tensions to the point of explosion.

It is because of deception that the definition of normal has been changed. The prophet Isaiah put it bluntly to the children of Israel, "Woe to those who call evil good, and good evil" (Isa. 5:20). What we are now witnessing, in America especially, is a total and complete role reversal. We are now living through a War on Words unlike any generation before us has experienced. This is our new normal!

I must also add a disclaimer here. I am not trying to say Americans suddenly decided to become wicked. Humanity has long wrestled with evil desires throughout its existence, beginning all the way back with

Adam and Eve in the Garden of Eden. Every time the Lord delivered Israel from bondage or persecution, they slipped back into these evil ways—from the golden calf at the foot of Mount Sinai to serving the Baals as soon as they settled into the Promised Land, and so on.

America, described by John Winthrop as a "city upon a hill," was no different.[9] What started as a nation consecrated to the Lord continued to slip further and further into darkness with each generation. Yet pastors and preachers did their best to keep their congregations on the straight and narrow. In the early days of Hollywood, a Catholic layman and a Jesuit priest intervened with studio executives to pave the way for the Hays Code. This code, a rigid list of principles and applications, was designed to keep morality afloat in motion pictures, promoting traditional values.[10] Today this code has been watered down to the simplified system we all easily recognize, ranging from G for acceptable for all audiences to R and NC-17 for the most violent or sexually charged films. Yet it no longer adequately prepares you for what is contained within each movie, as there is no simple rating for the sexual hints, drunkenness, selfish desires, and the other characteristics of an ungodly life that 2 Timothy 3 warns us about.

The corruption of modern mediums such as television, movies, and even social media is just one example. In the last decade alone, we saw the definitions of *marriage, gender,* and *identity* changed, along with the widespread acceptance, endorsement, and even *celebration* of abortion. Today, there is a massive push for Americans to accept pedophilia as normal or as a disability and not a criminal act.[11] The more the church continues to stay silent on the sidelines during these battles and transitions, the further this nation will continue to slip into the abyss.

One of the warnings the Lord gave to me on December 31, 2019, was that some Christians are already signing up for the antichrist system. We've all heard the warning from the pulpits and from evangelists on television. "Whatever you do, do not take the mark of the beast!" Even the pulpits of America who have avoided the Book of Revelation have quickly issued this warning to their congregations. "If you take the mark of the beast, you will not get into heaven," they warn, citing Revelation 20:4 and its reminder that the saints who are surrounding God at the final judgment are martyrs and the true Christians who stood for God and hadn't received the mark. Therefore, we go about our lives believing that we would never voluntarily sign up for something that would condemn us for all eternity.

What is not mentioned or taught, however, is a crucial verse from Revelation 19. Here, the enemy's troops are gathering for battle, and suddenly, the unthinkable happens.

> But the beast was captured and with him the false prophet who worked signs in his presence, by which he deceived those who received the mark of the beast and those who worshipped his image. These two were thrown alive into the lake of fire that burns with brimstone.
> —REVELATION 19:20

Notice what it says there? Those who received the mark of the beast were deceived. Look back at where it all begins:

> He causes all, both small and great, both rich and poor, both free and slave, to receive a mark on their right hand or on their forehead.
> —REVELATION 13:16

If you are specifically looking for the mark, you will not find it. Those who have been deceived by the antichrist system and are blindly following its actions may have already unwittingly signed up for it. The only way to know for sure whether you have, or are about to, take this mark is to continuously live in the Word of God, reform your life, and act according to the will of God.

Another of the warnings I received for 2020 was that soon you will be controlled by who you vote for, and you will not know you are part of a wicked, supernatural system. Paul describes the Antichrist in this manner:

> He will completely fool those who are on their way to hell
> because they have said no to the Truth; they have refused
> to believe it and love it and let it save them.
> —2 Thessalonians 2:10, tlb

What great consequence for those who choose not to believe! It is absolutely heartbreaking for those that refuse the Truth, for nothing awaits them but destruction. Of course, this rejection of the Truth is nothing new. We've seen it countless times in the Old Testament. In 1 Samuel, Israel had looked at the other nations and felt inferior to them because they did not have a human king to command them. Can you imagine how God felt? We don't have to imagine.

> But the thing was evil in the eyes of Samuel, because they
> said, "Give us a king to govern us." And Samuel prayed to
> the Lord. The Lord said to Samuel, "Obey the voice of
> the people in relation to all that they say to you. For it is
> not you they have rejected, but Me they have rejected from
> reigning over them. Just as all the deeds which they have
> done to Me, from the day I brought them up from Egypt
> even to this day, in that they have forsaken Me and have
> served other gods, so they are doing also to you now."
> —1 Samuel 8:6–8

God knew that Israel would turn away from Him, and He allowed it because it was necessary for His larger plan. Through Israel's independence, He would be able to strike a new and everlasting covenant. Throughout the generations, Israel saw kings and leaders who were mostly evil, who encouraged their occult practices and worship of multiple gods. Some kings, like Josiah, managed to bring the nation back to the Lord and bring revival across their land, much like many of us are praying in our pews and homes for! But that revival did not bear much fruit, forcing the Lord to bring judgment onto the land, and eventually, exile.

What have we seen in 2020 with our leaders? States like Michigan and California were absolutely locked down, forbidding any church to remain open lest COVID-19 continue to spread like wildfire. We saw states like New York install laws that allow for babies to be aborted up to birth! There is now talk about "deprogramming" conservative voices and voters.[12]

Millions of people blindly vote for candidates because they identify as a particular party. Neither party is perfect. There is as much infighting within the Republican party as there is the Democratic party. But what really matters is that millions upon millions of people are blindly following these organizations under false pretenses. Many of them view the church and Christians as those who believe and cast lies. Does this sound familiar, like a certain rider on a white horse who carries a bow but no arrows? Our country's destiny doesn't lie solely with leaders, nor does it lie exclusively with the church. It lies with those who can tie politics and Christianity together. This is why I continuously remind my viewers to research candidates and elect godly leaders into the White House, Congress, state capitals, and even your local city hall. You must vote your faith and vote it often.

But most importantly, you must continue to stand. To us, the battle looks impossible. But nothing is impossible for our God. Paul writes:

> Be not deceived. God is not mocked. For whatever a man sows, that will he also reap. For the one who sows to his own flesh will from the flesh reap corruption, but the one who sows to the Spirit will from the Spirit reap eternal life. And let us not grow weary in doing good, for in due season we shall reap, if we do not give up. Therefore, as we have opportunity, let us do good to all people, especially to those who are of the household of faith.
>
> —GALATIANS 6:7–10

Stand for truth. Stand for life. We must endure to see God's will through, especially since there are still two more stages to come.

STAGE 4: DEPRESSION

Deception will eventually cause depression. People will be in deep personal depression, and we will also see a tremendous global economic depression. I believe that we entered into this stage at the end of 2020. Thoughts of suicide, as well as feelings of hopelessness and helplessness, increased throughout the year.[13] Many believed that this pandemic would disappear as quickly as it came, but that did not happen.

We saw firsthand how deception truly fuels further deception and how pursuing one's lusts and fleshly desires only provides temporary gain. And when these gains end, depression quickly follows. My parents were inspired by a famous actor for my middle name, Orson. Shortly after I was born, Orson Welles released what is often regarded as one of America's greatest movies, *Citizen Kane*. This film follows a reporter who dives into the life of the recently deceased (and fictitious) Charles Foster Kane, a newspaper and media tycoon who had amassed incredible and inordinate wealth. The man had been known far and wide, but not a single soul knew what his final word, "Rosebud," meant. The reporter gives up his quest at the end of the film because no one could provide any insight. The viewer, however, is treated to the answer. All of Kane's fortune and belongings are being cataloged by the estate, and some items are selected to be destroyed, including an old snow sled, big enough for a small child. It's tossed into an active furnace. As flames engulf the sled, the camera zooms in to reveal a word written on it: Rosebud. Kane had spent his entire life climbing and fighting his way to the top for fame and fortune in the ultimate quest for happiness. In the end, he realized all too late that he could never again surpass his happiest moment when he was just a child sledding outside the family home.

This is the fate that awaits many. We saw earlier in 2 Timothy 4:3 that men are gathering more and more selfish desires and teachings to themselves, never finding satisfaction. My wife, Lori, had been a drug addict years before she and I met and married. She has told me many times about why drug addictions are so powerful: because of the euphoria they bring. Lori also shared that withdrawal periods and hangovers were among her worst experiences because the desire to keep that euphoria going forever was so strong. Eventually, there will not be anything humans can make or do to satisfy human desires. The deception that millions, perhaps billions, are living under will come to a head, and the result will be a total deadlock. Improvements will become impossible, and their insatiable desires must now look to desperate means in order to find measures of release.

This personal depression will be linked to economic depression as well. In 2020 we saw the foundation set for a massive collapse. Over twenty million jobs were lost in the American marketplace alone,[14] and hundreds of thousands of businesses, large and small, found themselves in jeopardy. This harkens back to an item from my original "31 Things" from 1999 when the Lord told me that there would be a deterioration in the world's most trusted stocks and brands. Companies such as J. C. Penney have filed for bankruptcy. Entertainment companies such as cruise lines and movie theaters have been brought to their knees.

The love of money has paved the way for destruction. In 1998, David Wilkerson made this very clear in his book *America's Last Call*. He wrote:

> Day after day, our prosperity here in America grows. Yet we have not humbled ourselves. We're storing up God's wrath against us—and soon he'll pour it out![15]

I believe this to be true. Before 2020, we could look around and see all the massive economic improvements around America. Our industries were returning from overseas. Factories, businesses, and restaurants were thriving, and there was no better time to be an entrepreneur. Today, as I write this, most of these opportunities are gone. The benchmarks we've looked to so that we might measure our success are nearly all removed. Across the nation, we've been reduced to businesses and positions considered "essential" in government officials' eyes. Don't they realize that every job is essential in order to maintain the livelihood of this nation and its people?

I applaud former President Trump, his team, and the members of Congress who stepped in to provide support to the American people. But the government can only go so far. As of this writing, the US national debt is well over twenty-seven trillion dollars, amounting to over $84,000 of debt per citizen and over $222,000 per taxpayer.[16] According to the US Census Bureau in 2019, the median household income was $68,703.[17] Assuming every household has one taxpayer and every person in America was paid equally and deferred all housing and living expenses, including food, it would take over three years to eradicate the national debt. Assuming every household has two taxpayers, it would take over six years. However, this figure does not include debts owed by every state and territory under the American flag, which altogether amount to several trillion dollars.[18] Simply put, America has overspent, and it will soon be time for the nations of the world to collect what they're owed.

For a nation built on the Word of God, we have ignored many warnings. "The love of money is the root of all evil," according to 1 Timothy 6:10. Jesus equally warns that:

> No one can serve two masters. For either he will hate the one and love the other, or else he will hold to the one and despise the other. You cannot serve God and money.
> —Matthew 6:24

Our nation's love of money has paved the broad path that is leading to its eventual destruction. We, my brothers and sisters, must follow the instructions of the apostle Paul:

> But you, O man of God, escape these things, and follow after righteousness, godliness, faith, love, patience, and gentleness. Fight the good fight of faith. Lay hold on eternal life, to which you are called and have professed a good profession before many witnesses....
>
> Command those who are rich in this world that they not be conceited, nor trust in uncertain riches, but in the living God, who richly gives us all things to enjoy. Command that they do good, that they be rich in good works, generous, willing to share, and laying up in store for themselves a good foundation for the coming age, so that they may take hold of eternal life.
> —1 Timothy 6:11–12, 17–19

STAGE 5: COLLAPSE

In 1999 I shared that there is a worldwide economic collapse coming. We are already teetering on the edge of the abyss, and we are about to fall over. Major crashes will occur worldwide as stock markets abruptly close for a final time and never reopen. Entire organizations, stores, banks, and even churches will shut their doors for good and never reopen. The resulting chaos will funnel people into the streets, sparking riots, demonstrations, looting, mass confusion, and eventually warfare.

This worldwide collapse is the final prerequisite, the last checkmark, the ultimate task that must be completed before the Antichrist can be revealed on this earth. Revelation 13:1 tells us that the beast (Antichrist) rises out of the sea, and the angel informs us later in 17:15 that this sea is "peoples and multitudes and nations and tongues." In other words, the beast must rise out of the ultimate instability and disorder (confusion) to claim his throne. But how does this happen?

In Revelation 17 the great harlot is first seen sitting on the back of this beast, shown to John the Revelator:

> One of the seven angels who had the seven bowls came and talked with me, saying to me, "Come, I will show you the judgment of the great prostitute who sits on many waters, with whom the kings of the earth committed adultery, and the inhabitants of the earth were made drunk with the wine of her sexual immorality."
>
> —REVELATION 17:1–2

Just a few chapters before, in Revelation 14:8, an angel first teased the destruction of mystery Babylon because "she made all the nations drink of the wine of the wrath of her sexual immorality." The sight of this harlot is so magnificent, so awe-inspiring, that the angel speaking to John has to snap him out of a trance! It is no wonder to John that this woman with all her features and power could have ensnared all humanity. And the most incredible thing happens. The destruction of the harlot occurs at the hand of the Antichrist and his world system.

> These ten horns and the beast which you saw will hate the
> prostitute; they will make her desolate and naked, and
> devour her flesh, and burn her with fire. For God has put
> in their hearts to fulfill His will, and to be of one mind,
> and to give their kingdom to the beast, until the words of
> God are fulfilled. The woman whom you saw is that great
> city, which reigns over the kings of the earth.
>
> —REVELATION 17:16–18

We know that the key to everlasting life and peace is unity through our Lord and Savior, Jesus Christ. He is the Way, the Truth, and the Life. Our ways are imperfect, but His ways are perfect. The ultimate salvation through Him yields an everlasting life free from sin and heartache. This truth is so universal that even the Antichrist knows it. Where there is no Christ, sin abounds, and unfortunately, that sin relies on a fractured society to flourish. The great harlot, this mystery Babylon, is the absolute embodiment of evil and corruption. To complete the great deception and render all nations and tribes under his control, the Antichrist must destroy the most powerful weapon in his arsenal.

And this isn't just a simple destruction. The harlot is stripped of everything that has made her seductive; she is cannibalized and burned, all on public display. In this one act, the Antichrist cements his power and gains control over the world.

I believe that this great harlot is none other than New York City. As I read the full breakdown in Revelation 18 and study each of the harlot's characteristics, I continue to stand more and more firm in this belief. And God's anger is burning so intensely that He is planning to "repay her double for her deeds" (v. 6). And indeed, no judgment doled out in Revelation has the fire, zeal, or even the description contained for what happens to the harlot. In one hour, mystery Babylon is eliminated, and everyone weeps. The kings of the earth, who lost all their wealth, weep (v. 9). The merchants of the earth weep for now they have nowhere to sell their wares no matter how luxurious, gaudy, delicious, and ornate they were (vv. 11–15). Even sea captains and seafaring men weep, for they now have no way to earn a living (vv. 17–18). Music, work, baking and cooking, light, buying, selling, and even celebrations of life never again appear because of this destruction (vv. 22–23).

There is a reason the World Trade Center was attacked on September 11, 2001. New York City long ago became the center of the world economic system. Its Stock Exchange is the cornerstone of the world economy and sets the standard for all to follow. Though the towers fell, the system endured. New York City's destruction, when it comes, will be the blow that will devastate all. Someone is already waiting to fill this void, and when it comes, only the return of Jesus Christ can stop what is implemented.

We are standing now at a crossroads, and there is still something you can do. First, heed the warning from above.

> Then I heard another voice from heaven saying: "'Come out of her, my people,' lest you partake in her sins, and lest you receive her plagues. For her sins have reached up to heaven, and God has remembered her iniquities."
>
> —Revelation 18:4–5

Second, do not conform to the things of this world. Think of godly matters and Scripture rather than the gossip surrounding sports stars, entertainers, and even your neighbors. Take a look at what Paul has to say in his second letter to the Corinthians:

> Do not be unequally yoked together with unbelievers. For what fellowship has righteousness with unrighteousness? What communion has light with darkness? What agreement has Christ with Belial? Or what part has he who believes with an unbeliever? What agreement has the temple of God with idols? For you are the temple of the living God. As God has said:
>
> "I will live in them and walk in them. I will be their God, and they shall be My people." Therefore, "Come out from among them and be separate, says the Lord. Do not touch what is unclean, and I will receive you."
>
> —2 Corinthians 6:14–17

The key to our survival is threefold: remain in Christ, keep His commandments, and remain in His body, the church. Escape is not an option. Endurance is our goal.

CHAPTER 11

WORLDWIDE JUDGMENT

T HE FOUR HORSEMEN are out of the barn and riding throughout the world. Our lives and values have been turned upside down, and as a result, we are living in a "new normal." Our society is teetering on the precipice of collapse. And the worst is still yet to come.

LOCATION, LOCATION, LOCATION

Several years ago on *The Jim Bakker Show*, my dear friend prophet Rick Joyner had flown in to tape several shows with us. On one of these broadcasts, he shared with our national audience that it would soon matter where they lived. We were to pray if we were to stay in our current home or if we needed to move elsewhere in preparation for what was coming to the earth. I think you need to pay close attention to where you live and make sure you have easy access to springs of water, food, and people who can help in a crisis.

Location matters. Real estate agents have made it their mantra for decades, seeing that home sales are more often attributed to location and the options in proximity to the home other than the features of the home itself.

Our Founding Fathers believed this as well. To them, America was a land of opportunity, a land of the free, a place to start anew. America was founded as a Christian nation, and when it has deviated from that foundation, we invited judgment. God has been shaking this nation repeatedly in recent years, trying to get this nation to repent and turn back.

My dear friend Rabbi Jonathan Cahn has also shared repeatedly on our broadcasts and around the world about *The Harbinger* and its dozens of shocking connections to the terror attack of September 11, 2001. The pattern God is following here is the same for Old Testament Israel before it was first invaded and its people exiled. I believe this is due to the constant commitments this nation has made to support Israel and the Jewish people and our efforts to urge them to compromise with their neighbors. Jonathan Cahn's book *The Harbinger II: The Return* reveals a fascinating connection between 9/11, the outbreak of COVID-19, and other events as part of this ongoing revelation.

People often wonder why a loving God would perform such incredible acts of destruction and violence. And it's not just our generation; it is a concept many Christians and nonbelievers have asked for millennia. The Book of Hebrews reminds us:

> My son, do not despise the chastening of the LORD, nor be discouraged when you are rebuked by Him; for whom the LORD loves He chastens, and scourges every son whom He receives.
> —HEBREWS 12:5–6, NKJV

God uses judgment to remind us of our true purpose and calling. And judgment can be averted if, like Nineveh, we truly repent and turn from wicked ways. We must pray for more than avoiding judgment in our cities and towns. Our leaders, mayors, sheriffs, board members, state and county officials, and even our governors need our prayers. We must earnestly pray that the person holding the office will execute their powers in a godly manner, each action in accordance with the Word of God and Christian and moral values, lest the great apostasy continue. Your location, where you live, matters now more than ever.

On December 31, 2019, and multiple times afterward, the Lord had me share several cities and locations that require urgent, unceasing, and fervent prayer.[1] I won't be able to share why judgment will come on these areas, as the Lord has not revealed His reasons to me, other than that they have continually cursed God.

Please pray for:

1. New York City

2. Long Island, New York

3. Towns in northern New Jersey

4. Los Angeles, California

5. Long Beach, California

6. Santa Ana, California

7. Bangkok, Thailand

8. Washington, DC

9. New Orleans, Louisiana

10. Tel Aviv, Israel

11. Puerto Rico

WORLDWIDE JUDGMENT

"God's judgment is coming, and it's coming around the world."[2] Immediately after I shared that on December 31, 2019, the studio audience fell silent. No one in the room needed to be told this was coming. It was something everyone had previously heard and believed. If anything, this word is a solemn reminder.

It is no longer about America. A worldwide judgment of God will come to place after place. For a lifelong student of the Word like me, this is not surprising. Anyone who has even a cursory knowledge of the Book of Revelation knows about the four horsemen of the apocalypse and the seven angels and their trumpets. The fourth horseman was given reign over a quarter of the earth, so why would these later events not continue to push the envelope?

The sad truth is that the Book of Revelation is rarely preached from the pulpit. Most preachers don't want anything to do with it, fearing it will chase their congregation out of the pews on Sunday. Nor does Revelation mesh with the widely accepted prosperity gospel. Others believe the church will be raptured away in a twinkling of an eye before any of this happens!

Regardless of your position, we can all agree on one thing: it will get worse in the world before the final battle and judgment. The night must get darker before the sun can dawn on the horizon. Already, the events of Revelation are in motion. Revelation 6 especially runs parallel to the signs of the times Jesus presents in the Olivet Discourse in Matthew 24, Mark 13, and Luke 21. We've already seen the four horsemen and the rise of deception. Ahead of us is the great tribulation, but what could be after that? Remember, each of the horsemen was loosed by the first four seals of Revelation 6. It's time to look at the fifth seal.

> When He opened the fifth seal, I saw under the altar the souls of those who had been slain for the word of God and for the testimony they had held. They cried out with a loud voice, "How long, O Sovereign Lord, holy and true, until You judge and avenge our blood on those who dwell on the earth?" Then a white robe was given to each of them, and they were told to rest a little longer, until the number of their fellow servants and brothers should be completed, who would be killed as they were.
>
> —REVELATION 6:9–11

The fifth seal is one of two that don't have actions associated with them. And it's also interesting that these souls under the altar of heaven, these great martyrs of the faith, are asking when the Lord will cast judgment on the earth. Does this mean that the four horsemen are not associated with judgment? If their actions are indeed parallel with Matthew 24, then surely we Christians must persevere through great tribulation before the day of the Lord.

It's important to note this as well. Each martyr is given a robe and commanded to rest for their number was not yet complete. More will continue to die for the faith, and this number will grow until Jesus returns. You, as a believer, need to buckle up because there are two choices before you. Either you can join the great deception, or you can continue to stand for Christ, knowing that the road ahead is straight and narrow and about to get rocky.

A SHAKING IS COMING

Make no mistake. God's judgment is not a singular event. It has been and will be a series of events carefully orchestrated to build on top of one another or work in tandem.

Pay attention to what Revelation 6 says next:

> I watched as He opened the sixth seal. And suddenly there was a great earthquake. The sun became black, like sackcloth made from goat hair, and the moon became like blood. And the stars of heaven fell to the earth, as a fig tree drops its unripe figs when it is shaken by a strong wind. Then the heavens receded like a scroll when it is rolled up, and every mountain and island was removed from its place.
> —REVELATION 6:12–14

Jesus tells us on at least three occasions that there will be great signs in the heavens, on the ground where we stand, and in our seas and oceans (Matt. 24:29–30; Luke 21:25; Rev. 8:3–12). Sixteen places in the Old and New Testaments warn us that the sun and moon will go dark; Isaiah 13:10, Job 9:7, Joel 2:10, Amos 8:9, Mark 13:24, and Acts 2:20 are just a few. If every scripture is inspired by God, and each word equally valuable, how much more critical does a warning become when repeated?

Do you remember Jules Verne's novel *Journey to the Center of the Earth*? In his tale, Professor Otto Lidenbrock launches an expedition to explore a crater in a dormant volcano that was rumored to lead to the earth's center. It's a good thing this book is fiction. Had it been real, then Professor Lidenbrock would have quickly been burned alive!

You see, our planet is covered by a series of tectonic plates, of which there are seven major plates, ranging from 30 to 125 miles in thickness.[3] These plates float on magma and are constantly moving, pushing against one another. These plates don't just push against each other; they slam one another. We can feel these events all the time. We call them earthquakes.

When I arrived in Los Angeles in 1997 to appear on *Larry King Live*, the Lord took me into a vision where I saw the city devastated by a vast earthquake. And then I saw how the earthquake happened. At the time, I could only describe this in a demonstration. I would place my fists together, intertwining my knuckles. I would gradually increase the pressure between my fists until one slipped and was thrust upward. Two years later, on March 5, 1999, the *LA Daily News* ran a headline, "Massive hidden fault threatens downtown."[4] In the article, I saw an illustration of a blind thrust fault for the first time, which perfectly explained what I had tried to demonstrate for years. When these two plates are pressing against each other, one will eventually slip and spring upward, and cause the great Los Angeles earthquake. I believe this earthquake will be coming very, very soon.

Many of us associate earthquakes with one region: the Ring of Fire in the Pacific Ocean. This particular set of plates covers the western coasts of North and South America, as well as the eastern coasts of Russia, Japan, New Zealand, and many of the Pacific islands in Asia and Alaska. We expect major earthquakes to occur in this area and occur often.

The United States Geological Society (USGS) has been monitoring earthquakes throughout the world for several years now, and their website is automatically updated whenever a new one strikes. Their logs are quite fascinating, especially since we can use them to identify trends. And what a trend I have discovered! In the year 2000, the USGS cataloged 61,328 earthquakes with a magnitude of 1.0 or greater, and 1,505 at or above the 5.0 range.[5] Just two years later, 79,049 of 1.0 or greater were registered with 1,341 at or above 5.0.[6] In 2010, a shocking amount of 89,945 of 1.0 or greater was recorded, with 2,383 at or above 5.0. 2018 holds the record with an incredible 137,158 of 1.0 or greater and 1,808 at 5.0 or greater recorded.[7]

What's even more shocking is that locations that normally don't see earthquakes, or areas that most believe to be earthquake-free, are being shaken. In 2020 alone, earthquakes have been recorded in places like Oklahoma, Arkansas, North Carolina, Iceland, and Puerto Rico. The quake that rocked North Carolina on August 9, 2020, registered at 5.1, the strongest quake to hit the area since 1916.[8] Puerto Rico has been experiencing an extremely unusual amount of seismic activity. Since 2001, the island has experienced at least 1,946 earthquakes that were above the 3.0 range. What's incredible is that over 1,400 of those earthquakes have occurred in 2020 or later. That's a span of eighteen months accounting for 73 percent of those major shakings since 2001![9] Even as I write this, earthquakes continue to occur in the most unusual of locations.[10] I believe we're seeing the fulfillment of Jesus warning us that there would be earthquakes in many places (Matt. 24:7).

The earth is trembling, travailing under great pressure. The fact that earthquakes are now appearing in unusual areas proves to me that a major shift is on its way. Circling back to Revelation 6:14, we see that every mountain and island will move from its place. Only by every single plate moving on this layer of molten rock is this possible. With all this energy building beneath our feet, it is only a matter of time before this becomes a reality.

FLAMES OF FIRE

On a broadcast in December 2015, I shared an alarming word that the Lord had given me. I saw a city on fire. All I could see was billowing smoke for what seemed like miles. The billows were a deep black color, and I instantly knew this represented cars and tires burning and oil tanks exploding. The fire and the smoke were so bad that people fled the city in whatever vehicle they could get into. All traffic lanes were jammed with people trying to flee. I looked inside a bus, and it seemed as if people were standing on top of one another. Tractor-trailers were trying to flee too, but not with their trailers. It looked as if fifteen people were in the front seat of those tractor cabs. Everyone was in a vehicle, and traffic was jammed and backed up. The atmosphere was one of extreme panic. Everyone—from all walks of life and every skin color—was screaming and fleeing for their lives.

When the riots began and city blocks were set ablaze in June 2020, it reminded me of this word, though I knew it would not be fulfilled this day. The same night I received this vision of fire, God told me to pray for Chicago, Illinois, and Minneapolis, Minnesota. I do not know if either of these cities were the ones I saw on fire, but I continue to pray for them nonetheless.

For weeks I watched from my sickbed as Minneapolis and other cities were torn apart from the inside out, entire city blocks set ablaze, police precincts burning to the ground, and people rioting in the streets and looting stores. After that, Minneapolis yielded to public pressure and began the process of dismantling its police department. Months later, news outlets reported that the crime rate was steadily increasing in Minneapolis.[11] I believe that one day soon Minneapolis will see a darker day than it already has.

I am not the only watchman who has seen such wanton destruction. David Wilkerson warned long ago that New York City would one day be ravaged by a thousand fires as a result of decades of falling away and turning its back on God.[12] I have long been on record that I believe New York City is the mystery Babylon from Revelation and will one day be uninhabitable.

Revelation 8:7 confirms that fire is a part of the last-day judgment:

> The first angel sounded, and there followed hail and fire
> mixed with blood, and they were thrown upon the earth.
> A third of the trees and all the green grass were burned up.

God told me before the start of 2020 that fire will be a part of His judgment. Massive fires will ripple around the world, more so than ever before. For the last several years, we have seen multiple fires ravage the nation's countryside and even abroad in other nations. For example, from June 2019 to March 2020, around forty-six million acres burned across the nation of Australia.[13] Other places, such as Arizona, saw 2,520 fires in 2020 with over 970,000 acres burned.[14]

Some states, such as California, experience large wildfires with such regularity that they now have wildfire seasons, much like the Midwest's tornado seasons and the East Coast's hurricane seasons. California experienced its largest wildfire season in history in 2020. The California Fire website estimates that over four million acres of the countryside have burned thanks to almost ten thousand incidents.[15]

I remember seeing live pictures of Los Angeles during the peak of the season. So much smoke had passed through the city, and the sky had turned a deep orange. It almost looked like a scene from a movie with incredibly rich colors.

WATER AND FLOODS

Our Father is a keeper of His promises. He promised that He would never again use a flood to wipe out His creation. Water and flooding, however, will still be a part of the end-time judgment. God even shared with me shortly before 2020 that water and floods will be a part of His judgment, but He assured me that it would not be anything like the days of Noah.

William Koenig, a White House correspondent for twenty years, has a keen eye for detecting the parallels between US presidents' actions to divide the land of Israel and natural disasters and other events that have taken place in our nation. For example, he states that Hurricane Katrina resulted from America pressuring and convincing Israel to withdraw from the Gaza Strip. Though nine thousand Israelis were evacuated in Israel, nearly one million Americans were forced from their homes during Katrina. These two events happened within two weeks of each other in August 2005.[16]

Koenig has drawn connections to other major events from 1991 to 2016, including the ten costliest insurance events, the ten costliest hurricanes, and five of the six largest tornado swarms in US history. Each of these events occurred within days or hours of American presidents' or dignitaries' attempts to pressure Israel into dividing its covenant land.[17]

But not all water-related disasters are connected to Israel. In 2011 we saw the damage inflicted on Japan by the earthquake-triggered tsunami. In 2004 we saw India, Indonesia, and Thailand overwhelmed by the Boxing Day Tsunami, leaving over two hundred thousand dead. Meanwhile, the American East Coast and Gulf Coast continue to see more hurricanes. In fact, 2020 produced a record of thirty named storms. Thirteen of those were upgraded to hurricanes, and twelve of them made landfall, breaking a record from 1916, when nine hurricanes made landfall in the United States.

Yet these are not the worst of what is to come. Revelation tells of four major events, all involving water, that are a part of God's judgment—the first of which comes to us from Revelation 8:8–9:

> Then the second angel sounded, and something like a great mountain, burning with fire, was thrown into the sea. A third of the sea became blood, a third of the living creatures in the sea died, and a third of the ships were destroyed.

How could a single event be so devastating? More importantly, is it even possible? Many scientists believe it isn't just possible but inevitable. The Canary Islands off the African coast are no stranger to seismic activity thanks to Cumbre Vieja, a massive volcano. This volcano cracked in 1949 and shifted toward the ocean. Enough seismic activity could exacerbate this crack and drop the west flank of the volcano into the Atlantic. Simulations estimate that a sudden drop of this magnitude could result in a tsunami with initial waves of over 328 feet in height and be propelled throughout the Atlantic Ocean, with 164- to 328-foot waves making landfall in Africa, 16- to 23-foot waves in Spain and England, 49- to 65-foot waves in South America, and 65- to 82-foot waves in Florida.[18] These waves could easily travel inland and devastate other coastal areas such as Boston, New York, and many Caribbean islands.

This may all sound like science fiction or a disaster movie. But I believe that these events from Revelation 8 will happen during this current generation on earth. As I've said before, we are living in the Revelation Generation.

FIRE FROM THE SKY

I've often remarked that Hollywood is the number one agency on the face of the earth when it comes to preaching the Book of Revelation. Studios have the resources, the budget, and the creativity to take the Scriptures and properly translate them to the silver screen for mass audiences to consume. The difference between Hollywood and the church is that the former uses these Revelation moments for pure entertainment. Over the course of two hours, movies such as *Deep Impact*, *2012*, or *Armageddon* depict humanity acting as God to overcome these larger-than-life celestial objects, save the planet, and start to rebuild, despite whatever destruction had been dealt.

But asteroids striking the planet are no act of fiction. Earth is repeatedly bombarded by asteroids and meteorites, most of which are small and burn up in our atmosphere before they can land and cause damage. To my knowledge, there are at least two that I call "dry runs" for this particular Revelation event.

The first is the 1908 Tunguska event in Russia. Early in the morning, a massive explosion rocked Siberia. It instantly flattened eight hundred square miles of forest, toppling eighty million trees. The area was sparsely populated, and therefore, there weren't many deaths connected to this strange event. Experts believe that an asteroid about 120 feet in size exploded a couple of miles above Earth's surface, tearing the asteroid apart with enough force to register a 5.0 on the Richter scale.[19]

The second event occurred not long ago, and this time in America, in 1871, with the Great Chicago Fire. On the evening of October 8, a fire broke out and rapidly grew, consuming much of the city over the course of a day before dying out, thanks to a rainstorm. Many blame Mrs. O'Leary's cow for knocking over a lantern, and while this is a good theory, it doesn't explain the countless other fires that occurred that same evening. Several cities across the lake in Michigan were devastated, including Holland, Manistee, and Port Huron.

The fires impacted another state. That night, 250 miles north of Chicago, the town of Peshtigo, Wisconsin, was destroyed by fire, killing between 1,200 and 2,500 people and devastating 1.2 million acres.[20] Despite the many fires on our West Coast in recent years, the Peshtigo Fire is still the deadliest on record. I once plotted each October 1871 fire with a set of pushpins on a map of the United States. To my amazement, I saw that a triangle formed, a wide end from Peshtigo to Chicago pointing to Michigan's thumb. I believe, as do others, that this event was caused by a meteor streaking down from the sky. I first learned of these events when watching the documentary *Fire From the Sky,* produced in 1997, which included interviews with Gene Shoemaker and David Levy, two of the Shoemaker-Levy 9 comet's discoverers.

The meteor crater near Flagstaff, Arizona, further proves that large celestial objects have indeed struck our planet. Popular theory still maintains that it was an asteroid strike that killed the dinosaurs. Our scientists routinely watch the skies for the next "Big One," a life-ending asteroid that would force humanity to the brink of extinction.

The year 2020 has seen the closest asteroid near-miss in recorded history, with a car-sized asteroid whizzing by the planet a staggering 1,830 miles away.[21] Another asteroid passed by Earth on November 2, just one day before Americans went to the polls and cast their ballots for the next president.[22]

Yet despite all these near misses, Bible prophecy still stands.

> The third angel sounded, and a great star from heaven, burning like a torch, fell on a third of the rivers and on the springs of waters. The name of this star is Wormwood. A third of the waters became wormwood, and many men died from the waters, because they were made bitter.
> —REVELATION 8:10–11

Scripture confirms that earth will one day again see an asteroid strike. One-third of our water supply will be tainted in the event, and many will die.

My friend and fellow student of Revelation, Dr. Tom Horn, recently published a book, *The Wormwood Prophecy*. Within its pages, he shares a series of reports and testimony from accredited scientists that the threat of an asteroid hitting the earth isn't just real but inevitable. So inevitable that one asteroid has been spotted and its trajectory plotted, which could impact earth within ten years.[23]

I firmly believe that all these things will happen, and happen soon. We entered the Revelation Generation a short time ago. All I can do is point to the Scriptures and the events of today and say that time is running out.

CHAPTER 12

PREPARING PHYSICALLY

H AVE YOU EVER been in a car accident?

Has your house or place of residence ever been burglarized or damaged by a natural event?

Have you fallen and broken a limb or required medical attention?

In all those situations first responders always make sure to tell you the same thing: to contact your insurance company right away (if you have it). Those without insurance know firsthand how crushing it can be when trying to recover from one of these events.

Perhaps you know what it's like to drive around with a damaged vehicle because you cannot afford to make necessary repairs. But what if your vehicle was totaled and you couldn't replace the car quickly? What if your home was destroyed in a tornado or hurricane, and you didn't have insurance to pay off what you still owe on your mortgage or start to rebuild your home? Even worse, imagine needing major surgery or treatment due to a life-altering issue, only to be turned away by doctors because you cannot afford to pay for a single night in the hospital.

Now think of the tens of millions of people who lost their jobs in 2020 due to the nationwide lockdown. US history has already recorded this singular event as the largest job loss in public record. Overnight, businesses deemed "non-essential" were shuttered, and unemployment offices were instantly overwhelmed by people looking for benefits. While our government did respond, it took precious time for federal actions to be implemented at the state and local levels simply because they could not keep up with the demand.

A 2015 prophecy from Heidi Baker was quickly realized.

> I had a vision in your church and it wasn't what I expected to see. But I saw…bread lines, soup kitchens, and I saw people wearing beautiful clothing…Their clothing was not worn out. Now in my nation [Mozambique] when people are hungry you can tell. I mean they are in shredded rags. They don't have shoes or they have flip flops. Most of them [have] no shoes. They're hungry; they know they are hungry. They come for food, not because they're beggars, but because they are hungry….
>
> And I saw all these people, and they had fancy cars, beautiful 4 x 4's and Lexus, Mercedes, BMWs, Toyotas. There they were, fancy shiny cars, and they were standing in line….
>
> I said, "Why are they so well dressed and standing in this line?"
>
> He said, "Because it's a suddenly. They're suddenly in need of food."[1]

In 2020, we saw lines of cars forming for miles in states such as California and Pennsylvania, awaiting their turn at a food bank, not knowing if they'd be able to receive food. It didn't matter if they were single parents, full families, or just individual people. The simple fact is that the demand for food suddenly skyrocketed.

Major grocery stores were emptied in a matter of hours. Perishable items such as milk, eggs, and meat, along with common household items such as cleaning supplies and toilet paper, became as rare as gold. Thanks to computerized inventory systems, most major retailers place an order with their distribution center at checkout, ordering just enough items to restock shelves within the next day or two. This "just-in-time" shipping method helps stores keep their costs down by limiting on-hand inventory and only stocking what will actually sell. The overwhelming demand, however, absolutely disrupted this system. Distribution centers themselves didn't have enough stock on hand to replenish their stores, causing retailers to sell out and remain sold out.

The most memorable example of this breakdown was the sudden toilet paper shortage.

Toilet paper is just but one example. With millions of people stuck at home, many turned to a common transportation staple to provide entertainment and exercise: bicycles. Major retailers were soon cleaned out, as well as outdoor shops and bicycle supply chains. Factories remained closed for months, meaning no one was able to manufacture new bicycles to refresh inventory. It took months and relaxation of pandemic lockdowns in multiple countries to restart production, but it will still be years before the industry recovers and inventory is fully restocked.

But what does this have to do with preparing? How can one prepare for the unexpected? In many ways, you are already doing it. First, if you have a car, you are required by law to have car insurance. Your state's department of motor vehicles will not register your car without it. When law enforcement pulls over your vehicle, they immediately ask for two things: your license and your proof of insurance. If you take out a mortgage on a home, you are required to maintain an insurance policy on the home for both your and your underwriter's benefit. In recent years, there has been a massive push for universal healthcare and insurance for all Americans.

Insurance aside, we are all aware of the tornado, hurricane, and fire seasons across the country. People living in those regions know where to go in their house (basement, storm shelter, or enclosed room in the middle of the house) should a tornado strike, or even know where to go should they have to evacuate suddenly. The Federal Emergency Management Agency (FEMA) recommends that everyone prepare a basic emergency kit with at least three days' worth of supplies such as water, food, toiletries, batteries, and more.[2]

So if you can prepare for unknowns in your transportation, health, and home in the event of a disaster, why can't you prepare for the last days?

A DIFFERENT KIND OF INSURANCE

I've often been ostracized for offering food through my television program. Many have likened me to a doomsday prophet, a preacher of doom-and-gloom who utilizes fear to trick people into buying buckets of thirty-year-shelf-life food to wait out the apocalypse.

First and foremost, I am not afraid of the end of the world. I've read the Bible cover to cover. The Book of Revelation isn't about despair; it's about hope. The very first chapter promises a blessing to those who hear and keep the words Revelation contains (Rev. 1:3). God did not give us the Book of Revelation so that we would fear the end of the world. He gave it to us so we could save those around us from being on the wrong side of judgment. God wants us to be mentally, physically, and spiritually prepared for all that is coming!

Both the prosperity gospel and the pretribulation rapture have promised that we as Christians will not see the days of judgment on this nation and the world at large. I submit to you, reader, that this simply is not true. I have already provided multiple chapters in this book to prove that that is simply not the case. Look back at Matthew 24. Jesus warns of deception (v. 4), war (v. 6), chaos, earthquakes, famines (v. 7), persecution (v. 9), betrayals, hatred (v. 10), more deception (v. 11), iniquity (v. 12), a great harvest (v. 14), the Antichrist (v. 15), tribulation (v. 21), even more deception (v. 24), and a terrible event in the heavens (v. 29).

And then we see Jesus return (v. 30). But that's not all.

The Ezekiel 38 War. The remainder of the seven seals. Trumpets. Bowls of wrath. The battle of Armageddon. These are events that are still about to come, and while I believe that the church will experience some of these events firsthand, and in some cases have a front-row seat, I know for certain that a fair portion of humanity will see it all. Luke 21:26 tells us that "Men's hearts failing them for fear" due to all the disasters happening around them (KJV). Multiple Revelation scriptures declare that huge swaths of the earth's population will fall at once with each event. Jesus reminds us that we must endure much for His sake and during these Revelation times (Matt. 24:13).

Therefore, I often ask people what it would hurt to have a little bit of food stored. It is called "Emergency Food" after all. During the pandemic, several of our partners and good friends lost their jobs. They didn't panic and instead pulled out what they had been encouraged to store. They were able to live off of that, in addition to what they could get from the grocery store, until they were able to get a new job and back on their feet. We have had many similar reports over the last decade where these food supplies got our partners through difficult times. This was all possible, thanks to their "food insurance."

I am not afraid of these upcoming events. Will I still be surprised when they happen? Probably. I knew of the events that transpired on September 11, 2001, but I was still shocked when I saw them on television. That day, my phone kept ringing as my closest friends, my family, and even people I'd admired called me to ask, "What is next?"

I believe in preparedness because of Matthew 24:13–14. It's the reason we are on television every day, bringing the voice of the prophets into your home.

> But he who endures to the end shall be saved. And this gospel of the kingdom will be preached throughout the world as a testimony to all nations, and then the end will come.
>
> —MATTHEW 24:13–14

In the middle of great trials and tribulation, we see the absolute reach of the gospel and salvation! Television is only just a piece of it. You will soon have a front-row seat as a participant in this harvest, but only if you are prepared for it. We have been prepared as the salt of the earth, given the Light in the darkness and the Comforter—all so we can be right there when those who are lost come looking for a home.

Knowing all that I know and having shared all that I've shared, I believe there are three very simple reasons you need to prepare for what's coming:

1. Famine

2. Lack of availability

3. Ministry

FAMINE

Famine removes the ability to produce food. If food cannot be produced, it cannot be sent to distribution centers. If the trucks stop running, food can't get to the grocery stores. If it can't get into your grocery store, it can't get into your pantry. If it can't get into your pantry, well, you can easily figure out where else it's not going.

Why not put a little bit of food away in your home for a rainy day or unexpected disaster?

If your income is limited, stock up slowly on canned goods. Most canned vegetables, for instance, have a shelf life of one to two years. When you buy new cans, place them in the back of your pantry and eat from your oldest cans to keep anything from spoiling. Continue to stock up as you are able or for however long you can safely store.

As I've mentioned before, think about where you live, especially for accessing water. A person can live weeks without food, but you can only live three to four days without water. Do you have access to creeks, rivers, or even springs? Consider adding rain barrels to your home and invest in pumps that can filter the dirt and sediment back out. If you don't own your home and you instead live in an apartment, condo, or shared living space, evaluate your water heater, toilets, and bathtub and how much water they can contain. From there, invest in a simple filtration system like a pitcher or set of bottles. Be sure to read the product labels carefully, as many common products are designed to work only within a certain set of circumstances and may not filter the water as well as you could hope.

LACK OF AVAILABILITY

Famine is not the only reason food shortages will appear. Again, as we saw with the early days of the COVID-19 pandemic, store shelves were quickly emptied, and some were not restocked in a timely manner. This lack of availability will limit your ability to restock on your own power. Let's look at two reasons this can happen.

First, consider the distribution networks and storage. In 2020, the entire world was turned upside down in a matter of days because we needed to limit human contact to slow (not stop) the spread of the virus. But what if a different approach had been taken? What if the lockdown was 100 percent? What if every store, restaurant, business, and office was shut down for thirty days? What if you weren't allowed to leave your home—and delivery drivers weren't able to bring your online orders and local restaurant deliveries to you—because it would have been the quickest and least devastating way to kill a deadly virus? Would you have been prepared to withstand the walls of your own home for that short period of time? Many of us can stomach a day or two, but beyond that, our home begins to feel like a prison. Not to mention, very few of us might have had thirty days of food in our own home when this began, and the stores in our area wouldn't have had the means to help us all prepare to shut ourselves in.

Take New York City, for example. I once heard it said that there is only enough food in New York City to feed its local population for just half a day. Let's do some math for a minute. The US Census Bureau, in 2018, estimated that roughly 8.4 million people reside in New York City.[3] Take this number, and multiply it by three for each meal of the day (breakfast, lunch, and dinner). Multiply that new number by thirty days. This amounts to 756 million meals. Now imagine trying to bring in that many meals for New York City's population in just a few hours.

In contrast, shortly after Hurricane Harvey, FEMA supplied three million meals over several days to regions devastated by the hurricane. Nearly 780,000 people in Texas had been forced to evacuate their homes.[4] New York City, by comparison, is much larger with a higher population density. The same can be said for cities such as Chicago and Los Angeles. But what about the country at large? It would take a feat of industry never seen before to provide thirty days' worth of food to every American in a matter of hours to enable an absolute, 100 percent lockdown. If this could have been done in February and March of 2020, I believe we would have seen it happen.

Second, let's consider the ability to purchase food. We've already established that there will be coming hyperinflation with the third horse from Revelation 6. We also looked at that rider's scales and their

Greek connection to an ox's or slave's yoke of bondage. I do not think this is that much of a stretch once you factor in the following verses:

> He causes all, both small and great, both rich and poor,
> both free and slave, to receive a mark on their right hand or
> on their forehead, so that no one may buy or sell, except he
> who has the mark or the name of the beast or the number
> of his name.
>
> —Revelation 13:16–17

We are all accustomed to purchasing our food at a store. Comparatively, few of us own and operate a farm and those who do often sell cattle or produce to a third party for butchering and distribution. But a day is coming when the only way to buy or sell is to have the mark of the beast. To buy, you will have to have a job, and that employer's only way of paying you is to pay into the antichrist system. So, if you can't even work, how can you pay? Or get paid?

My friend Rick Joyner has said that there will come a day where the church will have to barter for goods and services. Just think, there is a day coming where you can trade a can of green beans for a haircut. Bartering, however, only works when you have material of value to barter with. Gold and silver will one day be useless, according to Ezekiel 7:19. My wife, Lori, has always believed that common supplies such as toilet paper would become more valuable than gold.

And 2020 proved her right.

MINISTRY

Lori spent many years in the inner cities of Phoenix, Arizona, traveling to poor neighborhoods. No one wanted to hear the gospel just by her knocking on the door on a cold call. The way into their hearts was through their stomachs and their needs. Providing something as simple as a hot meal would open the hearts of the lost to be saved. Even today, we still hear from those families and their children whose lives were transformed because of Christ. I think of our own adopted children who, if they remained in the inner city, would have grown up into a very different lifestyle, one far away from hope and salvation. This wound up not being their future for one reason: the saving grace of Jesus Christ.

In the last days, when iniquity abounds and the love of many waxes cold, the world will be crying for answers. The Antichrist is alive and waiting in the wings, preparing to give them false answers and further twist his deception. Can you imagine the impact you will have for the kingdom of God if you show up with a warm meal? Or even if loved ones or strangers show up on your doorstep? This is why I believe that we are preparing to see the final and greatest harvest the church has ever seen, but that can only happen if we heed the watchman's call and prepare.

We must be able to take care of our families. We must do this today and all the more so as the days continue to darken. If you are praying for household salvation, have you also considered how vital a stocked pantry could be in this regard, especially when members of your family come to visit in a time of need?

> If you're a parent, make sure to have enough for your children and their grandparents.
>
> If you're a grandparent, make sure to have enough for your children and grandchildren.
>
> If you're an adult living on your own, make sure to have enough for your parents.
>
> If you have other loved ones or close friends or coworkers, have something on hand so that you can be a blessing to them.

Churches must be prepared for their members and must continue outreach to the lost. Pastors and elders, keep your church pantry stocked! Do not wait until a crisis comes to start opening your doors either.

Canvass your neighborhood and meet those who live near you. You never know where you'll find craftsmen, tailors, hairdressers, or even doctors and nurses. As I stated in the introduction to this book, God assured me that the only place of security in the last days is inside the body of Christ. Soon, we will have no choice but to rely on one another to get through difficult times.

The Bible very clearly states:

> Let us not forsake the assembling of ourselves together, as is the manner of some, but let us exhort one another, especially as you see the Day approaching.
>
> —Hebrews 10:25

The best example I've ever seen of how one person can make a difference in a crisis was one I observed in 2012 during Hurricane Sandy. Power was out for blocks all around, possibly miles. Yet one person had a gas generator. Rather than hide it away, they kept watch outside and kept it running for as long as they could. The only thing plugged into the generator was a surge protector. But what was plugged into the surge protector? Charging blocks and cables for everyone's phone in the neighborhood. Everyone took turns getting a little bit of charge for their phone so that they could keep in contact with the world and their families.

I do not know if this person was a Christian or a Good Samaritan, or both. But can you imagine what sort of influence that person would have had if the homeowner had a Bible? Souls would have been replenished that day, and not just cell phone batteries.

THE GREAT HARVEST

There are more than seven billion people in the world. According to a 2015 study conducted by the Pew Research Center, only 31.2 percent of the world's population, about 2.18 billion, profess to be Christian. That number is shrinking rapidly in continents such as Europe, and it certainly seems to be shrinking in places such as America.[5]

This isn't from a falling away; it is from a lack of evangelism. The Bible tells us:

> The time is coming, says the Lord GOD, when I will send a
> famine on the land, not a famine of bread, nor a thirst for
> water, but of hearing the words of the LORD.
>
> —AMOS 8:11

It's this famine of the Word that has allowed the antichrist spirit to run rampant. It is what allows the spirit of Leviathan to twist our words and wiggle into and disrupt our lives and families. Just as physical food replenishes and restores the body, the Bread of Life will sustain and revitalize the soul.

I experienced this firsthand in my final prison cell. A hunger for the Word had been spreading like wildfire among the incarcerated, and we could not get a single Bible to the prisoners. At the same time, I had the chance to speak with Ruth Bell Graham as I was in North Carolina. I shared the plight in my prison and how much I wished I could give any of them a Bible. Ruth's response wasn't just unexpected; it was overwhelming. She knew her husband, Billy Graham, had a library with dozens of unused, untouched Bibles that had been given to him throughout his many revivals and travels. Ruth sent them immediately to the prison, and every man there was able to begin reading the Scripture for themselves.

Start stocking away Bibles and multiple copies of Christian books that had a profound impact on your life. These materials are not for you! Just as you have been asked to store physical food away for your family, loved ones, and community, you must store spiritual food for them as well. When they arrive at your door hungry and tired, you will be able to feed their bodies and souls. By doing so, you are participating in the last days' harvest.

A SIMPLE CHECKLIST

Helping to prepare the church isn't just a calling or a mission I've been given. It's a clear directive. But you need to have more than just food on hand during a crisis. First, you need to have a plan. If you know you will have to leave your home, know first where you can go, whether it be to a family member's home or another location that you know well.

Or if your home will be where others will run to, make the appropriate arrangements.

Once those plans are settled, prepare your physical kits. There are many resources out there to help you prepare different kinds of kits for your home, based on where you live and the kinds of disasters that can strike your area.

One of the reasons people don't prepare is that they believe that it is an expensive undertaking. I'm not asking you to go out today and spend hundreds or thousands of dollars at once. Research the cost of each item on the list, and if you have to, buy one item at a time. Many of these items may even be available at your local discount stores. Preparation is easy when you can spread out your purchasing over several months, or even a year!

I urge you to have two different types of kits on hand.

First, prepare a grab-and-go bag for each person in your household that you can keep in your car or a closet. If you have to cut and run and only have a moment's notice, this bag will ensure you'll be able to survive until you get to your ultimate destination. Remember that this is not a long-term tool, just something to help you temporarily during a crisis. Make sure it contains:

- Food (nonperishable, if possible)

- Water bottle with filter

- Flashlight with extra batteries

- Toiletries such as toothbrush, toothpaste, and toilet paper

- Power bank for your phone

- Hand-crank radio

- Pocket or hunting knife

- Utility or work gloves

- First aid kit

- Whistle and mirror (to signal for help, if needed)

- Face masks and gloves

- Extra socks and personal undergarments

- Multi-tool

- Emergency poncho and/or solar blanket

- A copy of your previously prepared emergency plan

- Identification documents

- Local maps and compass

- Person-specific products (medication, baby formula, diapers, feminine products)

Second, collect and store the following items in a cool environment such as a basement or storm shelter in your home. If neither are available, find easily accessible places around your home that are protected from extreme heat and cold. Remember that these lists are only to help you get started. Pick an easy place on the list and make your purchases one at a time to make your preparation efforts affordable.

- Short-term food storage (canned goods, nonperishable items)

- Long-term food storage (prepackaged meals or recipes that need only one ingredient, such as water)

- Manual can opener

- Water bottles with extra filters

- Rain barrel and water pump

- Small power generator

- Solar panels and chargers

- Outdoor cooking stove and fuel (charcoal, propane)

- Flashlights with batteries

- Hand-crank radio

- Personal items (medications, toiletries, diapers)

- Hand tools (saws, drills, hammers, nails)

- Knives (pocket, Swiss army, utility, hunting)

- Baby items (diapers, formula, clothing)

- Air mattress(es) and blankets

- Identification records

- Cash and/or commodities

- Bartering items (coffee, specialty items)

- First aid kit with extra bandages and supplies

- Pet food and supplies

- Fire starters and extinguishers

- Duct tape, twine, and other fasteners

- Tarps and plastic sheeting

- Several Bibles

- Books and other informative materials

- Notepads, paper, and writing utensils

- Games and recreational items

- Gardening supplies (seeds, shovel, gloves)

A FINAL NOTE

God told me several years ago that His final time clock had started and that there would be no more stopping it. Now is the last season to get prepared. I do not know how long this season will last; therefore, I urge you to start now.

CHAPTER 13

PREPARING SPIRITUALLY

MY SON RICKY recently enlisted in the army. For weeks he endured basic training, some of the most vigorous physical conditioning known to Americans. Part of his training included jumping out of airplanes! We had intermittent contact with him throughout his training, and Lori and I had the pleasure of attending his graduation. Though I still saw my son in him, the man that greeted us was a new person. He was stronger and now a full member of the US Army. The army disciplined him into a fighting machine, ready to respond, no matter the crisis around the world, should he be called upon.

Army discipline has two purposes. The first is to take persons from various backgrounds, break them down, and rebuild them into a singular unit capable of responding quickly and accurately to orders following the chain of command, regardless of the situation they find themselves in. The second is to insulate their mental capacity as much as possible. This includes simulating a live battle environment as closely as possible.

How many of us can attest that we can retain our focus when the first shot gets fired? Have you ever been in such an experience? Even the best of soldiers, and the best of people, can easily be caught off-guard when the unexpected happens. The true test of our character is what happens when we are faced with these situations.

Consider the disciples. They had spent years following Jesus, watching Him perform miracle after miracle, bewildering the most intelligent of the age with His parables, and even acting on His behalf in different cities while He was still with us. Jesus was training them for His ministry, much like a soldier training for war. Yet during the last supper, He warned them that all of them would run away (Zech. 13:7; Matt. 26:31). And true to His word, in Matthew 26:56, when Jesus was arrested, Scripture attests, "Then all the disciples forsook Him and fled." Despite all their training and the miracles they had witnessed, the disciples had been shocked to their core and believed they had no choice but to run away.

The disciples had the best teacher that ever walked the earth, and they were still shocked when prophecy unfolded right before their eyes. Peter, the one Jesus deemed would be the rock upon which the church would be built, denied Jesus three times that very night! Their belief had been so shaken that the disciples fled and hid in the Upper Room, fearing they too would be killed. Even the appearance of their resurrected Savior frightened them. This experience ultimately strengthened their faith, and they all boldly went into the world to preach the gospel, sharing the love of Christ until their untimely end.

My friends, the Lord is calling us all to become shockproof. We know that the worst is still yet to come upon the earth, and we must be prepared. In addition to physical preparation to be a practical city on a hill, we must equally (if not more so) prepare ourselves spiritually for the days ahead.

SHOCKPROOF

If you think reading the Revelation events is shocking, experiencing them will be even more tremendous. Just as the disciples ran and hid after Jesus was crucified, the people of the earth will flee from the face of the One on the throne, and they will lament what they lost. You can also see this distress earlier within Luke's account of the Olivet Discourse.

> There will be signs in the sun and the moon and the stars;
> and on the earth distress of nations, with perplexity, the
> sea and the waves roaring; men fainting from fear and

expectation of what is coming on the inhabited earth. For the powers of heaven will be shaken.

—Luke 21:25–26

This verse specifically declares that there will be great stress and pressure among the nations and adds two very significant words: "with perplexity." The Greek word used for *perplexity* is ἀπορία or *aporia*, which means to have no way out, to be at a loss mentally and to stand in doubt.[1] Events will soon transpire that will be so utterly shocking and unbelievable that the human mind and heart will be unable to comprehend, leaving the person no choice but to be rendered utterly speechless or fall dead in bewilderment. Every event foretold in the Book of Revelation is catastrophic in its own right.

How can one become shockproof? The answer is simple; you must come to know the voice of the Lord and know what is coming.

People may ask why this matters. We've been told that the day and hour of the Lord's return is purposely left a mystery. Jesus has warned us that it will be sudden, and His true followers will be taken suddenly without warning (Matt. 24:36–44). But this is where the misconception begins.

Many worldwide believe that Jesus is coming like a thief in the night, with absolutely no warning. I have asked many congregations if they agree, and every time a vast majority of the parishioners will put up their hands. Sadly, every single person who agrees is mistaken. To understand, let us take a look at this passage:

> For you know perfectly that the day of the Lord will come like a thief in the night. When they say, "Peace and safety!" then sudden destruction will come upon them as labor upon a woman with child, and they shall not escape. *But you, brothers, are not in darkness so that this Day should overtake you as a thief.* You are all the sons of light and the sons of the day. We are not of the night nor of darkness. Therefore let us not sleep as others do. But let us be alert and sober.
>
> —1 Thessalonians 5:2–6, emphasis added

Paul makes it clear here. If we remain vigilant to the world around us, if we stay in His Word and know His voice, and if we listen to the prophets and the watchmen, we will know what is coming. In Matthew 5:14 we are called the "light of the world." Light and darkness do not mix; light casts out the darkness. Paul exhorts us, warning us to "not sleep as others do." In other words, we're not to blind ourselves to what is happening around us.

Why do you think the disciples asked Jesus what would be the signs of the end of the age? Why do you think we Christians are always looking ahead for the return of Jesus? We know that our world is temporary and that humanity keeps making a bigger mess than we can clean up on our own! Jesus is the only answer, even in the middle of these terrible events.

Jesus even says:

> But know this, that if the master of the house had known what hour the thief would come, he would have watched and not allowed his house to be broken into. Therefore you also be ready, for the Son of Man is coming at an hour you do not expect.
>
> —MATTHEW 24:43–44, NKJV

Think about that. If you knew that your house would be broken into on a certain day and time, would you not take adequate precautions to repel the criminal? Would you not do everything in your power to protect your home and those you love who dwell in it? This is why we must not live in darkness and must be on the lookout for the signs of His return. Only then can we become shockproof. We might not know exactly what will happen or how it will happen, but we will be able to recognize the forces behind the event and understand its purpose in these end-time events.

Do you need a final warning here? Jesus said to "Watch therefore, for you do not know what hour your Lord is coming" (Matt. 24:42, NKJV). Most accidents come when the driver's attention is diverted, even if just for a moment. Keep your eyes on Him, and you will be able to see what is coming.

AVOID THE FALLING AWAY

When I was growing up, my parents taught me a valuable lesson, which we know as the Golden Rule: "Do unto others as you would have them do unto you." I look at the news today, and I often wonder if we have an entire generation that could have benefited from learning that particular rule. As Christians, we are supposed to walk about our daily lives exuding what He called us to be. We must follow His example and walk in love.

But has today's church been walking in true love? Have we set ourselves up to be a judge, or have we given this world the wrong impression of our Savior? Christians are seen as racists or bigots. The Bible's truth is seen as hate speech. In Portland, Oregon, last year, we watched protestors burn the Bible. How could we have let this happen?

As I said before, the duplicity in our pulpits and our churches and the watering down of the gospel has caused massive damage to the church's reputation. Now that the curtain has been pulled back, the world is seeing the church's imperfections and rejecting its message. Many Christians themselves are giving up the faith. Others have forsaken the church and started focusing on personal spiritual walks.

Can we blame them? After all, how can a Christian remain a Christian with these unbelievable acts being committed in our churches? Recent years have been ripe with reports of sexual immorality in our pulpits and pews, not to mention embezzlement and other immoral acts that have forced the removal of many pastors and leaders.

Did we forget that King David, a man after God's own heart, committed adultery? What about Saul, who persecuted and killed members of the underground church before being saved by grace himself? The Holy Bible is filled with accounts of faithful individuals who committed terrible acts. Yet these people are a part of the lineage of the Son of Man. God can use anyone, but only if they repent and seek a godly life.

You are the salt of the earth. But if the salt loses its saltiness, how shall it be made salty? It is from then on good for

181

nothing but to be thrown out and to be trampled under-
foot by men.

—Matthew 5:13

Salt gives flavor to meat and prepared meals and even acts as a pre-
servative for raw food. But notice here what Jesus told those from His
Sermon on the Mount. If salt loses its saltiness, it loses its value. In the
eyes of the world, the church has lost its value. As a result, how can we
expect the world to embrace the church? We have a lot of work in front
of us. And it starts with you and me. The time for repentance is at hand.

THE THREE Rs

The most remarkable thing happened on September 11, 2001. In one
hour, nineteen people had shaken the country to its absolute core. For
the second time in sixty years, a foreign power had attacked the United
States on its own soil. Americans felt vulnerable and guilty, and they
knew there was only one place to go. And that was the church. Business
after business put up flags and put "God Bless America" on their mar-
quees and in their windows. America wanted God. Revival was beginning, or so it seemed.

Weeks later, churches were back to their regular attendance numbers. What could have been the greatest revival on a national scale had
quickly come to a halt.

This poor attempt at a revival lacked two things. The first was repentance, the prerequisite for any revival to take root. It was much like the
parable where the seeds fell on rocky ground with no good soil beneath
them with which to take root (Matt. 13:5). One must first repent to
invite true revival.

Once you have true *repentance* (the first R) and the start of *revival*
(the second R), there must be a final action, the most critical of all the
three Rs: *reformation*. This is something often overlooked in the revival
process. It is not enough to repent of wrongdoing and revive your faith.
You must be willing to reform your life. But what is the purpose of each
of these actions?

According to *The Oxford Dictionary*, *repentance* is to express sincere regret or remorse for one's actions.[2] Have you ever apologized to someone because you were told to? More often than not, your heart was not in that apology, and the other person recognized it immediately! To repent, you must truly believe, feel, and express your wrongdoing and sins to God.

Revival is seeking God with fervor in your spirit. It is allowing Him to cleanse you from that which you are repenting and fill those holes in your heart and spirit with His Word and the Holy Spirit. It is when you set your soul on fire for His will to be done and not your own. It is taking up your cross and following Him, dying to yourself daily, and fully devoting everything you are to Him.

But what about *reformation*? What is it, and what sets it apart from both repentance and revival? On December 31, 2019, New Year's Eve, my friend Lance Wallnau shared a comparison of revival and reformation and made them easy for everyone to understand. His illustration might be a bit crude, but it's the most effective one I have heard in my lifetime.

> Reformation is like Leah; revival is like Rachel. The church loves Rachel; nobody likes Leah. Leah was Jacob's unattractive other wife. Leah was the one however that produced for him all the children. Rachel was beautiful. Christians love revival. Reformation is dirty business because you have to go wading into the institutions where the world system is and you have to go in and that's where draining the swamp happens. That's where truth in media has to speak up and take the hits that come back. True speaking—that's where businesses got to be able to without compromise be able to build its wealth....In other words we have to move towards each one of these areas, and if we don't, it's already being occupied against us....So reformation is top down. Revival is bottom up. It's not either/or; you need both. It's a revived people who produce a reformation.[3]

Reformation is an act of true commitment to Jesus. It is a conscious decision to move forward in a new way of thinking and never returning to the one you came from. You must be willing to discard your past, forget your bad habits, and work daily toward a new normal, one that now reflects a godly lifestyle.

LET GO OF YOUR ANGER

Anger is a natural, albeit highly dangerous, emotion. When we let anger consume us, it begins to control us. You can perform swift and irreparable damage while your anger reigns supreme, such as compromising an important relationship with a loved one or employer or even destroying someone else's livelihood.

Many times in the Bible, God cautions us to manage our anger. Psalm 37:8, for instance, tells us that anger "surely leads to evil deeds." Ephesians 4:26 even warns us, "Be angry but do not sin. Do not let the sun go down on your anger."

While you are angry, you can be easily swayed by the evil one, the manipulating spirits that are running rampant, and even the great delusion that is on the world today. You are more easily deceived and convinced that the broad path is the better way, and you leave the straight and narrow. You will be blinded to the fact that the broad path will lead only to destruction.

A friend of mine once shared this powerful quote: "Bitterness is the poison you drink hoping the other person dies."

When you act in anger, it is difficult to listen to reason, much less the word of the Lord. You will miss the danger signs, and it could be too late! You will be unaware of the danger you inflict on yourself, your reputation, or others until your anger leaves you, and you are left in the wake of your own destruction.

Proverbs 14:29 says, "He who is slow to wrath is of great understanding, but he who is hasty of spirit exalts folly." Understanding what is to come will be your saving grace. Allowing your anger to blind you could condemn you.

How does one exactly get rid of anger and bitterness?

While Jesus walked with His disciples, He taught them many things. For some, He taught through parables and illustrations, and other times, through actions. In Jesus' early ministry, He made it a point to teach everyone how to pray, including this valuable portion of what is known as the Lord's Prayer.

> And forgive us our sins, as we forgive those who sin against us. And don't let us yield to temptation.
>
> —LUKE 11:4, NLT

In Matthew's version of the Lord's Prayer, Jesus expounds on forgiveness.

> For if you forgive men for their sins, your heavenly Father will also forgive you. But if you do not forgive men for their sins, neither will your Father forgive your sins.
>
> —MATTHEW 6:14–15

Forgiveness has incredible power. God is willing to forgive you for all your unrighteousness, all your sins, everything under the sun, and place it all under the blood of Jesus. But just as in praying for salvation, you must be the one to take the first and complete step. I learned this the hard way inside my prison cell. Forgiveness was the final barricade that had to be removed in my own life so I could begin my journey to restoration. To start my healing process, I had to forgive everyone who had wronged me from the bottom of my heart. Jesus commands:

> So also My heavenly Father will do to each of you, if from your heart you do not forgive your brother for his trespasses.
>
> —MATTHEW 18:35

Forgiveness was the key to my spiritual and physical freedom. Had I not been able to forgive, I would have been forever condemned to a spiritual and mental prison of my own making.

Why is forgiveness so powerful? And why must it be done? Anger, bitterness, and resentment take root in unforgiveness. Feuds between family members start with the inability to forgive a single wrong act. Conflicts within the church often begin when someone feels slighted by another church member or staff member. Unforgiveness will allow bitterness to fester and will harden the heart of the one who cannot forgive. How can we be expected to love one another when our hearts are as hard as diamonds and as cold as ice?

Hebrews 12:15 warns us that we must watch "diligently so that no one falls short of the grace of God, lest any root of bitterness spring up to cause trouble, and many become defiled by it." Proverbs 10:12 reminds us, "Hatred stirs up strife, but love covers all sins."

Finally, 1 John 4:16 states that "God is love. Whoever lives in love lives in God, and God in him." John goes on to say that "If anyone says, 'I love God,' and hates his brother, he is a liar. For whoever does not love his brother whom he has seen, how can he love God whom he has not seen?" (v. 20).

The inability or unwillingness to forgive will have drastic consequences, not just for you, but for all those whom you are supposed to reach for the kingdom of God. When you allow unforgiveness to build inside you, you unwillingly give the antichrist spirit and the rider on the red horse more freedom to work and operate unrestricted.

DEVOUR THE WORD

A good friend once asked me the top three things I learned in prison. I smiled and answered, "Jesus. Jesus. Jesus."

My friend immediately scoffed. "That's really one thing, Jim."

I supposed my friend was correct, so I gave him what he asked for. "Obedience. Obedience. Obedience." Anticipating another objection, I added, "And the Word. The Word. The Word."

Jesus

Obedience

The Word

Those are three incredibly simple and easy-to-grasp concepts. But they are most certainly a challenge to practice every day. Despite all the warnings I have given and all I've been through, I keep coming back to these three fundamental lessons. You cannot know Jesus without constantly staying in the Word. And you cannot continue consuming the Word without obeying what it says. Only by knowing the Word, knowing our Father's voice, can you navigate the tumultuous waters we are currently sailing in.

Stay in your Bible every day. Devour it as you would a hearty meal or decadent dessert. If you can, get a Bible with excellent study notes or even a thick concordance. Look for the parallels and patterns in Scripture to see God's amazing grace. Check every cross-reference in the Scripture and find those threads woven into this great tapestry. Take even care in reading those boring genealogy passages. These names often have fantastic meanings or even have been connected to incredible acts within Scripture. To me, these lists prove that every life has a purpose and that God does not forget who listens to Him and obeys His voice. Our names mean so much to Him that He writes them in the Book of Life in heaven (Rev. 3:5).

To help me study, I use specialized software on my computer to study the original Greek and Hebrew. Some translations are very poor renderings of the original Scriptures. Some words have been added by the translators, and other words have been improperly translated. In prison, I used special word study books with an interlinear Bible that shows every Greek and Hebrew word used in each scripture. These can be cross-referenced to other uses in the Bible to unlock what the Lord is teaching you. There are free resources available on the internet as well, especially with Greek and Hebrew meanings. Still, I highly recommend you invest in a pair of these word study books, as well as a few commentaries. Find a church whose pastor digs into the Word and brings new manna and revelation to every service.

No matter what, dig, dig, dig! His Word is inspiring and enriching every day and filled with new revelations and secrets just waiting for you to unlock.

WHAT IS YOUR CALLING?

God's final time clock is running. We are in, without a shred of doubt, the last days. When I delivered this set of warnings for December 31,

2019, I had no idea how quickly and how vastly they would transform our world. The horsemen are riding and working together. Various judgments are manifesting around the world as a result, and the skies are getting darker.

If you have been called to do something, make it a priority. The Master will soon return; don't let Him discover you buried His gift in the ground to keep it safe (Matt. 25:14–30).

If the Lord has called you to move to a different town or state, put your house up for sale and move.

If the Lord has called you to be a witness to your neighbor, be a witness.

If the Lord has called you to be a blessing to a family connected to your place of employment, be a blessing.

If the Lord has called you to use your gifts for His kingdom, use your gifts.

Time is running out, and you may not soon get the chance to do what you have been called to do.

STAY STRONG

It's not enough to be watchful for the things to come so that we won't be surprised or shocked, nor is it enough to continually devour the Word and take action in our communities. There is only one true way to stand against the strife created by the four horsemen, and that is to remain firmly rooted in the Lord. Paul says it best.

> Finally, my brothers, be strong in the Lord and in the power of His might. Put on the whole armor of God that you may be able to stand against the schemes of the devil. For our fight is not against flesh and blood, but against principalities, against powers, against the rulers of the darkness of this world, and against spiritual forces of evil in the heavenly places. Therefore take up the whole armor of God that you may be able to resist in the evil day, and having done all, to stand. Stand therefore, having your waist girded with truth, having put on the breastplate of righteousness,

having your feet fitted with the readiness of the gospel of peace, and above all, taking the shield of faith, with which you will be able to extinguish all the fiery arrows of the evil one. Take the helmet of salvation and the sword of the Spirit, which is the word of God.

Pray in the Spirit always with all kinds of prayer and supplication. To that end be alert with all perseverance and supplication for all the saints.

—EPHESIANS 6:10–18

Our battle is not with one another—not with our neighbor, our mayor, our governor, our congressmen, or our president. It is with Satan and his minions. It is the spiritual forces who have manipulated those on this earth to do their master's bidding in a massive attempt to corrupt and steal our Father's creation. I will not sit here and tell you the road will be easy. After eighty-one years of my own life, I can assure you that some days are harder than others. What has helped me stay the course has been a series of commitments I made to the Lord back in 1994, just before my release from prison. I have shared these commitments, which I call "My Daily Walk," with you in the appendix at the end of this book.

You must surround yourself with truth, live in righteousness, speak softly in love and peace, guard your faith, keep your mind on Christ, and be ready to fight the schemes of the evil one using the Scripture the Lord has armed you with.

And no matter what, do not waver. The storm will soon get worse, the boat will be rocked from side to side, and it will not let up. Stand firm in the Lord, and keep your strength up. Through your faithfulness and diligence, you will become a light in the darkness, and through you, many will come to know the truth and be saved.

I have read the end of the Bible. Revelation is not a tragedy. No, it's a story of hope and victory, the greatest love letter to the church! He has heard the cries of the saints and those who have not loved their lives, even unto death. One day the heavens will open. At the mouth of the heavens will be Jesus Christ on His white horse. At His side will be all the armies of heaven, and the final battle will begin. Our Savior will be victorious, and we will be reunited with our Father in heaven. A great reward awaits each of us, and it is more precious than anything this world can provide.

You can make it!

CHAPTER 14

BOLDLY GOING FORWARD

s WE CLOSE, a few of my family members wanted to share what they learned as we navigated our storm.

MARICELA

The year 2020 challenged everything about me. It challenged my life, my way of thinking, and the core values of my faith. I had learned immediately why Paul instructed Timothy to be ready both in and out of season (2 Tim. 4:2). Each trial that came upon us came suddenly and without warning. For different periods in 2020 we were overwhelmed. There were days I felt like Jesus' disciples in Matthew 14. They had just witnessed Jesus feed five thousand people and picked up the leftovers. Jesus then commanded the disciples to get into a boat, cross the sea, and meet Him on the other side. The disciples were obedient, yet a storm came around them in the middle of the sea and tossed them about. Late in the night, the disciples hadn't yet crossed the sea, yet Jesus came walking out to them on the water. Peter, encouraged by the Lord, got out of the boat and also walked on the water toward Jesus—only when he was reminded of the strong winds and looked down, he started to sink. When Jesus catches Peter in verse 31, He plainly asks, "O you of little faith, why did you doubt?"

There was a moment in 2020 when I felt like Peter. Though my eyes were fixed on Christ and I was walking in faith, I got swirled up into the dangers around me. I was overwhelmed by the legal actions and the issues with the credit card processors and even was worried about my dad when he had the stroke. But just as Jesus said to Peter, I heard Him say to me, "Why do you doubt?" A few weeks before this I had gathered the executives of the ministry and asked them if they were fully committed to seeing this ministry through its storm. I knew in my own ability I was not capable. Surrendering it all to God was my only option. I was even more encouraged when the rest of the executives agreed with me, that we all were trusting God to see us through.

That passage reminded me—no, it guaranteed me—that there would be storms in our lives. Jesus knowingly sent His disciples into it. He could have stopped the storm at any moment, just as He did elsewhere in Scripture. But the storm was designed to develop the faith of the disciples. The secret to navigating storms is not to be afraid of them but to keep your eye on Jesus, the prize of the high calling. Jesus is asking for our obedience and our gratitude while doing so. He is asking us to remain focused on Him. He will not let you stumble or fall, and He will enrich, fortify, and expand your faith!

This past year radically transformed my own way of thinking. My prayer each day is for God to show me His will in every action, whether that action is mine or taken by someone else. He has developed within me a patience that surpasses all human understanding and rewarded that with supernatural blessings and gifts. The storm might remain for now, but it is only temporary. My God and my peace are eternal. I have learned, without a doubt, that there is nothing my God cannot do.

MONDO

In 1999 I made a decision that would change my life. I was a former gang member that had been transformed by God. He gave me the opportunity to share my story with hundreds of thousands of people around the world in places that I could only have imagined. For so long I felt as if I had it all, but something was missing. When I first met Jim in Los Angeles, it all made sense. God asked me to serve Him by serving alongside Jim Bakker. I became his defender, his son, his best friend, and his "road dawg." In the church we call a person like this an armor bearer. Through my obedience and God's faithfulness, I have had the privilege of producing, directing, and now cohosting *The Jim Bakker Show*. But truly my greatest gift and lessons have come from my friendship with my "dad," Jim.

Let's be real; 2020 was tough. The pandemic forced all members of my family to stay at home. My wife, Elizabeth, was blessed to be able to work from home. She also took on the role of a teacher when the school where we sent our twins, Mila and Mateo, closed. COVID had us worried, especially since our twins have issues with asthma and my wife has lupus. But we knew faith was the key to getting through this challenging season.

And then April 2020 dealt a hard blow when Dad suffered his stroke. I was scared. My dad, my best friend, was hurting, and there was nothing I could do to help him. I had been by his side for more than twenty years, doing everything I could to protect him, only to be defeated by something I didn't see coming. I didn't know what the future held. I got down on my knees and cried out to the Lord, asking Him to help Dad get through this. There was no other option before me than to allow God to expand my faith. Through our faith we kept going.

Throughout the year, I kept hearing a song in my head, Andraé Crouch's "Through It All." Just as the song says, I had many tears, sorrows, and questions about the future. But God used every single one of these trials to make me and my faith stronger than ever. I've always trusted God, even in the most difficult times, and I have always encouraged other people to walk every day by faith. But this year especially, I can tell you by experience that the Bible is true when it says, "For we walk by faith, not by sight" (2 Cor. 5:7).

Every point in our lives, and every decision we make, sets us on the path toward our destiny. Hebrews 11:1 says that "faith is the substance of things hoped for, the evidence of things not seen." I also want to encourage you that even though you can't see it, faith is something you have to experience to fully understand. Until you do, faith is just a belief. Faith coupled with experience becomes knowledge. This knowledge and your obedience unlock your destiny. And your destiny will become a testimony to demonstrate to others the true power of our God.

God wants to speak to each and every one of us prophetically. He will do it through your actions as much as He will through the voices around you. Ground yourself in God's Word so that you will know His voice. Through it all we have learned to depend on His Word and to trust Him at every moment.

This destiny of mine came full circle for me during the pandemic. One day recently, after Dad had his stroke and had returned to television, I was helping him get dressed for a show taping. He was very weak that day. I could tell, though, that there was a glimmer of his former self in his eyes when he turned and asked me, "Mondo, you stayed my friend for all these years. Why?"

I didn't hesitate to answer. "I love you, man. God's calling in my life has always been to serve you."

To those who are reading: God is looking for our obedience in our service to Him. When we are obedient, God will bless us in return.

MY WIFE, LORI

The year 2020 taught me how much God is really in control. It is all too easy to say, "God's got this." But you can't speak those words when your own actions don't reflect that each and every day. God is the author and the finisher of our faith, but even then we have a choice whether we want to believe or trust that He will do the things that He says He will do. From the day I ran down the aisle at Phoenix First Assembly that Easter Sunday in 1989, I have lived every day pursuing God with all my heart. I wanted to be involved everywhere I could, from the bus ministry to missions trips to Masters Commission to so much more. God rewarded my faith and actions with several children and close friends from every aspect of my life and even allowed me to meet several people I've held in high regard, such as Ruth Bell Graham.

Every single step prepared me for that fateful April night. I wasn't ready to lose Jim, and it is still so difficult to think about that night. Jim's stroke reminded me that we are not guaranteed tomorrow and that we need to make every moment count for Him. Signing over Jim's life to doctors and specialists I did not know was one of the greatest steps of faith I've ever taken, and I was amazed with how it all worked out. I was amazed that every nurse and doctor who helped Jim was a Christian. I was amazed at how my husband was brought through his healing process and emerged stronger in faith than ever before. Jim thanks me every day for taking care of him. I always tell him that it's my honor to serve and that I do it because I love him so deeply.

I stand amazed at how God used every member of our family, as each one circled around us and fielded different duties to help Jim and me both work through our medical issues. It seems like yesterday that our children were little girls and boys wearing clean clothes for the first time. And now they're pillars in our family and ministry, educating and empowering their own children with what this experience has taught them. I don't think we could have ever known when we began the adoption process the master plan God had for these children, who had known only poverty. We have seen their struggles firsthand, their resistance to joining this family, and the trials we had to endure for each child. But to see what they have accomplished because of God? I have seen in action my life verse, Romans 8:28, which says, "We know that all things work together for good to those who love God, to those who are called according to His purpose."

I stand in full amazement at what God has done. I'm more than just awestruck with childlike wonder. I understand now when Jesus told His followers to welcome the children and not push them aside because they don't understand or don't belong. It's more than just their innocent mindset; it's the fact that they hadn't been tainted by worldly experience. As an adult, it is so easy to say that something can't be done. It is our doubts that compromise our faith. But a child—a child has a better ability to see truth and to have the faith most adults lack.

The trials we had suffered brought validation for decades of walking in faith. This past year, I had the pleasure and privilege of seeing my faith become more than reality. My faith became my life, and I have no greater reason to rejoice.

MY REFLECTIONS

The circumstances and situations I have seen and experienced in the last year are extraordinary. But I have to believe that what we endured as a family and a ministry was for reasons greater than I can understand. We know of persecution and betrayal because the Bible tells us so.

But we also know that these unfortunate acts are not exclusive to those in the public eye. We are living in a day and age where true Christianity is not accepted. Culture is asking us to either compromise or abandon our beliefs when the world needs Jesus the most. This is why prophets and watchmen exist, and this is why we and our partners have been targeted.

James 1:2–4 tells us to count it all joy when facing many trials and tribulations. Trials such as these test our faith, creating within us an ability to persevere. They mature us and complete our spirit.

The closer you move into the center of God's will, the greater the attack becomes. This is why Jesus warned that you must give up your life to save it (Matt. 10:39), and why Paul continually reminded us of the trials and responsibilities we have been commissioned for (Rom. 5:1–11; 12:9–21; 2 Timothy; and others). Eventually this persecution will reach global levels, as the mark of the beast will control all commerce and trade! People who go through these drastic and extreme situations are a twofold testimony to you. First, you will receive persecution for His name's sake one way or another. It will cost you platforms, finances, security, family, and more. Second, no matter what you experience, you must remember that you can make it!

As Jesus began preparing His disciples for His death and resurrection, He declared to them what it would truly mean for them to continue following Him.

> Then Jesus said to His disciples, "If anyone will come after Me, let him deny himself, and take up his cross, and follow Me. For whoever would save his life will lose it, and whoever loses his life for My sake will find it. For what will it profit a man if he gains the whole world and loses his own soul? Or what shall a man give in exchange for his soul?"
> —M<small>ATTHEW</small> 16:24–26

The apostle Paul wrote to the Corinthians that he had to "die daily" for the sake of the gospel (1 Cor. 15:31). To truly become a follower of Christ, one must be willing to sacrifice. "Deny yourself," Jesus told His disciples. Yes, there is joy in following Christ. There are miracles, wondrous teaching, revelation, and security in the body of Christ. But there is a high cost. We must die to the flesh to be born of the spirit. We must suffer persecution to endure to the end and victory.

But persecution is just one of the many things we will experience in the days ahead. COVID-19, for instance, was tragic for many. The loss of life deeply saddens me, from personal friends to major prophetic teachers such as Dr. Irvin Baxter, and even loved ones tied to our staff and community. My heart goes out to the hundreds of thousands of families who found tragedy in the virus.

When I step back and reflect on 2020, I can see that if it weren't for COVID, we wouldn't have been sued. If it weren't for the lawsuits, there wouldn't have been petitions. If it weren't for the petitions, I wouldn't have had my stroke. And if I hadn't had my stroke, the ministry would never have restructured itself the way it needed to for the future.

God purposely designed 2020 to be a year of restructuring for the future of our ministry. Over the last decade, we have experienced all sorts of difficult situations. Each one was a different level of transition and preparation in accordance with our ministry's purpose and mission. There were times we simply needed to refocus. There were also times we had to shift entire departments to meet a growing need in the ministry. The lessons that we learned from our external pressure and strife brought some needed changes to how we produce television so that we do not compromise the gospel and the validity of the prophets we bring to our platform.

Throughout this whole process, not only have I delighted so much more in the Lord, but I've found tremendous joy within my family. The love that they continually share with me never ceases to astound me. It would have been easy for any of them to give up and walk away, but no one did. In fact, I've seen more of my children and grandchildren in the last few months than I have in years. If it were not for COVID, I wouldn't have had this fantastic blessing.

I am still weak from my stroke. But I have more deeply learned that "when I am weak, then I am strong" because God's strength is made perfect in weakness (2 Cor. 12:10). His strength sustained both my physical body and my soul. Not a single action was performed because

God wanted to take me out of the picture. I was ready and willing for the Lord to take me home, but at each turn, He assured me that He wasn't done using me yet. My continued dependence on the Lord has yielded fruit and blessings more wonderful than any material means. I have seen fresh manna from heaven and fulfillment of promises that stretch back for decades. Every day, I see the signs my children placed throughout my home with the words, "My Story Isn't Over Yet." I love how true that is because I know that God isn't through using me.

I believe that He will fulfill all the promises on my life, including the miracles that are still yet to happen at Morningside with the great Voice of the Prophets network. Morningside is meant to be a hub for the prophets. I believe that this pandemic will disappear just like all the other pandemics in history, and when it does, Christians will once again travel to hear directly from the prophets. Not only will prophets come to Morningside, but multitudes will come to be commissioned with prophetic gifts and opportunities.

On my eighty-first birthday, I decided to demonstrate my faith again and act on this promise, despite my slow recovery. It was a bitterly cold day, and it was snowing! But it did not stop my wife and me from walking on a plot of land behind our Grace Street facility. My children stood alongside us, along with their spouses and children, and many faithful family members, friends, staff members, and residents of Morningside. As snow flurries fell around us, we broke ground for our next facility, the Hall of the Prophets Studio. We know that through God, the building will be finished. All odds might seem to be against us, but I know without a shadow of a doubt that nothing is impossible for our God.

DO NOT IGNORE THE WARNINGS

You have heard the warnings from the Lord. You have seen the struggles I have experienced for the sake of the gospel. At any point, I could have refused. I could have refused to share the warning. I could have walked away from the struggles. If I did, I would not have seen the fulfillment of the many promises He placed on my life and those on my family. My walk with Christ would not have become as strong as it is now. I would not have seen the victorious moments (and there have been many moments of victory).

I hope my testimony will serve as both an inspiration and a reminder to you of what God has promised will soon transpire on the earth. Darkness grows all around us, not just in our nation but in the entire world. God has not revealed His secrets to scare us, but to warn us of the coming judgments. These warnings are not for me. These warnings are for all of us. The knowledge of these warnings comes with an important responsibility. Let us recall the Lord's command in Ezekiel 33.

> Son of man, speak to the children of your people and say to them: If I bring a sword upon a land, and the people of the land take a man from among them and set him for their watchman, and he sees the sword come upon the land and blows the trumpet and warns the people, then whoever hears the sound of the trumpet and does not take warning, and a sword comes and takes him away, his blood shall be upon his own head. He heard the sound of the trumpet yet did not take warning. His blood shall be upon himself. But he who takes warning delivers his soul. But if the watchman sees the sword come and does not blow the trumpet and the people are not warned and a sword comes and takes a person from among them, he is taken away in his iniquity. But his blood I will require from the hand of the watchman.
>
> —EZEKIEL 33:2–6

That portion of Ezekiel refers to the position and duties given to His appointed watchmen. It is our job to look past the gates of our communities, cities, and nation to spot the coming dangers. When we see them, it is our job to sound the alarm, no matter how strange or unusual these things must appear. But the watchman's duty doesn't stop once we've shared what we've seen. That duty is passed along to every person who hears.

This next portion of Ezekiel refers to the responsibilities you have been given for hearing the Word. It is not enough to simply hear the

Word. Faith without works is dead (Jas. 2:17), and we have a responsibility once we hear the Word of the Lord and take appropriate action. We cannot be like the five bridesmaids whose oil ran out before the bridegroom came (Matt. 25:1–13) or the servant who hid his master's talents in the ground (vv. 14–28). God wants to be clear about this responsibility given in Ezekiel 33, so He repeats it!

> Now as for you, son of man: I have set you a watchman to the house of Israel. Therefore you shall hear a word from My mouth and warn them from Me. When I say to the wicked, "O wicked man, you shall surely die," and you do not speak to warn the wicked from his way, that wicked man shall die in his iniquity. But his blood I will require from your hand. Nevertheless, if you on your part warn the wicked to turn from his way and he does not turn from his way, he shall die in his iniquity. But you have delivered your soul.
>
> —Ezekiel 33:7–9

This charge, this responsibility, is absolutely serious. You cannot pray for household salvation and not be ready to ensure your loved ones are prepared to learn the Word. You cannot witness to those in need and not help them prepare for the dark days ahead. It is not enough to say, "Jesus loves you," with your mouth and let your actions and behaviors say something opposite. Do not let your salt become tasteless and then be discarded and ignored (Matt. 5:13). Paul warns us clearly:

> But if any do not care for their own, and especially for those of their own house, they have denied the faith and are worse than unbelievers.
>
> —1 Timothy 5:8

Every day, we must continue to stand for Christ. Do not let your light fade in front of your family, loved ones, neighbors, or even the person who just cut you off on the highway. As long as you are on this earth, radiate the love of Christ and share what God is doing. Get deeply involved in your church and your community. Don't stand on the sidelines, shouting to a crowd that is purposely ignoring you. Only when you meet the needs of those around you will they be receptive to hearing Christ's magnificent love.

And remember, God has no secrets from those who love Him! Surely the Lord God will do nothing without first telling the prophets (Amos 3:7). We know He shares these things so that we will not be caught unaware and unprepared for the days that are soon to come. Don't you forget that we have the end of the book! We know how it all ends!

As Christians, we are all ambassadors for Christ. We are always on duty, and the world will judge us based on our every action. More importantly, the world will judge the body of Christ as a whole by the actions of a few. I sadly know this firsthand due to my own experience. This is why I am so emboldened to continue pushing forward every day with the message the Lord has given me, no matter the physical opposition that comes from the enemy. We must all collectively work to fulfill Jesus' final command, to go into all the world, to share the gospel, and to make disciples of all nations (Matt. 28:19).

Paul commands Timothy to be a good minister of Christ Jesus.

> Until I come, give attention to reading, exhortation, and doctrine. Do not neglect the gift that is in you, which was given to you by prophecy, with the laying on of hands by the elders. Meditate on these things. Give yourself completely to them, that your progress may be known to everyone. Take heed to yourself and to the doctrine. Continue in them, for in doing this you will save both yourself and those who hear you.
>
> —1 TIMOTHY 4:13–16

We know that the days ahead will be difficult. They're trying now, but what lies ahead will be rockier than anything we've experienced before. The darkness grows only darker before the sun dawns on the horizon. English author Charles Dickens penned the perfect description of our current society more than a century ago. "It was the best of times, it was the worst of times."[1] Despite all the strife, trouble, heartache, and grief, we are living in the days that Jesus foretold. This is a time to rejoice! Out of all eternity, God determined that this was the era you were destined to live in and experience. You have been chosen and designed for these days, and your role is incredibly important in the events to come. Clothe yourself in the armor of God so that you can do just as I have, stand firm against the schemes of the devil and planted firmly in the Word of God.

I can't wait to sit with Moses, Elijah, the Apostles, and so many more to interview them about their experiences here on earth and what's not shared in the Bible. I know they are sitting in heaven, cheering on the saints. They're cheering for you because they know what you are about to do! You and I have been chosen to be a part of this Revelation Generation.

This is the last season to get prepared. The stroke of midnight is near, and the clock can no longer be stopped. We do not act in fear, but we continue to move forward in the authority of our Lord and Savior, Jesus Christ. He will return very soon for those who love Him. Until then, we must remain as vigilant as the five bridesmaids. Keep your lamp oiled and your light burning.

The end is near, but there is still so much more ground to cover before we hit the official end of the road. There will come a time when the true Word will be hard to come by, the mouth of the prophets hard to hear, and the call of the watchman faint. God will not forsake you in the days to come. I've been on the highest of mountains and the lowest of valleys, so I can say with confidence that you can make it through the valley of the shadow of death (Ps. 23:4). God will be right there beside us, and we shall emerge victorious. He will never leave us, nor will He forsake us (Heb. 13:5). Jesus Himself promises:

> And remember, I am with you always, even to the end of the age.
>
> —MATTHEW 28:20

Why? Because God loves you! He really does!

JIM BAKKER'S "MY DAILY WALK"

O<small>N</small> J<small>ULY</small> 1, 1994, shortly before my release from prison, I began to write a series of commitments I would make to Jesus on a daily basis. These commitments have enabled me to maintain my walk with Him in the last twenty-seven years.

I encourage you to keep this list, or one similar to it, and follow it each day. You might be able to adopt this as a simple fifteen-day devotional. With each step, I have included several scriptures that I either read or pray to help me stay the course.

As I learned in prison, the Word is ever living and ever inspiring, and it is needed more and more for the days ahead.

1. I will humble myself and walk daily in humility before God.

Scriptures to read

- 1 Peter 5:5
- Matthew 23:12
- 2 Chronicles 7:14
- James 4:1–10
- Isaiah 57:15
- Matthew 18:3–4
- 1 Samuel 15:17
- Proverbs 6:16–17

- Proverbs 16:5–8
- 2 Chronicles 32:24–26
- 2 Samuel 15:30
- 2 Chronicles 34:27
- Numbers 12:3
- Philippians 2:1–8
- Ephesians 4:1–3

2. I will seek my God today and every day and do nothing without consulting Him.

Scriptures to read

- 1 Chronicles 10:13
- Philippians 4:4–7
- 2 Chronicles 26:5
- Matthew 6:33
- John 16:13–15
- Acts 6:4
- Psalm 118:8–9
- 1 Corinthians 2:9–16
- Revelation 8:3–4
- 1 Thessalonians 5:17
- 2 Samuel 21:1
- 1 Samuel 23:1–4
- James 1:5–6
- 1 Timothy 2:8
- Hebrews 4:14–16

- 2 Samuel 5:19–25

- James 5:16

- 2 Samuel 2:1–2

3. I will read, study, and meditate on God's Word today and every day and implement it.

Scriptures to read

- Psalm 1:1–3

- 2 Timothy 2:15

- Romans 10:17

- Psalm 119:133

- Psalm 119:11

- John 8:32

- John 1:1–3

- 2 Chronicles 34:30

- 1 Timothy 4:13–16

- Revelation 1:3

- 2 Timothy 3:14–17

- 1 John 2:3–6

- Deuteronomy 17:18–20

4. I will have no other gods or idols or place anything before my God.

Scriptures to read

- Galatians 5:1

- Philippians 4:8

- 1 Timothy 4:1–2

- 1 John 2:15–19

- 1 John 5:21

- Exodus 20:3

- 1 Corinthians 10:1–14

- 1 Corinthians 3:16–17

- Deuteronomy 5:7

- 1 Corinthians 15:33–34

- Galatians 1:6–9

- Galatians 4:7–9

- 2 Chronicles 33

- Hebrews 12:1–22

- 2 Chronicles 34:1–4

- Deuteronomy 6:14

5. I will love, trust, praise, and worship my God with all my heart today and every day.

Scriptures to read

- 1 Timothy 4:10

- Matthew 22:37

- 2 Samuel 15:32

- John 9:31

- Romans 10:8–10

- Hebrews 13:15

- 1 Peter 2:9

- Psalm 37:1–9

- Job 13:15

- Isaiah 12:2

- 2 Samuel 22:1–7

- Psalm 52:8

- 1 Thessalonians 5:18

- 2 Samuel 7:22

- 2 Samuel 12:20

6. I will today, and every day, show mercy, forgiving all, and love my neighbor as myself.

Scriptures to read

- Galatians 5:13–14

- Matthew 5:7

- Matthew 22:39

- Matthew 5:44

- Matthew 6:14–15

- Matthew 9:9–13

- Matthew 18:35

- Matthew 25:32–46

- John 13:34–35

- 1 John 3:10–24

- 1 John 4:7–21

- Galatians 6:1–10

- Ephesians 4:32

- 2 Samuel 22:26

- 1 Peter 3:8–12

- Job 42:10

7. I will abide in Christ and allow His Word to abide in me and keep His commandments.

Scriptures to read

- Philippians 4:13
- John 15
- Colossians 1:26–28
- 2 John 9
- John 6:51–58
- John 8:31
- John 14:1–24
- 1 Timothy 6:14
- 1 John 2:3
- 1 Corinthians 12:26–27
- 2 Corinthians 6:14–18
- Ephesians 3:17
- 1 John 2:22–29
- 1 John 4:4

8. I will crucify my flesh and die to it daily, fleeing temptation and sin.

Scriptures to read

- Romans 6
- Romans 7:18–25
- Romans 8:1–15
- Galatians 5
- 1 Timothy 6:1–12

- 1 Corinthians 15:20
- 1 Corinthians 10:14
- Romans 13:14
- 1 Corinthians 15:31
- Matthew 16:24–26
- 1 Corinthians 9:27
- 2 Corinthians 7:1
- John 12:24–26
- Galatians 2:19–21
- 2 Timothy 2:22
- 2 Corinthians 12:1–10
- Colossians 3:1–4
- 1 Peter 2:11
- 2 Peter 2:9–22

9. I will accept the trial of my faith as more precious than gold, knowing whom God loves He chastises.

Scriptures to read

- Acts 14:22
- 1 Peter 1:7
- Hebrews 12:6–8
- Colossians 1:24
- John 16:33
- Revelation 3:17–19
- Romans 8:16–18
- 2 Corinthians 4:7–11

- James 1:2–3
- 2 Timothy 2:10–13
- 2 Corinthians 6:1–10
- 2 Timothy 3:12
- James 5:10–11

10. I will always confess that Jesus Christ is Lord, my Master, Owner, Possessor.

Scriptures to read

- Hebrews 9:11–28
- Philippians 2:11
- Revelation 17:14
- John 3:16–18
- Romans 1:16
- Romans 10:91
- John 4:15
- 1 Corinthians 2:2
- 1 Corinthians 12:3
- Philippians 3:7–10
- 2 Timothy 1:12
- Hebrews 13:81
- John 5:1–14

11. I will keep my heart right toward God, confessing my sins and never lying to the Holy Spirit.

Scriptures to read

- Ephesians 4:30

- 1 Kings 2:3
- Matthew 12:31–37
- Acts 5:1–6
- Matthew 22:37
- 2 Corinthians 4:2
- 2 Corinthians 7:10–11
- 2 Corinthians 10:3–5
- Hebrews 10:22
- James 5:8
- 1 Samuel 12:20
- 1 Samuel 16:7
- Hebrews 3:7–15
- 1 Samuel 13:14
- 2 Samuel 24:10

12. I will live by the total counsel of God's Word.

Scriptures to read

- Matthew 4:4
- Philippians 2:16
- Psalm 119:133
- Acts 4:31
- Hebrews 4:12
- Acts 17:11
- Ephesians 6:10–20
- Colossians 3:16
- James 1:22

- Psalm 119
- 2 Chronicles 24:20
- 1 Corinthians 2:13
- 1 Corinthians 4:2
- 2 Timothy 3:16
- 2 Timothy 4:3–4
- 2 Peter 1:1–10

13. I will not judge others, lean on my own understanding, or trust the arm of the flesh.

Scriptures to read

- 1 Peter 1:22–25
- Matthew 7:1
- Proverbs 3:5
- Romans 2:1
- Romans 12:1–2, 19–21
- 2 Chronicles 32:8
- Romans 14:12–13
- James 4:11–17
- Romans 7:18
- Jeremiah 48:7
- Jeremiah 17:5
- Psalm 146:3
- John 7:24
- Psalm 44:6
- Psalm 49:6–7

- Ezekiel 33:13

14. I will demonstrate love, joy, peace, long-suffering, gentleness, goodness, faith, meekness, and temperance.

Scriptures to read

- Galatians 5:22–25
- Matthew 7:16–27
- 1 Corinthians 13
- Ephesians 4:1–2
- Hebrews 11
- Colossians 3:12–15
- Matthew 3:10
- Matthew 13:18–23
- Colossians 1:10–11
- 1 Timothy 1:16
- Ephesians 5:8–12
- Hebrews 12:14
- Nehemiah 8:10
- 1 Peter 4:8
- James 3:17–18
- 2 Peter 1:6

15. I will keep my eyes on heaven, the mark of the prize of the high calling in Christ Jesus.

Scriptures to read

- Philippians 3:14
- 1 John 3:3

- 2 Corinthians 5:2–8
- 2 Peter 3:12
- Philippians 1:23
- Luke 12:33
- Hebrews 11:10–16
- Matthew 6
- Matthew 25:13
- 1 Thessalonians 4:16–18
- Ecclesiastes 9:11–12
- 1 Corinthians 9:27
- 2 Timothy 4:7–8
- Hebrews 12:1

NOTES

INTRODUCTION

1. Nancy G, "PTL and David Wilkerson," YouTube, May 30, 2015, https://www.youtube.com/watch?v=EMbles5npus.
2. The Jim Bakker Show, "David Wilkerson on PTL," YouTube, April 9, 2015, https://www.youtube.com/watch?v=UJyoSuDzCTQ.
3. The Jim Bakker Show, "David Wilkerson on PTL."
4. The Jim Bakker Show, "David Wilkerson on PTL."
5. *Merriam-Webster*, s.v. "iniquity," accessed February 9, 2021, https://www.merriam-webster.com/dictionary/iniquity.
6. Blue Letter Bible, s.v. *"anomia,"* accessed February 9, 2021, https://www.blueletterbible.org/lang/lexicon/lexicon.cfm?Strongs=G458&t=KJV.

CHAPTER 1

1. Greg Gittrich, "Massive Fault Threatens Downtown," *Los Angeles Daily News*, March 5, 1999. See also Deborah Netburn, "Earthquake Fault Long Thought Dormant Could Devastate Los Angeles, Researchers Say," *Los Angeles Times*, August 31, 2019, https://www.latimes.com/california/story/2019-08-31/an-earthquake-fault-long-thought-dormant-could-devastate-los-angeles-reseachers-say.
2. G. F. Wieczorek et al., "Debris-Flow and Flooding Hazards Associated With the December 1999 Storm in Coastal Venezuela and Strategies for Mitigation," United States Geological Survey, 2001, https://pubs.usgs.gov/of/2001/ofr-01-0144/; Tamotsu Takahashi et al., "Flood and Sediment Disasters Triggered by 1999 Rainfall in Venezuela; A River Restoration Plan for an Alluvial Fan," *Journal of Natural Disaster Science* 23, no. 2 (2001): 65–82, https://jsnds.sakura.ne.jp/jnds/23_2_2.pdf.
3. Editors of Encyclopaedia Britannica, "Hurricane Katrina," *Encyclopaedia Britannica*, updated September 23, 2020, https://www.britannica.com/event/Hurricane-Katrina.
4. John P. Rafferty, "Japan Earthquake and Tsunami of 2011," *Encyclopaedia Britannica*, updated March 27, 2020, https://www.britannica.com/event/Japan-earthquake-and-tsunami-of-2011.
5. Rafferty, "Japan Earthquake and Tsunami of 2011."

CHAPTER 2

1. "The Next 31 Things: Part 2," *The Jim Bakker Show*, January 9, 2020, https://jimbakkershow.com/watch/?guid=3838R.

2. Blue Letter Bible, s.v. *"eirēnē,"* accessed February 10, 2021, https://www.blueletterbible.org/lang/lexicon/lexicon. cfm?Strongs=G1515&t=KJV.

3. "The Next 31 Things: Part 2," *The Jim Bakker Show*.

4. Blue Letter Bible, s.v. *"ethnos,"* accessed February 10, 2021, https://www.blueletterbible.org/lang/lexicon/lexicon. cfm?Strongs=G1484&t=KJV.

5. See, for example, Christi Carras, "Hollywood Condemns Amy Coney Barrett Confirmation: '6-3 Doesn't Represent Me,'" *Los Angeles Times*, October 27, 2020, https://www.latimes.com/ entertainment-arts/story/2020-10-27/amy-coney-barrett-confirmation-supreme-court-celebrity-tweets; Christian Toto, "Hooray for Hollywood—Unless You're a Conservative," *The Hill*, March 15, 2020, https://thehill.com/opinion/technology/487640-hooray-for-hollywood-unless-youre-a-conservative.

6. FAO, IFAD, UNICEF, WFP, and WHO, "The State of Food Security and Nutrition in the World 2020: Transforming Food Systems for Affordable Healthy Diets," Food and Agriculture Organization of the United Nations, 2020, https://doi. org/10.4060/ca9692en.

7. "As Famines of 'Biblical Proportion' Loom, Security Council Urged to 'Act Fast,'" UN News, April 21, 2020, https://news. un.org/en/story/2020/04/1062272.

8. David Njagi, "East Africa Is Seeing Its Worst Swarms of Locusts in Many Decades. How Can These Ravenous Pests Be Stopped?," BBC, August 6, 2020, https://www.bbc.com/ future/article/20200806-the-biblical-east-african-locust-plagues-of-2020; Andrew Freedman, "Extreme Weather Patterns Are Raising the Risk of a Global Food Crisis, and Climate Change Will Make This Worse," *Washington Post*, December 9, 2019, https://www.washingtonpost.com/weather/2019/12/09/ extreme-weather-patterns-are-raising-risk-global-food-crisis-climate-change-will-make-this-worse/.

9. "Unemployment Rate Rises to Record High 14.7 Percent in April 2020," Bureau of Labor Statistics, May 13, 2020, https://www.bls. gov/opub/ted/2020/unemployment-rate-rises-to-record-high-14-point-7-percent-in-april-2020.htm.

10. Blue Letter Bible, s.v. *"zygos,"* accessed February 10, 2021, https://www.blueletterbible.org/lang/lexicon/lexicon.cfm?Strongs=G2218&t=KJV.

11. Reuters Staff, "Court Outlaws Wal-Mart de Mexico Worker Vouchers," Reuters, September 5, 2008, https://www.reuters.com/article/mexico-walmex/court-outlaws-wal-mart-de-mexico-worker-vouchers-idUSN0546591320080905.

12. Blue Letter Bible, s.v. *"thanatos,"* accessed February 10, 2021, https://www.blueletterbible.org/lang/lexicon/lexicon.cfm?page=2&strongs=G2288&t=NASB#lexResults.

13. Blue Letter Bible, s.v. *"thanatos."*

14. Paul M. Sharp and Beatrice H. Hahn, "Origins of HIV and the AIDS Pandemic," *Cold Spring Harbor Perspectives in Medicine* 1, no. 1 (September 2011): a006841, https://www.ncbi.nlm.nih.gov/pmc/articles/PMC3234451/.

15. Sharon N. DeWitte and Maryanne Kowaleski, "Black Death Bodies," *Fragments* 6 (2017), http://hdl.handle.net/2027/spo.9772151.0006.001.

16. Evan Andrews, "6 Devastating Plagues," History, updated August 22, 2018, https://www.history.com/news/6-devastating-plagues.

17. "Plague—Madagascar," World Health Organization, November 27, 2017, https://www.who.int/csr/don/27-november-2017-plague-madagascar/en/.

18. "Archived: WHO Timeline—COVID-19," World Health Organization, April 27, 2020, https://www.who.int/news/item/27-04-2020-who-timeline---covid-19.

19. Associated Press, "Timeline: China's COVID-19 Outbreak and Lockdown of Wuhan," ABC News, January 22, 2021, https://abcnews.go.com/Health/wireStory/timeline-chinas-covid-19-outbreak-lockdown-wuhan-75421357.

20. "Databases, Tables & Calculators by Subject: Unemployment Rate, 1948–2021," Bureau of Labor Statistics, accessed February 10, 2021, https://data.bls.gov/pdq/SurveyOutputServlet.

21. Stephanie Soucheray, "US Food Processing Plants Become COVID-19 Hot Spots," CIDRAP, April 27, 2020, https://www.cidrap.umn.edu/news-perspective/2020/04/us-food-processing-plants-become-covid-19-hot-spots.

22. John M. Barry, *The Great Influenza* (New York: Penguin, 2004), 4, 361, https://archive.org/details/greatinfluenzaep00barr/page/4/mode/2up.

23. "The Next 31 Things: Part 2," *The Jim Bakker Show.*

24. "The Next 31 Things: Part 1," *The Jim Bakker Show*, January 9, 2020, https://jimbakkershow.com/watch/?guid=3837R.

25. John H. Boman IV and Owen Gallupe, "Has COVID-19 Changed Crime? Crime Rates in the United States during the Pandemic," *American Journal of Criminal Justice* (July 8, 2020): 1–9, https://www.ncbi.nlm.nih.gov/pmc/articles/PMC7340780/; Mark É. Czeisler et al., "Mental Health, Substance Use, and Suicidal Ideation During the COVID-19 Pandemic—United States, June 24–30, 2020," *CDC Morbidity and Mortality Weekly Report* 69, no. 32 (August 14, 2020): 1049–1057, https://www.cdc.gov/mmwr/volumes/69/wr/mm6932a1.htm.
26. Sharon Cohen, "Millions of Hungry Americans Turn to Food Banks for 1st Time," Associated Press, December 7, 2020, https://apnews.com/article/race-and-ethnicity-hunger-coronavirus-pandemic-4c7f1705c6d8ef5bac241e6cc8e331bb.

CHAPTER 3

1. Lori Graham Bakker, *More Than I Could Ever Ask* (Nashville: Thomas Nelson, 2000), 161, https://archive.org/details/morethanicouldev00bakk/page/160/mode/2up.

CHAPTER 4

1. Yanan Wang, "China Reports 2nd Death From Virus Behind Pneumonia Outbreak," Associated Press, January 17, 2020, https://apnews.com/article/a9bf5807be39651eac6612263da3b24b.
2. Associated Press, "What's New Today in the China Virus Outbreak," Associated Press, January 21, 2020, https://apnews.com/article/8cb0160641755ec3a792e65d7644a71b.
3. "Taiwan Urges China to Release All Information on New Virus," Associated Press, January 22, 2020, https://apnews.com/article/1a90ab8517d2cdfaf6b66fadb681ce4e.
4. Ken Moritsugu, "Chinese City Stops Outbound Flights, Trains to Fight Virus," Associated Press, January 22, 2020, https://apnews.com/article/902c9f9f551d55b227b3d754f42aad50.
5. Barry, *The Great Influenza*, 4.
6. "Statement on the Second Meeting of the International Health Regulations (2005) Emergency Committee Regarding the Outbreak of Novel Coronavirus (2019-nCoV)," World Health Organization, January 30, 2020, https://www.who.int/news/item/30-01-2020-statement-on-the-second-meeting-of-the-international-health-regulations-(2005)-emergency-committee-regarding-the-outbreak-of-novel-coronavirus-(2019-ncov).

7. "Research," American Biotech Labs, accessed February 12, 2021, https://silverbiotics.com/research/.

8. R. Roy et al., "Ultradilute Ag-aquasols With Extraordinary Bactericidal Properties: Role of the System Ag–O–H$_2$O," *Material Research Innovations* 11, no. 1 (2007): 3–18, https://doi.org/10.1179/143307507X196167.

9. A. de Souza, D. Mehta, and R. W. Leavitt, "Bactericidal Activity of Combinations of Silver–Water Dispersion™ With 19 Antibiotics Against Seven Microbial Strains," *Current Science* 91, no. 7 (October 2006): 926–929, https://www.researchgate.net/publication/237743031_Bactericidal_activity_of_combinations_of_Silver-Water_Dispersion_with_19_antibiotics_against_seven_microbial_strains.

10. M. A. Munger et al., "An In Vivo Human Time-Exposure Investigation of a Commercial Silver Nano-Particle Solution," *Clinical Pharmacology and Therapeutics* 91 (March 2012), https://www.researchgate.net/publication/294304578_AN_IN_VIVO_HUMAN_TIME-EXPOSURE_INVESTIGATION_OF_A_COMMERCIAL_SILVER_NANO-PARTICLE_SOLUTION.

11. P. L. Tran et al., "Efficacy of a Silver Colloidal Gel Against Selected Oral Bacteria In Vitro," *F1000 Research* 8, no. 267 (March 7, 2019), https://doi.org/10.12688/f1000research.17707.1.

12. Robert J. Holladay and William D. Moeller, "Antiviral Colloidal Silver Composition," US Patent and Trademark Office, June 17, 2014, http://patft.uspto.gov/netacgi/nph-Parser?Sect1=PTO2&Sect2=HITOFF&p=1&u=%2Fnetahtml%2FPTO%2Fsearch-bool.html&r=1&f=G&l=50&col=AND&d=PTXT&s1=%22Antiviral+Colloidal+Silver+Composition%22&OS=.

13. Christopher Tseng, "Virucidal Activity of ARB 03-6534" (unpublished study, November 5, 2003), PDF; Christopher Tseng, "Virucidal Activity of ARB 03-6533" (unpublished study, November 5, 2003), PDF.

14. G. Pedersen and B. M. Hegde, "Silver Sol Completely Removes Malaria Parasites From the Blood of Human Subjects Infected With Malaria in an Average of Five Days: A Review of Four Randomized, Multi-Centered, Clinical Studies Performed in Africa," *The Indian Practitioner* 63, no. 9 (September 2010): 567–574, https://cdn2.hubspot.net/hubfs/211377/Silver%20Sol%20Malaria%20The%20Indian%20Practitioner.pdf.

15. "MALARIA AND TB: IMPLEMENTING PROVEN TREATMENT AND ERADICATION METHODS," US House of Representatives,

April 26, 2005, http://commdocs.house.gov/committees/intlrel/hfa20915.000/hfa20915_0f.htm.

16. Paul K. Carlton Jr., "Letter to Tom Ridge," Last Chance Treatment Foundation, November 10, 2003, https://lastchancetreatment.org/blogs/news/the-strongest-immune-supplement-available.

17. Tseng, "Virucidal Activity of ARB 03-6534"; Tseng, "Virucidal Activity of ARB 03-6533."

18. "Attorney General James Takes Action Against Coronavirus Health Scams, Issues Guidance to New Yorkers," New York Attorney General, March 5, 2020, https://ag.ny.gov/press-release/2020/attorney-general-james-takes-action-against-coronavirus-health-scams-issues.

19. Letitia James, "Cease and Desist Notification," New York Attorney General, March 3, 2020, https://ag.ny.gov/sites/default/files/bakker_cease_and_desist_letter_notification.pdf.

20. William A. Correll and Richard A. Quaresima, "Warning Letter," Federal Trade Commission, March 6, 2020, https://www.ftc.gov/system/files/warning-letters/fda-covid-19-letter-jim-bakker.pdf.

21. Gregory J. Holman, "Missouri AG Files Suit Against Jim Bakker Show, Says Stop Selling Coronavirus 'Cure,'" *Springfield News-Leader*, March 10, 2020, https://www.news-leader.com/story/news/local/ozarks/2020/03/10/jim-bakker-coronavirus-cure-claim-missouri-attorney-general-files-suit/5009377002/.

CHAPTER 5

1. "Drop Televangelist for Selling Fake Coronavirus Cure," Faithful America, April 6, 2020, https://act.faithfulamerica.org/sign/bakker-coronavirus/. This article was later updated (May 8).

2. "Drop Televangelist for Selling Fake Coronavirus Cure," Faithful America.

3. Stephen Strang, "Why I Believe Jim Bakker Is Being Unfairly Attacked Online," Charisma News, April 21, 2020, https://www.charismanews.com/opinion/80850-why-i-believe-jim-bakker-is-being-unfairly-attacked-online.

4. CBN News, "Is 'Faithful America' the Voice of Christians? Who Are They?," YouTube, May 1, 2020, https://www.youtube.com/watch?v=6Qf8TLTyBcY.

CHAPTER 9

1. Lexico.com, s.v. "edify," accessed February 16, 2021, https://www.lexico.com/definition/edify.

CHAPTER 10

1. Blue Letter Bible, s.v. "*mᵊhûmâ*," accessed February 17, 2021, https://www.blueletterbible.org/lang/lexicon/lexicon.cfm?Strongs=H4103&t=KJV.

2. Blue Letter Bible, s.v. "*akatastasia*," accessed February 17, 2021, https://www.blueletterbible.org/lang/lexicon/lexicon.cfm?Strongs=G181&t=KJV.

3. "The State of Abortion in the United States: January 2021," National Right to Life Committee, January 2021, 5, https://www.nrlc.org/uploads/communications/stateofabortion2021.pdf.

4. *Merriam-Webster*, s.v. "explosion," accessed April 5, 2021, https://www.merriam-webster.com/dictionary/explosion.

5. Blue Letter Bible, s.v. "*anomia*," accessed February 21, 2021, https://www.blueletterbible.org/lang/lexicon/lexicon.cfm?Strongs=G458&t=KJV.

6. International Crisis Group, "Preventing Boko Haram Abductions of Schoolchildren in Nigeria," OCHA, April 12, 2018, https://reliefweb.int/sites/reliefweb.int/files/resources/b137-preventing-boko-haram-abductions.pdf.

7. Bradford Betz, "Shaun King: Statues of Jesus Christ Are 'Form of White Supremacy,' Should Be Torn Down," Fox News, June 22, 2020, https://www.foxnews.com/media/shaun-king-jesus-christ-statues-white-supremacy.

8. "Fire Franklin Graham, or Resign," Faithful America, January 15, 2021, https://act.faithfulamerica.org/sign/franklin-graham-insurrection/.

9. John Winthrop, "A Model of Christian Charity," Casa Charter School, https://www.casa-arts.org/cms/lib/PA01925203/Centricity/Domain/50/A%20Model%20of%20Christian%20Charity.pdf.

10. Thomas Doherty, "Pre-Code Hollywood: Sex, Immorality, and Insurrection in American Cinema, 1930–1934," *New York Times*, 1999, https://archive.nytimes.com/www.nytimes.com/books/first/d/doherty-hollywood.html?_r=1&scp=10&sq=hays%2520office&st=cse.

11. See, for example, Margo Kaplan, "Pedophilia: A Disorder, Not a Crime," *New York Times*, October 5, 2014, https://www.nytimes.com/2014/10/06/opinion/pedophilia-a-disorder-not-a-crime.html.

12. Tony Perkins, "Couric to Conservatives: Get With Deprogram," Family Research Council, January 19, 2021, https://www.frc.org/updatearticle/20210119/couric-conservatives.

13. Czeisler et al., "Mental Health, Substance Use, and Suicidal Ideation During the COVID-19 Pandemic."

14. "Employment Situation Summary," Bureau of Labor Statistics, February 5, 2021, https://www.bls.gov/news.release/empsit.nr0.htm.

15. David Wilkerson, *America's Last Call* (Lindale, TX: Wilkerson Trust Publications, 1998), 12, https://archive.org/details/americaslastcall00wilk/page/12/mode/2up.

16. "US National Debt," US Debt Clock.org, accessed February 17, 2021, https://www.usdebtclock.org/.

17. Jonathan Rothbaum, "Was Household Income the Highest Ever in 2019?," Census Bureau, September 15, 2020, https://www.census.gov/library/stories/2020/09/was-household-income-the-highest-ever-in-2019.html.

18. "US National Debt," US Debt Clock.org.

CHAPTER 11

1. "The Next 31 Things: Part 3," *The Jim Bakker Show*, January 10, 2020, https://jimbakkershow.com/watch/?guid=3839R.

2. "The Next 31 Things: Part 1," *The Jim Bakker Show*.

3. "What Is a Plate?," Geological Society, accessed February 18, 2021, https://www.geolsoc.org.uk/Plate-Tectonics/Chap2-What-is-a-Plate.

4. Gittrich, "Massive Fault Threatens Downtown."

5. "USGS Earthquakes: 1.0+, 2000," USGS, accessed February 18, 2021, https://earthquake.usgs.gov/earthquakes/map/?extent=-88.77768,-270&extent=88.76259,630&range=search&timeZone=utc&search=%7B%22name%22:%22Search%20Results%22,%22params%22:%7B%22starttime%22:%222000-01-01%2000:00:00%22,%22endtime%22:%222000-12-31%2023:59:59%22,%22minmagnitude%22:1,%22orderby%22:%22time%22%7D%7D.

6. "USGS Earthquakes: 1.0+, 2002," USGS, accessed February 18, 2021, https://earthquake.usgs.gov/earthquakes/map/?extent=-88.77768,-270&extent=88.76259,630&range=search&timeZone=utc&search=%7B%22name%22:%22Search%20Results%22,%22params%22:%7B%22starttime%22:%222002-01-01%2000:00:00%22,%22endtime%22:%222002-12-31%2023:59:59%22,%22minmagnitude%22:1,%22orderby%22:%22time%22%7D%7D.

7. "New Earthquakes Hazards Program: Lists, Maps, and Statistics," USGS, accessed February 18, 2021, https://www.usgs.gov/natural-hazards/earthquake-hazards/lists-maps-and-statistics; "USGS Earthquakes: 1.0+, 2018," USGS, accessed February 18, 2021, https://earthquake.usgs.gov/earthquakes/

map/?extent=-88.77768,-270&extent=88.76259,630&range=sea
rch&timeZone=utc&search=%7B%22name%22:%22Search%20
Results%22,%22params%22:%7B%22starttime%22:%222018-
01-01%2000:00:00%22,%22endtime%22:%222018-12-31%20
23:59:59%22,%22minmagnitude%22:1,%22orderby%22:%22time
%22%7D%7D.

8. "Information by Region—North Carolina: All Earthquakes 1900–Present," USGS, accessed February 18, 2021, https:// earthquake.usgs.gov/earthquakes/map/?extent=22.106,- 108.58887&extent=46.49839,-52.33887&range=search&bas eLayer=terrain&timeZone=utc&search=%7B%22name%2 2:%22Search%20Results%22,%22params%22:%7B%22start time%22:%221900-01-01%2000:00:00%22,%22maxlatitude% 22:36.644,%22minlatitude%22:33.761,%22maxlongitude%22:- 75.597,%22minlongitude%22:-85.331,%22minmagnitude%22:0,% 22orderby%22:%22time%22%7D%7D.

9. "Earthquake Catalog: Puerto Rico, 2001-02-11—2021-02-18," USGS, accessed February 18, 2021, https://earthquake.usgs.gov/ earthquakes/map/?extent=17.33491,-68.18665&extent=19.11403,- 64.67102&range=search&sort=largest&timeZone=utc&se arch=%7B%22name%22:%22Search%20Results%22,%22pa- rams%22:%7B%22starttime%22:%222001-02-11%20 00:00:00%22,%22endtime%22:%222021-02-18%20 23:59:59%22,%22maxlatitude%22:18.554,%22 minlatitude%22:17.897,%22maxlongitude%22:- 65.533,%22minlongitude%22:-67.324,%22minmagnitude%22:1,% 22orderby%22:%22magnitude%22%7D%7D.

10. For example, the 5.6 magnitude earthquake in Guyana on January 31, 2021; see "M 5.6 - 82 km SSE of Lethem, Guyana," USGS, accessed February 18, 2021, https://earthquake.usgs.gov/ earthquakes/eventpage/us6000ddge/executive.

11. Jemima McEvoy, "Minneapolis Cuts Millions From Police Budget Amid Crime Spike," *Forbes*, December 10, 2020, https://www.forbes. com/sites/jemimamcevoy/2020/12/10/minneapolis-cuts-millions- from-police-budget-amid-crime-spike/?sh=c860aa0701ee; Libor Jany and MaryJo Webster, "New Look at Police Stats Shows the Spread of Violent Crime Across Minneapolis This Summer," *Star Tribune*, September 21, 2020, https://www.startribune.com/analysis-poorer- mpls-areas-bear-the-brunt-of-rising-violence/572466101/.

12. David Wilkerson, "An Urgent Message," World Challenge, March 7, 2009, http://davidwilkersontoday.blogspot.com/2009/03/urgent- message.html.

13. Alexander I. Filkov et al., "Impact of Australia's Catastrophic 2019/20 Bushfire Season on Communities and Environment. Retrospective Analysis and Current Trends," *Journal of Safety Science and Resilience* 1, no. 1 (September 2020): 44–56, https://doi.org/10.1016/j.jnlssr.2020.06.009.

14. "Arizona's 2020 Wildfire Season Among Worst in Past Decade," Associated Press, January 27, 2021, https://apnews.com/article/forestry-fires-arizona-wildfires-858c6f1695983e55d80dc07a24dd4c17.

15. "2020 Incident Archive," Cal Fire, accessed February 18, 2021, https://www.fire.ca.gov/incidents/2020/.

16. "2020 Incident Archive," Cal Fire, accessed February 18, 2021, https://www.fire.ca.gov/incidents/2020/.

17. William Koenig, *Eye to Eye* (McLean, VA: Christian Publications, 2017), 406–12.

18. Steven N. Ward and Simon Day, "Cumbre Vieja Volcano—Potential Collapse and Tsunami at La Palma, Canary Island," *Geophysical Research Letters* 28, no. 17 (September 1, 2001): 3397–3400, https://agupubs.onlinelibrary.wiley.com/doi/epdf/10.1029/2001GL013110.

19. Tony Phillips, ed., "The Tunguska Impact—100 Years Later," NASA, June 30, 2008, https://science.nasa.gov/science-news/science-at-nasa/2008/30jun_tunguska; Chris Trayner, "The Tunguska Event," *Journal of the British Astronomical Association* 107, no. 3 (June 1997): 117–130, http://articles.adsabs.harvard.edu//full/1997JBAA..107..117T/0000117.000.html.

20. "Major American Fires: Peshtigo Fire," University of Illinois, accessed February 18, 2021, https://guides.library.illinois.edu/c.php?g=348303&p=2346981.

21. Chelsea Gohd, "A Car-Sized Asteroid Made the Closest Earth Flyby a Space Rock Has Ever Survived," Space.com, August 18, 2020, https://www.space.com/closest-asteroid-flyby-of-earth-recorded.html.

22. Hannah Osborne, "Election Day Asteroid Didn't Hit—NASA Says 2 More Will Pass Earth Today," *Newsweek*, November 3, 2020, https://www.newsweek.com/nasa-election-day-asteroid-earth-1544348.

23. Tom Horn, *The Wormwood Prophecy* (Lake Mary, FL: Charisma House, 2019), 24, https://www.amazon.com/Wormwood-Prophecy-Horn/dp/1629997552.

CHAPTER 12

1. "'Well Dressed People in Bread Lines All Over America, BUT It Will Come With Miracles!, Heidi Baker Shares About a Vision She Was Given While Ministering at a Church in America,"

Greg Lancaster Ministries, February 25, 2016, https://vfnkb. com/2016/02/heidi-bakers-prophetic-vision-bread.html.

2. "How to Build a Kit for Emergencies," FEMA, June 12, 2020, https://www.fema.gov/news-release/20200716/how-build-kit-emergencies.

3. "Current Estimates of New York City's Population for July 2018," NYC Department of City Planning, accessed February 18, 2021, https://www1.nyc.gov/site/planning/planning-level/nyc-population/current-future-populations.page.

4. "Historic Disaster Response to Hurricane Harvey in Texas," FEMA, September 22, 2017, https://www.fema.gov/news-release/20200220/respuesta-historica-al-huracan-harvey-en-texas.

5. Conrad Hackett and David McClendon, "Christians Remain World's Largest Religious Group, but They Are Declining in Europe," Pew Research Center, April 5, 2017, https://www. pewresearch.org/fact-tank/2017/04/05/christians-remain-worlds-largest-religious-group-but-they-are-declining-in-europe/.

CHAPTER 13

1. Blue Letter Bible, s.v. "*aporia*," accessed February 19, 2021, https://www.blueletterbible.org/lang/lexicon/lexicon. cfm?Strongs=G640&t=KJV; *Merriam-Webster*, s.v. "aporia," accessed February 19, 2021, https://www.merriam-webster.com/ dictionary/aporia.

2. Lexico, s.v. "repentance," accessed February 19, 2021, https:// www.lexico.com/definition/repentance.

3. "We Need Reformation More Than Revival," *The Jim Bakker Show*, January 13, 2020, https://jimbakkershow.com/ watch/?guid=3840R.

CHAPTER 14

1. Charles Dickens, *A Tale of Two Cities* (London: Bancroft Books, 1969), 7, https://archive.org/details/taleoftwocities0000dick_i2p2/ page/n9/mode/2up.

ABOUT THE AUTHOR

Pastor Jim Bakker, host and founder of *The Jim Bakker Show*, is a pioneer of Christian television. From humble beginnings, he rose to build one of the largest ministries in the world. His life is proof of the power of God's restoration and grace.

As a young man, Jim was called to "make Jesus real" to the world. During the golden era of television, he was divinely inspired to use this new medium. In the 1960s he joined the Christian Broadcasting Network under the direction of Pat Robertson. Jim developed one of the first daily one-hour kids' shows for Christians called *Come On Over*. He also later became the first host of a groundbreaking talk show called *The 700 Club*, featuring many of the top ministers and singers of the day.

After eight years at CBN, the Lord led Jim back into a traveling ministry, helping to plant and start many television ministries around the country. Jim and his family soon joined Paul and Jan Crouch in California to pioneer a new television ministry. Jim was the first president and a founder of Trinity Broadcasting Network, which today still beams around the world with twenty-four-hour-a-day Christian programming.

In 1974 Pastor Jim relocated to Charlotte, North Carolina, to birth several of the most dynamic ministries the world has ever known, including *The PTL Club*, The Inspirational Network, and a state-of-the-art Christian retreat center called Heritage USA. Through these ministries they recorded over ten million salvations through phone calls, feedback cards, and on-campus ministry.

After thirteen years of developing and expanding Heritage USA, Pastor Jim Bakker was forced to resign. PTL, under new management, soon found its way into bankruptcy. Jim became the target of a lawsuit, and in 1989 he was indicted and sentenced to forty-five years in prison.

While in prison Jim turned to his Bible and found a deeper walk with the Lord than he ever experienced before. Throughout five years Jim intensely studied the Book of Revelation and received a call from God to be a watchman, always looking ahead for the return of the Lord.

A few years later, thanks to the efforts of men such as Alan Dershowitz and James Albert, Jim's appeal was won. On July 1, 1994, Jim was released on parole after serving five years in prison. Jim was invited to many churches to share his testimony and to begin sharing what he had learned in the Book of Revelation.

In 1998, while working in the inner-city ministry of the Dream Center of Los Angeles, Jim met Lori Graham. They married that year and have totally dedicated their lives to ministry.

In 2002, Jim and Lori were blessed with the happiness of expanding their family with nine children from the inner city of Phoenix, where Lori had ministered for years. In that same year, Jim and Lori were offered the opportunity to move to Branson, Missouri, where they would begin *The New Jim Bakker Show.*

In 2003, sixteen years to the date that Pastor Jim had made his last broadcast from PTL, he and Lori launched their new television ministry. Today, *The Jim Bakker Show* is broadcast throughout the United States, Canada, and the entire world through DirecTV, DISH Network, Roku, livestreaming on jimbakkershow.com, and many more outlets, reaching a potential audience of 1.6 billion people.

The show is broadcast from a Christian Retreat Center called Morningside USA, located just outside Branson, Missouri. This seven-hundred-acre property is a thriving Christian community that also serves as the back lot for *The Jim Bakker Show* and other outreach ministries, including Lori's House, a safe, supportive home for pregnant women in difficult situations.

Pastor Jim is considered one of today's experts on the Book of Revelation. Since prison he authored *I Was Wrong, The Refuge, Prosperity and the Coming Apocalypse,* and *Time Has Come.* In 2020 Jim launched the PTL: Voice of the Prophets Network, a twenty-four-hour-a-day network carrying the most important messages from the prophets and watchmen of today.

Millions relate to Pastor Jim's and Lori's testimonies of the redemptive power of love. If God can put Pastor Jim's and Lori's lives back together, then He can do it for anyone.